INTERSECTIONALITY AND HUMAN RIGHTS LAW

This collection of essays analyses how the diversity in human identity and disadvantage affects the articulation, realisation, violation and enforcement of human rights. The question arises from the realisation that people who are severally and severely disadvantaged because of their race, religion, gender, age, disability, sexual orientation, class etc, often find themselves at the margins of human rights; their condition seldom improved and sometimes even worsened by the rights discourse. How does one make sense of this relationship between the complexity of people's disadvantage and violation of their human rights? Does the human rights discourse, based on its universal and common values, have tools, methods or theories to capture and respond to the difference in people's lived experience of rights? Can intersectionality help in that quest? This book seeks to inaugurate this line of inquiry.

Intersectionality and Human Rights Law

Edited by
Shreya Atrey
and
Peter Dunne

•HART•
OXFORD • LONDON • NEW YORK • NEW DELHI • SYDNEY

HART PUBLISHING

Bloomsbury Publishing Plc

Kemp House, Chawley Park, Cumnor Hill, Oxford, OX2 9PH, UK

1385 Broadway, New York, NY 10018, USA

HART PUBLISHING, the Hart/Stag logo, BLOOMSBURY and the Diana logo are
trademarks of Bloomsbury Publishing Plc

First published in Great Britain 2020

First published in hardback, 2020

Paperback edition, 2021

A catalogue record for this book is available from the British Library.

Library of Congress Cataloging-in-Publication data

Names: Atrey, Shreya, 1988- editor. | Dunne, Peter, editor.

Title: Intersectionality and human rights law / edited by Shreya Atrey and Peter Dunne.

Description: Oxford, UK ; New York, NY : Hart Publishing, an imprint of Bloomsbury Publishing, 2020. |
Includes bibliographical references and index.

Identifiers: LCCN 2020032752 (print) | LCCN 2020032753 (ebook) |
ISBN 9781509935291 (hardback) | ISBN 9781509935314 (ePDF) | ISBN 9781509935307 (Epub)

Subjects: LCSH: International law and human rights. | Human rights—Social aspects. |
Intersectionality (Sociology)

Classification: LCC KZ1266 .I5887 2020 (print) | LCC KZ1266 (ebook) | DDC 342.08/5—dc23

LC record available at https://lccn.loc.gov/2020032752

LC ebook record available at https://lccn.loc.gov/2020032753

ISBN: PB: 978-1-50994-225-1
       ePDF: 978-1-50993-531-4
       ePub: 978-1-50993-530-7

Typeset by Compuscript Ltd, Shannon

To find out more about our authors and books visit www.hartpublishing.co.uk.
Here you will find extracts, author information, details of forthcoming events
and the option to sign up for our newsletters.

FOREWORD

This collection of essays is a welcome addition to the intersectionality discourse. The collection is ambitious, provocative, stimulating and forward-looking – a rewarding read in these troubled times. In their various ways, the contributing authors seek to illuminate the points of collision and combination between strands of intersectionality and human rights law in order to identify a framework for understanding the relationship between the two in a more systematic way. The chapters are compelling voices in the argument that intersectionality may be considered part of the human rights canon and deserves to be elevated beyond the realm of discrimination law alone.

As a young black woman, my introduction to intersectionality came via Black Feminist theory, lived experience and social activism. In later years, as a lawyer practising in the fields of equality and human rights law, I encountered intersectionality primarily as a critique of discrimination law. I recognised the validity of the complaint that discrimination law premised on a single-axis logic ignored the complexity of disadvantage associated with multiple grounds of identity and disadvantage. As a practitioner, I have often been brought up short by the limitations of the tools at my disposal to articulate, enforce and seek redress for violations of individual rights. In terms of the provision of practical, effective remedies, the presence of overlapping protected characteristics or identities is largely inconsequential in UK discrimination law.

I have long considered that the law is a poor vehicle for reflecting the reality of intersectionality and a poorer one still for mitigating its disadvantageous consequences. Yet discrimination and equality law have tended to be the main routes by which intersectional concerns have been examined. This book seeks to demonstrate that the idea and field of intersectionality transcend the technical constraints of equality and discrimination law, and are relevant to a broader human rights debate.

This book places centre stage the insight that people who are 'severally and severely disadvantaged' often find themselves at the margins of human rights. As Atrey observes, their conditions are seldom improved and are sometimes worsened by the human rights discourse. The authors point out that the reality of the lived experience that flows from the collision of disadvantages and vulnerabilities implicit in intersectionality is a matter of human rights. Intersectionality affects the realisation and attainment of human rights. Thus, the common goal for the contributing authors is to rationalise intersectionality in human rights law.

The relationship of intersectionality with other human rights has not yet been systematically or widely explored – this notwithstanding the fact that there is ample territory to explore. What insights might an examination of intersectional concerns and human rights case law in relation to the prohibition on torture, the right to liberty and security, the right to protection for private and family life or freedom of thought, conscience or religion bring? As the reach of the state grows as it legislates to introduce emergency measures to tackle the COVID-19 pandemic, might an integrated analysis provide a more nuanced understanding of the structures, systemic obstacles and lived experiences that lead to breaches of rights? Is it too much to hope that an integrated analysis might in turn lead to a greater respect for rights, more effective enforcement of rights and better remedies?

The central argument of these works is that intersectionality has both a theoretical and practical appeal in human rights law.

The authors remain true to the disruptive force present in much intersectional analysis. With a clear-sighted energy, they address questions of theory and practice which have nagged away in the corners of our thinking, as well as questions which have never occurred to us but which, once posed, we recognise are urgent and transfixing. The style of the works is discursive, creating space for debate, reflection and reframing rather than seeking to definitively identify an account of the relationship between intersectionality and human rights law. In this way, the reader is drawn into an engaging and dynamic conversation.

One of the frustrations often expressed in relation to the notion of intersectionality is that it is an ever-expanding field that defies classification or exact definition. Its mutability may be both its blessing and its curse. In their engagement with intersectionality, the authors try to make best use of the mutability of intersectionality to adapt it to the human rights framework. As we read our way through these chapters, we begin to understand the significance of this exercise in understanding intersectionality as well as its implications for a better, fuller understanding of rights.

This book does not mark just another staging post on the all-conquering march of intersectionality. The authors are not in uncritical thrall to the idea or practice of intersectionality. They identify the risks and the opportunities that exist on this journey. One author records the challenges involved in developing an intersectional approach to poverty-related concerns, noting the risk that each discourse may be diluted, but also the possibility of meaningful gains. Another considers the limits of intersectionality in human rights law and warns that constructing a relationship between intersectionality and human rights law is not a panacea for all concerns.

As well as providing theoretical 'food for thought', the chapters in this book consider how intersectionality might affect the experience of specific human rights such as rights to sexual and reproductive health, the right to housing and the right to education. There is so much in this innovative collection to consider and enjoy.

ACKNOWLEDGEMENTS

As editors, we owe a significant debt of gratitude to many individuals and institutions without whose support, guidance and generosity this book would not have been possible.

We are grateful for the support of the Faculty of Social Sciences and Law at the University of Bristol and the Society of Legal Scholars (SLS) in organising an exploratory workshop in November 2018 on the topic of this book. We are also grateful to the Bristol Human Rights Implementation Centre and the Bristol Centre for Law at Work for co-sponsoring the workshop. Jacqueline Nichols, Ellie Claypole and Jay Nash at the Bristol Law School Executive Office provided extraordinary assistance in organising the workshop, while Max Tsu Jiun and Hysan Woo who are undergraduate students at the Bristol Law School, were our pillars in running the workshop. Above all, we are grateful to the participants at the workshop whose reflections have shaped the contours of this book.

Colleagues at the Bristol Law School have tirelessly engaged with the project in numerous ways. We wish to thank Lois Bibbings, Alan Bogg, Joanne Conaghan, Paula Giliker, Lee McConnell, Joanna McCunn, Rachel Murray, Ken Oliphant, Jane Rooney and Tonia Novitz for their exceptional generosity in engaging with our ideas and in steering us in imagining, and ultimately completing, this project as a book.

We have received unrivalled editorial assistance from our colleagues at Hart Bloomsbury Publishing, whose consistent professionalism, expert guidance (and welcome patience!) have made this book possible. Many thanks are due to Sinead Moloney, Sasha Jawed and Tom Adams in particular.

And, finally, our greatest debt is owed to the authors who have contributed outstanding chapters to this book. We are inspired by your depth of thought and commitment to the project. We have learnt a great deal from working with each of you. Thank you for collaborating with us, for sharing your invaluable insights and for your unending goodwill.

SA and PD
August 2020

CONTENTS

LIST OF CONTRIBUTORS

Shreya Atrey is Associate Professor of International Human Rights Law at the University of Oxford.

Meghan Campbell is Senior Lecturer in Law at the University of Birmingham.

Gauthier de Beco is Reader in Law at the University of Huddersfield.

Fiona de Londras is Chair of Global Legal Studies at the University of Birmingham.

Peter Dunne is Senior Lecturer at the University of Bristol.

Sandra Fredman is Rhodes Professor of the Laws of the British Commonwealth and the United States at the University of Oxford.

Colm O'Cinneide is Professor of Constitutional and Human Rights Law at University College London.

Geraldine Van Bueren is Professor of International Human Rights Law at Queen Mary, University of London.

TABLE OF CASES

UK (including England and Wales, Northern Ireland and Scotland)

United Nations Human Rights Treaty Bodies

Committee on Economic, Social and Cultural Rights

Committee on the Elimination of Discrimination against Women

US

TABLE OF STATUTES

US

Introduction

Intersectionality from Equality to Human Rights

SHREYA ATREY

This book is about understanding how the complexity of human identity and disadvantage affects the articulation, realisation, violation and enforcement of human rights. The interest in this topic arises from the realisation that people who are severally and severely disadvantaged because of their race, religion, sex, gender, age, disability, sexual orientation, language, class etc often find themselves at the margins of human rights, their condition seldom improved and sometimes even worsened by the rights discourse. The Covid-19 crisis is but a reflection of this; it affects everyone and yet affects disadvantaged groups more severely. Though lockdown, isolation, social distancing and quarantine are deemed necessary to prevent the spread of the virus, the same measures aggravate human rights abuses of vulnerable populations like people of colour, women, children, disabled persons, refugees, asylum seekers, homeless persons, migrant workers and, within these, especially those who belong to two or more of these groups at the same time. For example, intimate-partner violence, domestic abuse and sexual exploitation are worsened by the crisis and affect poor women, disabled women, migrant women, refugees and asylum seekers more than others. At the same time, these groups have diminished access to services, including pregnancy and maternal healthcare. Frontline workers, from midwives and nurses to pharmacists and cleaners, care workers, and homemakers looking after children and the elderly, are disproportionately women, often of migrant and working-class backgrounds. They face significant consequences of overwork while being underpaid. Women, who make up the majority of the workers in informal economies throughout the world, face similar precarity, struggling for basic interests of clothing, shelter, food, water and sanitation to be met. The education of girls, disabled children and children of ethnic minorities is also in peril.[1] So, while the crisis affects everyone, it

---

[1] See reports from the early days of the crisis: OHCHR, 'States Must Combat Domestic Violence in the context of COVID-19 Lockdowns', 27 March 2020, https://www.ohchr.org/FR/NewsEvents/Pages/DisplayNews.aspx?NewsID=25749&LangID=E; UN Women, 'In Focus: Gender Equality

does not affect everyone equally. Grave inequities exist in the extent to which the rights to life, liberty, security, home, privacy and health seem compromised across groups straddling several forms of disadvantage. How does one make sense of the relationship between various rights and such complex intersectionality? The book pursues this line of inquiry.

In law, intersectionality has primarily developed as a critique of equality and discrimination law. As famously argued by Kimberlé Crenshaw, premised on a 'single-axis' logic, discrimination law often ignores the complexity of disadvantage associated with multiple grounds of identity and disadvantage.[2] Discrimination lawyers have since argued for expanding the basis of discrimination to one which is capable of addressing intersectional disadvantage.[3] Beyond this, intersectionality has had a limited purchase in law. The relationship of intersectionality with rights, other than the right to equality and non-discrimination, remains unexplored and under-theorised.[4] There is some research connecting, on the one hand, established discourses in intersectionality studies and, on the other hand, discourses in

Matters in COVID-19 Response', https://www.unwomen.org/en/news/in-focus/in-focus-gender-equality-in-covid-19-response; Human Rights Watch, 'Human Rights Dimensions of COVID-19 Response', 19 March 2020, https://www.hrw.org/news/2020/03/19/human-rights-dimensions-covid-19-response; Human Rights Watch, 'COVID-19 Law Puts Rights of People with Disabilities at Risk', 26 March 2020, https://www.hrw.org/news/2020/03/26/uk-covid-19-law-puts-rights-people-disabili ties-risk; Council of Europe, 'COVID-19 Confinement: For Many Women and Children, the Home is Not a Safe Place', 24 March 2020, https://www.coe.int/en/web/genderequality/-/for-many-women-and-children-the-home-is-not-a-safe-place.

[2] KW Crenshaw, 'Demarginalizing the Intersection of Race and Sex: A Black Feminist Critique of Antidiscrimination Doctrine, Feminist Theory and Antiracist Politics' (1989) *University of Chicago Legal Forum* 139.

[3] S Fredman and E Szyszczak, 'The Interaction of Race and Gender' in B Hepple and E Szyszczak (eds), *Discrimination: The Limits of the Law* (Mansell, 1992); K Abrams, 'Title VII and the Complex Female Subject' (1993) 92 *Michigan Law Review* 2479; N Duclos, 'Disappearing Women: Racial Minority Women in Human Rights Cases' (1993) 6 *Canadian Journal of Women and the Law* 25; N Iyer, 'Categorical Denials: Equality Rights and the Shaping of Social Identity' (1993) 19 *Queen's Law Journal* 179; E Carasco, 'A Case of Double Jeopardy: Race and Gender' (1993) 6 *Canadian Journal Women and Law* 142; M Eaton, 'At the Intersection of Gender and Sexual Orientation: Towards a Lesbian Jurisprudence' (1994) 3 *Southern California Review of Law and Women's Studies* 183; S Hannett, 'Equality at the Intersections: The Legislative and Judicial Failure to Tackle Multiple Discrimination' (2003) 23 *Oxford Journal of Legal Studies* 65; A McColgan, 'Reconfiguring Discrimination Law' [2007] *Public Law* 74; J Conaghan, 'Intersectionality and UK Equality Initiatives' (2007) 23 *South African Journal on Human Rights* 317; E Bonthuys, 'Institutional Openness and Resistance to Feminist Arguments: The Example of the South African Constitutional Court' (2008) 20 *Canadian Journal of Women and Law* 1; M Pieterse, 'Finding for the Applicant? Individual Equality Plaintiffs and Group-Based Disadvantage' (2008) 24 *South African Journal on Human Rights* 397; I Solanke, 'Putting Race and Gender Together: A New Approach to Intersectionality' (2009) 72 *Modern Law Review* 723; D Schiek and A Lawson (eds), *European Union Non-discrimination Law and Intersectionality* (Ashgate, 2011); D Schiek and V Chege (eds), *European Union Non-discrimination Law: Comparative Perspectives on Multidimensional Equality Law* (Routledge-Cavendish, 2008).

[4] Some notable exceptions include J Squires and H Skjeie, *Institutionalizing Intersectionality: The Changing Nature of European Equality Regimes* (Palgrave Macmillan, 2012); H Potter, *Intersectionality and Criminology: Disrupting and Revolutionizing Studies of Crime* (CRC Press, 2015); J Kantola and E Lombardo, *Gender and the Economic Crisis in Europe: Politics, Institutions and Intersectionality* (Palgrave Macmillan, 2017).

human rights law.[5] While impactful, these interventions remain solitary and are seldom woven into the fabric of human rights law tout court. One exception is the recalcitrant issue of violence against women, which, because of Crenshaw's initial contribution to the same, remains committed to intersectional analyses.[6] Again, these thematic interventions are often viewed as *specific* intersectional problems rather than problems of human rights law *generally*. By and large, discrimination law happens to be the mainstay for channelling intersectional concerns, with the theory and doctrine of human rights law, domestically or internationally, merely dabbling with intersectionality.

Intersectionality is obviously not just a matter of equality and discrimination law. Given its activist roots in Black feminism in the US and the way it has developed over a long course of intellectual history of nearly 200 years and across disciplines and continental boundaries, intersectionality seems hardly confined to the technical limits of equality and discrimination law.[7] In fact, it has continued to develop *despite* the technical limitations of the field, which were the subject of Crenshaw's initial critique. Intersectionality has since emerged as the go-to idea for making sense of disadvantage which cannot be neatly segregated into silos of racism, sexism, homophobia, transphobia, xenophobia, ableism, ageism etc.[8] It thus has a wide import in human rights law, for example, to illuminate how particular interests in life, liberty, security, education, housing, health etc are subjectively transformed by people's multiple identities and the disadvantages associated with them. If multiple and compounding disadvantages make a difference to the experience of human rights, as intersectionality shows that they do, there must be a broad and sustained way of connecting the discourses in intersectionality and human rights law to address such disadvantage or violation of human rights.

---

[5] LA Crooms, 'Indivisible Rights and Intersectional Identities or, "What Do Women's Human Rights Have to Do with the Race Convention?"' (1996) 40 *Howard Law Journal* 619; J Bond, 'International Intersectionality: A Theoretical and Pragmatic Exploration of Women's International Human Rights Violations' (2003) 52 *Emory Law Journal* 71; J Bond, 'Intersecting Identities and Human Rights: The Example of Romani Women's Reproductive Rights' (2004) 5 *Georgetown Journal of Gender and the Law* 897; M Satterthwaite, 'Women Migrants' Rights under International Human Rights Law' (2004) 77 *Feminist Review* 167; A Vakulenko, '"Islamic Headscarves" and the European Convention on Human Rights: An Intersectional Perspective' (2007) 16 *Social and Legal Studies* 183; N Taefi, 'The Synthesis of Age and Gender: Intersectionality, International Human Rights Law and the Marginalisation of the Girl-Child' (2009) 17 *International Journal of Children's Rights* 345; M Campbell, 'CEDAW and Women's Intersecting Identities: A Pioneering Approach to Intersectional Discrimination' (2015) *Revistia Diretio GV* 479; G de Beco, 'Protecting the Invisible: An Intersectional Approach to International Human Rights Law' (2017) 17 *Human Rights Law Review* 633.
[6] K Crenshaw, 'Mapping the Margins: Intersectionality, Identity Politics, and Violence against Women of Color' (1991) 43 *Stanford Law Review* 1241; S Atrey, 'Lifting as We Climb: Recognising Intersectional Gender Violence in Law' (2015) 5 *Oñati Socio-legal Series* 1512; PH Collins, 'On Violence, Intersectionality and Transversal Politics' (2017) 40 *Ethnic and Racial Studies* 9; L Sosa, *Intersectionality in the Human Rights Legal Framework on Violence against Women: At the Centre or the Margins?* (Cambridge University Press, 2017).
[7] A-M Hancock, *An Intellectual History of Intersectionality* (Oxford University Press, 2016).
[8] See especially K Davis, 'Intersectionality as Buzzword' (2008) 9 *Feminist Theory* 67.

The central argument of this book, as advanced through each of the individual chapters, is that intersectionality has a theoretical and practical appeal in human rights law. At the theoretical level, the chapters explore the contestations and possibilities in engaging intersectionality and human rights law together and lay out some preliminary framework considerations for examining the relationship between the two. For example, theoretically, intersectionality is said to transform the universal basis of human rights into one which appreciates difference *as a matter* of universality of human rights. The book also picks up on particular concepts and tries to place them within the existing scheme of human rights law. For example, it assesses the influence of the use of intersectionality in conceptualising the impact of poverty, class and socio-economic disadvantage in human rights law. The purpose is to determine whether and how intersectionality may better serve poverty-related concerns which have hitherto been elided in both human rights and discrimination law. Herein, the chapters, taken as a whole, argue that intersectionality can be rather helpful in addressing poverty-related concerns in human rights law because it is better suited to understanding both the nature of such concerns (which are essentially intersectional in character) and also has tools (such as its emphasis on 'vulnerability' and 'systems' or 'structures' of disadvantage) to address them squarely. At the practical level, the chapters explore how intersectionality affects the experience of specific human rights. This involves applying intersectionality to understand the basis of violations and to find ways of redressal and realisation of rights that are appreciative of this intersectional experience of rights. The right to education and women's rights are two areas which are explored at length and across the chapters. The uptake here is that a disjunct reading of rights or the interests associated with them, and the multiple and cross-cutting positionalities (identities, disadvantage, geography etc) that shape the experience of those rights or interests, has affected the way in which human rights are enjoyed or not. Violations of human rights are thus deeply embedded in these complex causalities, which are best understood in intersectional terms. To avert such violations, intersectionality needs to be centred and engaged with fundamentally in the practice of human rights law.

The rest of this introduction elaborates on each of these claims in order to explain further their context, meaning and purpose in relation to the book. In particular, it will elaborate on three clusters of inquiries alluded to above. First, it justifies the move from equality and discrimination law to human rights law generally, as a move intended not only to make the most of intersectionality theory in law, but also to make the most of human rights itself. Second, it expands on the contours of this book and the central argument outlined above to give the reader tools for navigating the chapters that follow. Finally, it lays out the book's relationship with intersectionality as an idea and as a field, ie, it lays out the meaning of intersectionality invoked herein and the engagement with intersectionality literatures.

***

[I]ntersectionality is far broader than what most people, including many of its practitioners, imagine it to be. We have yet to fully understand the potential of the constellation of ideas that fall under the umbrella term *intersectionality* as a tool for social change.[9]

In *Intersectionality as Critical Social Theory*, Patricia Hill Collins aptly captures the boundless state in which intersectionality exists. Far from being capable of being set out in clear definitional terms, intersectionality challenges every project that invokes it with its sheer profundity. Invoking it leaves its interlocutor to confront some seemingly basic but otherwise deep questions. What is intersectionality? Is it an idea,[10] a concept,[11] a metaphor,[12] a theory and praxis,[13] a research paradigm,[14] a heuristic and analytic tool,[15] a methodological approach and epistemological stance,[16] or an analytical and political orientation?[17] Where does it truly belong? To sociology, gender studies, literature, political theory, political science, sociology, anthropology, history, policy studies or law? Is it about identities, disadvantage, power, oppression, vulnerabilities, systems, structures or the social world generally? Which categories does it pertain to? Race, sex, gender, religion, language, age, sexual orientation, disability, trans-status etc? Is it about Black women, its original purveyors, or does it go beyond them and into geographical contexts far beyond the US? The questions only multiply.

Coming from one of its chief thinkers, the admission of our less-than-full grasp of intersectionality is thus sobering. It shows that no matter how clear we may be in our answers to these questions, intersectionality may still be broader. As an ever-expanding and expansive field, intersectionality may defy neat boundaries, exact definitions or finite applications.

But if such is the nature of intersectionality, how is it that it has been narrowly confined in law mainly to the field of discrimination law? Law is a vast field, especially the field of human rights or, more broadly, public law, a discourse that has to do with the power of state and public bodies and the implications of the exercise of such power on people. Discrimination law is but one field within this much larger universe. Why then does the reach of intersectionality in law seem to arise from and subside within discrimination law?

This question and the claim within – prompting us to go beyond discrimination law – requires some unpacking. The reason that discrimination law is the first

[9] PH Collins, *Intersectionality as Critical Social Theory* (Duke University Press, 2019) 2.

[10] S Atrey, *Intersectional Discrimination* (Oxford University Press, 2019) ch 2.

[11] A Carastathis, 'The Concept of Intersectionality in Feminist Theory' (2014) 9 *Philosophy Compass* 304.

[12] A Garry, 'Intersectionality, Metaphors, and the Multiplicity of Gender' (2011) 25 *Hypathia* 826.

[13] PH Collins and S Bilge, *Intersectionality* (Polity Press, 2016).

[14] L McCall, 'The Complexity of Intersectionality' (2005) 30 *Signs* 1771.

[15] DW Carbado et al, 'Intersectionality: Mapping the Movements of a Theory' (2013) 10 *Du Bois Review* 303.

[16] S Cho, 'Post-intersectionality: The Curious Reception of Intersectionality in Legal Scholarship' (2013) 10 *Du Bois Review* 385.

[17] VM May, *Pursuing Intersectionality: Unsettling Dominant Imaginaries* (Routledge, 2015).

port of call for intersectionality is obvious. In 1989, Crenshaw coined the term 'intersectionality' in the context of discrimination law.[18] We know that intersectionality has existed both before and after this moment of coinage, well beyond the strictures of discrimination law.[19] Yet, because the coinage was supplemented by a trenchant account of what intersectionality really is, it made the coinage as well as the immediate context of it – discrimination law – rather potent. Crenshaw's contribution has thus come to define intersectionality as an idea and as a field of intersectionality studies. Because discrimination law was so central to her contribution – its focus being the critique of single-axis framework of discrimination law – it naturally took centre stage in addressing intersectional concerns in law generally. Since then, discrimination law has maintained this foothold. Discrimination lawyers have continued to populate the field with intersectional analyses from around the world and for vulnerable groups beyond Black women.[20] While discrimination law still continues to be highly resistant to intersectionality, over 30 years after Crenshaw's initial contribution, *this* too explains the enduring interest in cracking the problems with discrimination law above all and resisting its single-axis framework with continued vehemence.[21]

In 1991, Crenshaw's second contribution extended the intersectional critique to the issue of violence against women, especially women of colour.[22] Again, her contribution here was not limited to the specific issue of violence against women; it was the *analyses* of the issues involved, particularly her *conceptualisation* of intersectionality as structural, political and representational, that captured the moment of growing interest in the concept in the early 1990s. For example, she showed in careful detail the way in which immigration law and policy trapped women of colour in violent and abusive relationships, not only because of racism and sexism, but also because these women were often poor, economically dependent, of dependent immigrant status and non-English speaking.[23] It was the combination of the many intersecting positions of vulnerability that defined what was generically termed 'violence against women' when it came to women of colour. Violence against women of colour or minority women has since been amongst the more researched areas at the cross-section of intersectionality and human rights law and policy.[24]

---

[18] Crenshaw (n 2).

[19] Hancock (n 7); Collins and Bilge (n 13).

[20] See references in n 3.

[21] For a comparative analysis of the collective failures of legislatures and courts, see Atrey (n 10) ch 1. Much more can be said about intersectionality's relationship with discrimination law and where it stands today, but that is a topic for other works on discrimination law. Here, with our human rights law hats on, what we are trying to do with this book is to conceive of intersectionality as relevant *also to* human rights law. For that reason, it should suffice to say that discrimination law, relevant as it is, hardly exhausts the domain of law for the purposes of intersectionality.

[22] Crenshaw (n 6).

[23] ibid 1246–50.

[24] B Moradi et al, 'Mapping the Travels of Intersectionality Scholarship: A Citation Network Analysis' (2020) (44) *Psychology of Women Quarterly* 151 (a citation analysis of intersectionality literatures in 17 'clusters', not including law, though violence against women is included explicitly).

This focus is reflected in basic search results. A combination of intersectionality and equality/discrimination/anti-discrimination/non-discrimination as keywords returns over 10,000 results on Google Scholar, while a combination of intersectionality and violence against women returns 33,000 results. In contrast, a combination of intersectionality and human rights law returns about 6,000 results. The difference is particularly stark given that the field of human rights law is broader and includes the discourses in equality, discrimination and violence against women. A glance at the search results confirms that broader considerations of classical rights, like the right to life, liberty and security, or freedoms, such as freedom of movement, association, religion, home, family and private life, or the rights pertaining to education, housing, health, food and water, get comparatively less attention either individually or systematically *as* issues of human rights law, ie, to be addressed within the theoretical and doctrinal framework of human rights law, whether international, regional or comparative.

As a general idea, intersectionality represents the complexity of disadvantage people suffer when they belong to two or more vulnerable groups, such as Black women, who are both Black and female at the same time. Black women in the US are less employed, paid less and suffer exponential levels of sexual harassment at work.[25] But they are also incarcerated and killed at a much higher rate than white people, and on a comparable scale as Black men,[26] have diminished access to reproductive justice (despite a staggering rate of abortion),[27] face insurmountable barriers to educational attainment[28] and lead more households with or without children while facing greater levels of income insecurity.[29] Surely, all of this is a matter of human rights squarely and not only a matter of discrete claims of individual discrimination to be addressed via discrimination law. In other words, while systemic discrimination defines Black women's intersectional disadvantage,

[25] Economic Policy Institute, United States Census Bureau, https://www.census.gov/newsroom/press-releases/2018/income-poverty.html; A Hegewisch, 'The Gender Wage Gap: 2017; Earnings Differences by Gender, Race, and Ethnicity', Institute for Women's Policy Research, https://iwpr.org/publications/gender-wage-gap-2017.

[26] See especially '#SAYHERNAME Movement', *African American Policy Forum*, https://aapf.org/shn-campaign; K Crenshaw, 'From Private Violence to Mass Incarceration: Thinking Intersectionally about Women, Race, and Social Control' (2012) 59 *UCLA Law Review* 1418.

[27] SA Cohen, 'Abortion and Women of Color: The Bigger Picture' (2008) 11 *Guttmacher Policy Review*, https://www.guttmacher.org/gpr/2008/08/abortion-and-women-color-bigger-picture; Centre for Reproductive Rights, 'Women's Reproductive Rights in the United States', a Shadow Report Prepared for the Eighty-Seventh Session of the Human Rights Committee (2006).

[28] H Hartmann, C Childers and E Shaw, 'Toward Our Children's Keeper: A Data Driven Analysis of the Interim Report of the My Brother's Keeper Initiative Shows the Shared Fate of Boys and Girls of Color', Institute for Women's Policy Research, 25 February 2015, https://iwpr.org/publications/toward-our-childrens-keeper-a-data-driven-analysis-of-the-interim-report-of-the-my-brothers-keeper-initiative-shows-the-shared-fate-of-boys-and-girls-of-color; National Women's Law Centre, 'When Girls Don't Graduate, We All Fail' (2007), www.nwlc.org/sites/default/files/pdfs/when_girls_dont_graduate.pdf.

[29] K Patrick, 'Black Women Lead Families But Still Lag behind in Jobs and Wealth', National Women's Law Centre, 4 August 2017, https://nwlc.org/blog/black-women-lead-families-but-still-lag-behind-in-jobs-and-wealth.

it affects not only those issues classified as 'discrimination' for the purposes of discrimination in employment or access to goods and services, but life chances at a broader scale and as pertaining to interests spanning all human rights. The fact that intersectionality affects human rights attainment thus seems to be an insight, both trite and critical, at the same time.

∗ ∗ ∗

This then is what motivates this book. The common goal for the authors is to rationalise intersectionality in human rights law. This is carried out in both general and particular ways – ie, the contributions delineate the conceptual and doctrinal issues in human rights law broadly – with the aim of systematising the relationship of intersectionality with human rights law, and also provide intersectional readings of discrete issues or rights, such as the Grenfell fire tragedy, reproductive justice, the right to housing and the right to education.

The issues chosen in pursuing this goal are rather discursive. The goal of sketching the relationship between intersectionality and human rights law, though writ large, does not purport to be comprehensive by any measure. There is no attempt to present *an account* of intersectionality and human rights law; instead, the attempt is to inaugurate the line of inquiry which may lead to such an account in the future. The field is far too young to try to exert an account yet without caution. The discursive themes explored in and across the chapters are thus meant to get the conversation rolling by defining the terms of the debate, which may in turn define the development of the conversation. To summarise, the themes explored herein are: the theoretical basis of universal human rights and its capacity to accommodate intersectionality fundamentally; the relevance of a systems-based understanding of intersectionality in interpreting two or more international human rights treaties or sets of norms together (such as disability rights and children's rights); the development of a vulnerability-based analysis in social rights adjudication to hone in on intersectionality; the relevance of class in intersectionality and human rights law; the relevance of substantive equality as a bridge between intersectionality and human rights; the engagement with the particularities of intersectional positions in human rights law, especially subaltern groups such as rural women; and the dilemmas of intersectional activism in social movements and law reform. The specific human rights considered in the chapters include: the right to life, liberty and security; the right to housing; the right to education; reproductive rights; and, of course, the right to equality and non-discrimination as a crosscutting right across all issues. Some intersectional groups animate the discussion in particular viz Black women, disabled children, Black and minority children, rural women, trans and non-binary persons, and immigrant women. All of these specific positions of issues, rights and groups serve as points of analysis for both general and particular conclusions presented in the individual chapters. They are thus treated as instantiations to illuminate something about the relationship of intersectionality with human rights and do not purport to be either the only or even the main areas of interest for human rights lawyers. Just as intersectionality remains boundless, one can expect its instantiation in human rights law to be of a similar character.

In this vein, dualities such as theory and doctrine, international and comparative law or civil-political and socio-economic rights are transcended in an attempt to show just how inseparable these are in practice and how intersectionality helps make sense of the links between them. That said, the discussion in each chapter is naturally defined by a precise set of human rights laws as applicable to a particular issue in a given geographical location. These locations include Ireland, South Africa, the UK and the US. References to other jurisdictions, including, France, Germany, Spain and Canada, are also found at relevant points of discussion in the chapters. Domestic human rights norms, as applicable to specific issues under consideration, are examined, especially in light of the states' international obligations in human rights treaties, such as the International Covenant on Civil and Political Rights (ICCPR),[30] the International Covenant on Economic, Social and Cultural Rights (ICESCR),[31] the Convention for the Protection of Human Rights and Fundamental Freedoms (ECHR),[32] the European Social Charter (ESC),[33] the Convention on the Elimination of All Forms of Racial Discrimination (CERD),[34] the Convention on the Elimination of All Forms of Discrimination against Women (CEDAW),[35] the Convention on the Rights of the Child (CRC)[36] and the Convention on the Rights of Persons with Disabilities (CRPD).[37] The legal references are not meant to be exhaustive, but merely illustrative in canvassing the theoretical and doctrinal issues relevant to each contribution. Thus, the discussion is meant to show the possibilities of practical engagement with international and domestic human rights issues in an intersectional way, and we hope that this exercise provides cues for developing this analysis further in the specific geographical contexts discussed, but also beyond.

The following overview of the individual chapters should help make clear the remit of each of the contributions and the book as a whole.

***

Chapter 1 is an elaborate and abstract meditation on the nature of universal human rights. It explores just how much of the liberal theory sees diversity and difference in human identity as part of, but not central to, the universality of rights. This is

[30] 999 UNTS 171 (opened for signature 16 December 1966, entered into force 23 March 1976).
[31] 993 UNTS 3 (opened for signature 16 December 1966, entered into force 3 January 1976).
[32] ETS No 005 (opened for signature 4 November 1950, entered into force 3 September 1953).
[33] ETS No 035 (opened for signature 18 October 1961, entered into force 26 February 1965).
[34] 660 UNTS 195 (opened for signature 21 December 1965, entered into force 4 January 1969).
[35] 1249 UNTS 13 (opened for signature 18 December 1979, entered into force 3 September 1981).
[36] 1577 UNTS 3 (opened for signature 20 November 1989, entered into force 2 September 1990).
[37] 2515 UNTS 3 (opened for signature 30 March 2007, entered into force 3 May 2008).

clear in the way in which the right to equality and non-discrimination is embedded in human rights as a framework which aims to discount rather than account for the complexity in human identity. There appears to be little in human rights theory that makes space for the kind of politics of difference imagined by intersectionality. However, there is Hannah Arendt's view of identity and the eternal commitment to difference, which seems to ground human rights a bit differently. Arendt's view comports with intersectionality in its focus on difference as the only universal basis for rights. Chapter 1 suggests replacing the conventional understanding of universality with this refined basis of human rights, one which it calls 'intersectional universality'. The aim is to exhume the essential force of intersectionality in justifying the theory of human rights law.

In Chapter 2, Gauthier de Beco considers possibilities of unlocking intersectionality's full potential in human rights law. With the example of the right to education of children with disabilities, he explains how intersectionality may help understand systems and structures of disadvantage better. However, this requires going beyond the limited identity-based understanding of intersectionality and instead focusing on a systems-based understanding of intersectionality. The chapter shows that this understanding is not only in line with intersectionality literature more broadly, but also helpful in enforcing human rights across international treaties. Thus, according to him, this would be particularly useful in promoting human rights of those who are seemingly protected under two or more international treaties, viz disabled children, who are protected under the CRC as children and under the CRPD as disabled persons, but who may slip through the cracks of both, since they do not belong exclusively to either.

Through the example of socio-economic rights adjudication, in Chapter 3, Colm O'Cinneide considers how intersectionality has been mobilised, in particular, to understand and address poverty-related concerns which are otherwise often sidelined in rights adjudication. Intersectionality, he argues, serves as a credible interpretive tool for capturing the material inequality at play in socio-economic rights violations. This approach is salient in European jurisprudence (under the ECHR and the ESC), where the concept of 'group vulnerability' has been used to make sense of intersectionality in adjudication. However, there are also conceptual traps that need to be avoided to actually harness intersectionality. O'Cinneide traverses the labyrinth of the embryonic social rights adjudication in Europe and systematises the potential and pitfalls of engaging intersectionality on a sustained basis.

In Chapter 4, Sandra Fredman approaches the subject of poverty from the opposite viewpoint. She problematises the nature of poverty itself as too complex for any one paradigm – intersectionality, equality and discrimination law or human rights law – to have addressed fully or easily. With the example of the right to education as an amplifier right, she explains the nature of poverty as inherently intersectional and thus highlights the inevitability of understanding it in terms of intersectionality theory, but also, in human rights law, in terms of equality, especially the framework of substantive equality. Her compelling examples from the right to education cases in the US and South Africa allow us to appreciate how the human rights discourse either misses poverty or misses race without an intervening force like intersectionality. She argues that substantive equality provides a bridge between intersectionality and human rights law, which helps connect intersectional issues (of poverty and race) with the goal of realising human rights (such as the right to education).

In Chapter 5, Geraldine Van Bueren agrees that while poverty-related concerns may be addressed via intersectionality in human rights law, material concerns which are class-related and not characterised by extreme deprivation may still fail to be examined through this lens. She thus presents us with a cautionary tale for constructing the relationship between intersectionality and human rights law as a panacea for all concerns, including class-based inequality. Using Grenfell as an example, she explains why class discrimination falls by the wayside of both intersectionality and human rights law, and may need to be redressed on its own terms. Her intervention argues for a paradigm of addressing class discrimination not as subsumed within intersectionality, or individual human rights like the right to housing or the right to life and security, but as self-standing and complementing these other paradigms to prevent grave violations like Grenfell.

In Chapter 6, Fiona de Londras provides us with an extraordinary view of the dynamics of intersectionality praxis. Through the example of the 'Repeal the 8th' campaign for reforming abortion laws in Ireland, she gives a rare instance in which intersectionality became the fulcrum of solidarity amongst different groups. But this apparent moment of solidarity for transformative politics did not seem to translate into a transformative law which appreciated intersectionality; in fact, trans and non-binary persons, as well as migrant women, have been pushed to the margins of law reform. How then could one bridge the divide between successful intersectional campaigning in social movements on the one hand, and human rights laws and policies which emerge as a result of those campaigns and social movements, on the other? De Londras explores these questions in a deeply reflective contribution based on her own involvement with abortion law reform in Ireland.

In Chapter 7, Meghan Campbell continues with the theme of reproductive justice and explores how the right to sexual and reproductive health is actually experienced by rural women. In this final chapter, she argues that the appreciation of the complexity of lives of rural women matters in understanding their experience of human rights. She argues that it is particularly important to understand the intersectionality of their position as rural women in order to make sense of the content of rights and international obligations in their context. This chapter thus excavates the meaning of Article 14 CEDAW, which is targeted at recognising and redressing the position of disadvantage of rural women in accessing their human rights.

* * *

One of the threads running through the chapters in this edited collection is the realisation that intersectionality is ubiquitous yet latent in human rights discussions, even within the existing jurisprudence. Prominent cases such as *Brown v Board of Education*[38] can be read from an intersectional perspective as affecting the right to education not merely because of race, but perhaps because of poverty and gender too.[39] The implications of such a reading need to be unravelled for a better understanding of rights – their content, the interests at stake, the reasons for which they matter, the reasons for their violation, and their modes of redressal and possible remedies. Emphasising the primordial significance of intersectionality in this way consolidates the idea that intersectionality is relevant to human rights law beyond the individual and discrete questions of discrimination or as a matter of equalising access to or enjoyment of rights. Intersectionality appears to be central to these, but also widely to all other issues of human rights.

Yet what is this intersectionality being referred to throughout? It would be useful to say a bit more about intersectionality itself and the way in which the central insights of this book may impact intersectionality scholarship at large. The understanding of intersectionality employed by each of the authors is distinct in emphasis but united in its thrust. Thus, the starting point, in implicit or explicit ways, is the canonical text of Crenshaw from 1989, especially the traffic metaphor:

> Consider an analogy to traffic in an intersection, coming and going in all four directions. Discrimination, like traffic through an intersection, may flow in one direction, and it may flow in another. If an accident happens in an intersection, it can be caused by cars traveling from any number of directions and, sometimes, from all of them. Similarly, if a Black woman is harmed because she is in the intersection, her injury could result from sex discrimination or race discrimination.[40]

The traffic metaphor does not seem to enlist important concepts in intersectionality that are to do with systems of power or structures of disadvantage or, as Hill Collins describes, a 'matrix of domination' in understanding the implications of intersecting patterns.[41] It neither says much about what brings about intersections to exist in the first place or how they are dismantled, nor does it explain what the intersections themselves mean. It is thus considered to be a well-cited but ultimately incomplete reference for understanding intersectionality.[42]

---

[38] *Brown v Board of Education* 347 US 483 (1954) (US Supreme Court).
[39] See Sandra Fredman, ch 4 in this volume.
[40] Crenshaw (n 2) 149.
[41] PH Collins, 'The Difference That Power Makes: Intersectionality and Participatory Democracy' (2017) 8(1) *Revista de Investigaciones Feministas* 19, 22: 'The matrix of domination refers to how political domination on the macro-level of analysis is organized via intersecting systems of oppression. Heteropatriarchy, neo-colonialism, capitalism, racism, and imperialism constitute forms of domination that characterize global geopolitics, that take different forms across nation-states and that influence all aspects of social life. Intersectionality's emphasis on intersecting systems of oppression suggests that different forms of domination each have their own power grid, a distinctive "matrix" of intersecting power dynamics.'
[42] A Carastathis, 'Basements and Intersections' (2013) 28 *Hypathia* 698.

Yet, the metaphor does a lot more for the purposes of human rights law than one might imagine. It brings to fore the causal complexity that is at play in violations of human rights at the intersection for groups like Black women.[43] Its vivid description makes it easy to grasp the major uptake of intersectionality: that things happen because some people are caught in the throes of many disadvantages at once and in a way that it is impossible to gauge the independent impact of each. As a descriptor of causal complexity, the traffic metaphor is pithy and does an apt job in getting us started in thinking about problems in human rights law. In their individual contributions, Sandra Fredman and Meghan Campbell both work through human rights doctrine in comparative and international law, respectively, to see how this causal complexity has been hitherto undermined in even good jurisprudence which has served some groups well. But in undermining an intersectional perspective of rights, viz the right to education (Fredman) and women's reproductive rights (Campbell), both domestic and international law seems to have botched an understanding of the inner workings of human rights in terms of the complex processes through which they come to be violated.

The originating context of intersectionality – Black women in the US – and the literatures expounding their position inspire the extensions of intersectionality in human rights law to other disadvantaged groups in different geographical contexts. This is because this context is internal to the logic of intersectionality. It is difficult to imagine how intersectionality can be taken up otherwise without committing fatal violence to its transformative roots embedded in anti-racism and Black feminist struggle.[44]

Much of the forthcoming discussion makes use of intersectionality in specific and pointed ways not captured by a single manoeuvre. One of these is the reference to intersectionality's social justice and social movement roots in praxis. Scholarship often glosses over these roots which preceded itself; the interest of academia in intersectionality only succeeded what was already an established discourse in practice.[45] The nineteenth-century examples of Sojourner Truth, Maria Stewart and Anna Julia Cooper show that intersectional thinking was key to Black women's activism, even before the term 'intersectionality' came into existence. The fact that intersectionality continues to be wielded, from the Combahee River Collective in 1977 to Tarana Burke's original conception of #MeToo in 2006, makes it clear that intersectionality exists out there and beyond the text which defines its scholarship. Fiona de Londras' exceptional telling of the intersectional dilemmas in Ireland's recent abortion rights campaign bears out intersectionality's activist rendering most distinctly in this book. This rendering stays true to Patricia

[43] A-M Hancock, 'When Multiplication Doesn't Equal Quick Addition: Examining Intersectionality as a Research Paradigm' (2007) 5 *Perspectives on Politics* 63.
[44] See S Bilge, 'Intersectionality Undone' (2013) 10 *Du Bois Review* 405; B Tomlinson, 'To Tell the Truth and Not Get Trapped: Desire, Distance, and Intersectionality at the Scene of Argument' (2013) 38 *Signs* 993; VM May, *Pursuing Intersectionality: Unsettling Dominant Imaginaries* (Routledge, 2015).
[45] Collins and Bilge (n 13).

Hill Collins' formulation that intersectionality is broader than what it is imagined to be, even by its practitioners.

The contributions in this volume also pick on explicit aspects of intersectionality with a view to centring them in human rights law. For example, one of the themes in intersectionality has been its focus on transformation for social change, thus disrupting the intersectional dynamics of disadvantage that the discourse reveals. As Rita Dhamoon describes, intersectionality scholarship 'serves to not simply describe and explain complex dynamics of power in specific contexts and at different levels of social life but also critique or deconstruct and therefore *disrupt* the forces of power so as to offer alternative worldviews' (emphasis in original).[46] This view to disrupt is carried over into the field of human rights law. Chapter 1 thus interrogates the settled ways of justifying the universal basis of rights. In Dhamoon's words, it 'disrupts the normalization of what is seen as necessary, natural, and universal'[47] in human rights and instead refocuses attention on that which is yet more fundamental (intersectionality), but has hitherto remained marginal. It thus presents a worldview of rights from the standpoint of a world which is already complex as viewed through intersectionality, rather than a world where complexity is flattened out for the sake of universality.

The discussion in the forthcoming chapters also maps onto wider debates in intersectionality literature about *intersectionality* as such.[48] The tension between intersectionality's invocation of identities and its use of identity politics, and wider analysis of structures of disadvantage or systems of power associated with them, is one such area which straddles both the literature on intersectionality and its applications like the present one. Gauthier de Beco's contribution to resolving this tension in the context of international human rights law seems to be purposefully aligned in feeding back into intersectionality scholarship which impresses on a meaning that focuses on a systems-based understanding that is not all about identities per se. On the other hand, Colm O'Cinneide's chapter adds to this scholarship a rendering which has been particularly developed in human rights law in Europe: of group vulnerability. His trenchant account of the European social rights jurisprudence, which has developed an intersectional thinking through the lens of vulnerability, shows that pre-existing concepts in human rights doctrine (like vulnerability) can be mobilised in terms of bringing in new and urgent forms of analyses (intersectionality). This seems to thus serve not only human rights law, but also intersectionality – in being developed through its instantiations in particular discourses.

---

[46] RK Dhamoon, 'Considerations on Mainstreaming Intersectionality' (2011) 64 *Political Research Quarterly* 230, 240.

[47] ibid 241.

[48] Emphasis is Collins' in the original quote (n 9), which I take to mean an emphasis on the concept of intersectionality as such, distinct from broader debates and applications that fall under the umbrella of intersectionality studies as a field. This book is an example of the latter, though it touches on debates on *intersectionality*, as would any project that invokes the concept.

However, this is not risk-free. Geraldine Van Bueren recounts the difficulty in channelling all material concerns and inequalities, such as those related to class, via intersectionality. In fact, she reasons that no one solution may on its own attend to class-based issues in human rights. Class cannot simply be just a matter of discrimination or of a particular right like housing or health; a more layered, albeit intersectional, reading of human rights may be preferable instead.

This eclectic mix of engagement with intersectionality as an idea and its literatures thus defines the book's treatment of intersectionality. It desists from setting a fixed point of reference for intersectionality and instead works through its many renditions and concepts relevant to it, bringing out its full wherewithal in the context of human rights law. While this book does not aim to contribute squarely to *intersectionality*, it does hope to contribute to its meaning and relevance in human rights law by clarifying the terms of their engagement with each other. Following Patricia Hill Collins' refrain, we must admit that we are yet to fully understand the potential of the constellation of ideas that may define the interface between intersectionality and human rights law. This book hopes to dispatch some of them and perhaps act as a conduit to others in the future.

1

Beyond Universality

An Intersectional Justification of Human Rights

SHREYA ATREY

Introduction

Where, after all, do universal rights begin? In small places, close to home – so close and so small that they cannot be seen on any maps of the world. Yet they are the world of the individual person; the neighborhood he lives in; the school or college he attends; the factory, farm or office where he works. Such are the places where every man, woman, and child seeks equal justice, equal opportunity, equal dignity without discrimination. Unless these rights have meaning there, they have little meaning anywhere.

– Eleanor Roosevelt[1]

In a small but plush part of the world, Grenfell Tower had been home to 350 residents since 1967. The residents were, according to data published in 2015, amongst the top 10 per cent most-deprived sections in the country, nestled in one of the wealthiest neighbourhoods in London – Kensington and Chelsea.[2] When Grenfell caught fire in the early hours on 14 June 2017, not all could escape. Seventy-two individuals lost their lives.[3] Grenfell's victims were overwhelmingly poor, Black, Muslims, first-generation immigrants and refugees – many of them inhabiting all of these characteristics at the same time. Amongst those who died, 18 were children, including one stillborn infant. Seven were persons with disabilities.

---

[1] 'The Great Question', remarks delivered at the United Nations, New York, 27 March 1958.

[2] 'English Indices of Deprivation 2015', https://www.gov.uk/government/statistics/english-indices-of-deprivation-2015.

[3] The official number of deaths is believed to be vastly underestimated. See A Gentlemen, 'Scepticism Persists over Grenfell Death Toll Despite Met's Final Figure' *The Guardian* (16 November 2017), https://www.theguardian.com/uk-news/2017/nov/16/scepticism-persists-over-grenfell-death-toll-despite-mets-final-figure.

The number of women outnumbered men. People from 19 other nationalities lost their lives alongside seven white Britons and over 20 non-white Britons. Twenty-one were from Africa and 15 from the Middle East and Asia. There were also diverse professionals – artists, chambermaids, chefs, electricians, retailers, waiters, taxi drivers, lorry drivers and porters all among them.[4]

Tragedy, calamity and disaster could strike anywhere. Yet, Grenfell was anything but accidental. The local council had only recently (in 2016) renovated Grenfell Tower with poor-quality cladding. In 2015, it was warned that the fire barriers were ineffective and could put lives at risk. The Council instead chose to save £693,161 with cheaper cladding. But the demographics of Grenfell's victims are telling and the implication is clear: that those disadvantaged at multiple levels have cheaper lives still. Their rights to life, liberty, security, housing, family and livelihood are negotiable; their poverty, race, religion, gender, age, disability, nationality and employment status, determinative of their life conditions and in fact, the existence of life at all.

The charred skeleton of Grenfell now stands as a reminder of the hollow and despondent location where rights did not inhabit the homes and lives of its residents. A distant reality compared to that which Eleanor Roosevelt had imagined for universal human rights. How did that come to be? Why did rights have no meaning in the lives of the Grenfell residents? If rights are universal and guaranteed equally to everyone, how come the Grenfell residents so obviously fell through the cracks?

The Grenfell tower tragedy is a poignant example of how the diversity of human lives bears on the experience of universal human rights. Poverty, race, religion, gender, age, disability, nationality, employment status etc all played a part in how the panoply of rights of the Grenfell residents – to life, liberty, security, home, family and livelihood – came to be violated. How does one make sense of the relationship between the complexity of people's disadvantage and the violation of their human rights? Does human rights law, based on its universal values, have tools to capture and respond to the difference in people's experiences of rights? Can intersectionality help in this quest?

This chapter explores these questions. It seeks to square the emphasis on the universality of human rights with the rich diversity of the experience of human rights. It argues that the norms of equality and non-discrimination may be limited in recognising such diversity. Instead, such diversity, and its full complexity, may be appreciated via intersectionality theory. Intersectionality provides a framework for mediating the universality of human rights and in fact modifies the normative basis for which rights matter. This basis, referred to as 'intersectional universality', may in turn have a significant impact on human rights practice. It is argued

---

[4] M Rice-Oxley, 'Grenfell: The 72 Victims, Their Lives, Loves and Losses' *The Guardian* (14 May 2018), https://www.theguardian.com/uk-news/2018/may/14/grenfell-the-71-victims-their-lives-loves-and-losses.

that the most significant impact may be on resurrecting the waning discourse on causation in human rights.

A few remarks are necessary to clarify what this chapter is not about. It is not about the diversity of rights themselves. As such, it is not a challenge to the universality of the range of equal and similar rights of all persons around the world. Consequently, it is not about the oft-repeated challenge to universality – that of cultural relativism.[5] Instead, it is about the diversity in the experience of human rights based on different identities and conditions which define human life, but not necessarily cultures. It thus does not speak to the debate over group versus individual rights.[6] Equally, it is not about the universality of human nature or human essence as the basis of human rights.[7]

In fact, the chapter seeks to underscore the relevance of seeing human life aside of, or beyond, the fact of its common humanity because it has an influence on human rights, especially their justification. Even in the most homogeneous of cultures or societies, such difference can and will exist – there will be men and women; they will be of different ages; they may belong to many genders; some of them will be straight and others gay; some will be disabled and some not; and there may be several classes, ethnic groups, religions, languages, professions and political opinions which define them. What makes up common humanity are these internal differences. What difference do these differences make and how does the complexity of difference come to be reflected in universality once we accept it as the premise of human rights?

This chapter ponders over this rather discursive theme. It does not go into the specific ways in which specific differences are recognised in the form of the right to freedom of association, freedom of religion, collective rights, right to self-determination and so forth. The concern is more general than that – that rights, such as the right to life, which are general and non-specific, tend to remain at that level rather than relating to the specific identities, positions, contexts and experiences which breathe life into it. Defined in formal terms and confined to status-identities, the general guarantee of the right to non-discrimination also remains at this rather superficial level when it comes to recognising the full complexity and character of human life. The chapter proposes that this full complexity can be reckoned with as a matter of intersectionality. That said, the

---

[5] JAM Cobbah, 'African Values and the Human Rights Debate: An African Perspective' (1987) 9 *Human Rights Quarterly* 309; Y Ghai, 'Human Rights and Asian Values' (1998) 40 *Journal of the Indian Law Institute* 67; N Othman, 'Grounding Human Rights Arguments in Non-Western Culture: Shari'a and the Citizenship Rights of Women in a Modern Islamic State' in J R Bauer and D A Bell (eds), *The East Asian Challenge for Human Rights* (Cambridge University Press, 1999).

[6] C. Taylor, 'The Politics of Recognition' in A Gutman (ed), *Multiculturalism: Examining the Politics of Recognition* (Princeton University Press, 1994); W Kymlicka, 'Individual and Community Rights' in J Baker (ed), *Group Rights* (University of Toronto Press, 1994); A Buchanan, 'Liberalism and Group Rights' in JL Coleman and A Buchanan (eds), *In Harm's Way: Essays in Honor of Joel Feinberg* (Cambridge University Press, 1994).

[7] For the many meanings of universality in human rights law, see E Brems, *Human Rights: Universality and Diversity* (Martinus Nijhoff Publishers, 2001).

chapter is not an exposition of intersectionality theory or its defences per se.[8] There is little space here to engage with the vast breadth of what has come to be 'a field of intersectionality studies'.[9] The immediate purpose of enlisting intersectionality here is to exhume it in human rights law by going beyond its invocation in the vastly important but limited site of discrimination law. More specifically, the purpose is to have intersectionality speak directly to the theory of human rights in terms of conceiving universal human rights as they are experienced by one and all. The references to intersectionality are thus going to be directed to serving that purpose. With all that, the exploration of the links between the foundations of human rights and intersectionality theory remains rudimentary, open to critique and amendment.

I. Universality

Universality, it may be said, is the first amongst first principles of human rights law. The Universal Declaration of Human Rights (UDHR) in 1948 opened with the proclamation that 'all human beings are born with equal and inalienable rights and fundamental freedoms'.[10] This was followed in 1950 by the European Convention on Human Rights (ECHR), which aimed at 'securing the universal and effective recognition and observance' of rights.[11] In 1965, the incoming Convention on the Elimination of All Forms of Racial Discrimination (CERD) reiterated the UDHR in that 'all human beings are born free and equal in dignity and rights and that everyone is entitled to all the rights and freedoms set out therein, without distinction of any kind, in particular as to race, colour or national origin'.[12] Soon after in 1966, the International Covenant on Civil and Political Rights (ICCPR) and the International Covenant on Economic, Social and Cultural Rights (ICESCR) both recognised the 'inherent dignity and ... equal and inalienable rights of all members of the human family'.[13] In fact, it would be futile to look for a human rights treaty which begins without echoing the commitment to universality in some form.

---

[8] Such accounts may be found in: S Atrey, *Intersectional Discrimination* (Oxford University Press, 2019); A-M Hancock, *An Intellectual History of Intersectionality* (Oxford University Press, 2016); P Hill Collins and S Bilge, *Intersectionality* (Polity Press, 2016); A Carastathis, *Intersectionality: Origins, Contestations, Horizons* (University of Nebraska Press, 2016); VM May, *Pursuing Intersectionality: Unsettling Dominant Imaginaries* (Routledge, 2015).

[9] S Cho, KW Crenshaw and L McCall, 'Toward a Field of Intersectionality Studies: Theory, Applications, and Praxis' (2013) 38 *Signs* 785.

[10] UN General Assembly, Universal Declaration of Human Rights (10 December 1948) 217 A (III).

[11] European Convention on Human Rights and Fundamental Freedoms (opened for signature 4 November 1950, entered into force 3 September 1953) ETS 5, preamble.

[12] United Nations International Convention on the Elimination of All Forms of Racial Discrimination (opened for signature 21 December 1965, entered into force 4 January 1969) 660 UNTS 195, preamble.

[13] International Covenant on Civil and Political Rights (opened for signature 16 December 1966, entered into force 23 March 1976) 999 UNTS 171, preamble; International Covenant on Economic, Social and Cultural Rights (opened for signature 16 December 1966, entered into force 3 January 1976) 993 UNTS 3, preamble.

But universality is hardly of preambular significance alone. Theorists have posited moral, ethical and political accounts of human rights based on universality. Human rights are described as 'rights that one has simply because one is a human being'[14] or 'rights possessed by all human beings (at all times and in all places), simply in virtue of their humanity'.[15] They are said to arise from the 'minimum fact of human origin'.[16] To call them 'human' rights is to 'characterize the scope of the claims being made, [that is] … to universality and a commitment to equality and non-discrimination'.[17] In fact, equality/non-discrimination is the corollary of universality. Recognising that rights rest upon common humanity, universality debars the denial of common humanity and thus any form of inequality or discrimination in the status of human beings as human beings or as bearers of rights. In this way, rights are guaranteed not just to all human beings, but to all human beings *equally*. Egalitarianism is thus an essential feature of universal human rights.[18] This is reflected in the preponderance of equality guarantees in human rights instruments. These take the form of the right to equality and non-discrimination proclaiming not only that everyone is entitled to all rights equally, but also specifically that rights are guaranteed to everyone without distinction or discrimination based on certain characteristics, often included in a list of grounds, such as race, colour, sex, gender, language, religion, disability, age, sexual orientation, political or other opinion, national or social origin, and property.[19]

Given that the history of the world is saturated with inequality, where human beings have been denied equal status as human beings and as deserving of equal moral worth and concern as another human being, the commitment to 'radical political egalitarianism' is believed to be 'a central achievement of the human rights movement'.[20] It is an achievement because in reality, equality was not in any way a given; it is the result of the process gone through by humanity and hence arrived at.[21] In Hannah Arendt's vivid words: 'We are not born equal; we become equal as members of a group on the strength of our decision to guarantee ourselves mutually equal rights'.[22] Yet, importantly for Arendt, equality is a constant reminder of

---

[14] J Donnelly, *Universal Human Rights: In Theory and Practice*, 3rd edn (Cornell University Press, 2013) 10.

[15] A J Simmons, *Justification and Legitimacy: Essays on Rights and Obligations* (Cambridge University Press, 2001) 185.

[16] H Arendt, *The Origins of Totalitarianism* (Harvest, 1973 [1959]) 300.

[17] J Waldron (ed), *Nonsense upon Stilts: Bentham, Burke and Marx on the Rights of Man* (Methuen, 1987) 163.

[18] A Buchanan, *The Egalitarianism of Human Rights* (2010) 120 *Ethics* 679.

[19] UDHR, art 7; ICCPR, arts 2(1), 26; ICESCR, art 2(2).

[20] J Donnelly, 'The Social Construction of International Human Rights' in T Dunne and NJ Wheeler (eds), *Human Rights in Global Politics* (Cambridge University Press, 2012) 96.

[21] This is a historical claim about the reality of denial of equality and the efforts made in actually having equality being extended and applied to all.

[22] Arendt (n 16) 301. See also K Booth, 'Three Tyrannies' in Dunne and Wheeler (n 20) 51–52: 'The point is that humans are not essentially born, they are socially made, and that human rights are part of what might make them at this stage of world history. We have human rights not because we are human, but because we want the species to become human.'

the difference and diversity of humans. The distinctiveness of their individuality and their condition is what is typically human about humans. For Arendt, 'we are all the same, that is, human, in such a way that nobody is ever the same as anyone else who ever lived, lives, or will live'.[23] On this view, the claim about universality is one about the equality of difference. Thus, universal human rights matter because they affirm both the differences in humans and the equality in the fact of such difference.

Arendt contemplates humans in their full complexity and more than *just* humans. She thus doubts the idea that human rights accrue to humans even when they are stripped of all other attributes and thus are simply nothing but bare humans.[24] This was particularly true in the case of Jews, for whom appeals to abstract humanness were worthless.[25] It was *because* they were stripped of all other attributes – their religion, culture and nationality – and thus rendered nothing but their bare selves that they became dispensable. To Arendt: 'It seems that a man who is nothing but a man has lost the very qualities which make it possible for other people to treat him as a fellow-man'.[26] For her, the differences in human condition, identity and life were significant in grounding human rights.

From a similar perspective on universal human rights, David Beetham considers that 'it is the negotiation of difference, not the assertion of similarity, that becomes the most pressing political imperative'.[27] Susan Mendus makes a related point about political theory and its role in grounding human rights:

> If we take social and historical facts seriously, then we may understand human rights as representing an acknowledgement of the contentiousness of boundaries and identities. Rights begin from the political and social realities of all our lives, and address problems about the forms which negotiation may take in circumstances where such boundaries are disputed, or identities fragmented.[28]

The important point is that this acknowledgement and negotiation of difference does not undercut universality. In fact, it changes the meaning that we attach to it, in that it no longer stands for homogeneity or sameness in the persons to whom it applies. Instead, it stands for the recognition that the fact that we are all so different from one another may itself be a unifying ground for equality for the application of universal standards of human rights. So, to reason backwards that universality implies commonality would be a fallacy. Ken Booth explains this analogy well: 'Just because an examination sets standards (for example, requiring certain

---

[23] H Arendt, *The Human Condition* (Chicago University Press, 1958) 7–8. This was strongly connected to her ontological claim about natality as the basis of the right to have rights; see P Birmingham, *Hannah Arendt and Human Rights: Predicament of Common Responsibility* (Indiana University Press, 2006).

[24] Arendt (n 16) 299–300.

[25] In Arendt's words: 'The survivors of the extermination camps, the inmates of concentration and internment camps, and even the comparatively happy stateless people could see … that the abstract nakedness of being nothing but human was their greatest danger' (ibid 300).

[26] ibid.

[27] D Beetham, 'Introduction: Human Rights in the Study of Politics' (1995) XLIII *Political Studies* 1, 2.

[28] S Mendus, 'Human Rights in Political Theory' (1995) XLIII *Political Studies* 10, 18.

minimum levels of grammar, logic and knowledge) it does not mean that every essay on Shakespeare has to be identical ... universal standards may indeed sustain diversity rather than the opposite.'[29] But following Arendt's logic, universality in human rights may not just sustain, but may itself be grounded in diversity.[30] The difference is non-marginal and can be appreciated in contrast with major liberal works in human rights. For example, in his influential account of universal human rights, Jack Donnelly writes that:

> Human beings are seen as equal and autonomous individuals rather than bearers of ascriptively defined social roles. Individuals are also members of families and communities, workers, church-goers, citizens and occupants of numerous other social roles. A human rights conception, however, insists that essential to their dignity, and to a life worthy of a human being, is the simple fact that they are human beings.[31]

Donnelly's reliance on 'the simple fact' of being human is noted frequently throughout his work.[32] He mediates this fact by admitting 'some degree' of individuality, because for him, 'basic moral equality of all human beings, once accepted, logically requires that each person be specially recognised as an individual'.[33] Yet, his difference thesis merely acknowledges that difference may be inescapable because each human being *is* different, but it does not treat difference as constitutive of 'the simple fact' of humans *being* humans.

In fact, Arendt's version of universality as embedded in difference remains an outlier in liberal human rights theory. The human in human rights has somehow 'flattened', as if the ontological facts of humans stopped mattering cognitively once they were incorporated into human rights. The theory of human rights has instead been arrested by 'higher' moral, ethical and political facts about humans, which seem to provide a better justification for universal human rights that are to do with dignity,[34] ethnical communities,[35] human interests,[36] human nature[37] or the idea of wrongs.[38]

---

[29] Booth (n 22) 55.

[30] Susan Mendus ((n 28) 23) shares this view: 'human rights are bulwarks against evil, borne of an acknowledgement of difference, not harbingers of goods consequent upon a commitment to similarity, whether created or discovered'.

[31] Donnelly (n 20) 80.

[32] Donnelly (n 14) 1, 7, 10 and 14.

[33] ibid 8.

[34] W Moka-Mubelo, 'Human Rights and Human Dignity' in *Reconciling Law and Morality in Human Rights Discourse* (Springer, 2016); L Valentini, 'Dignity and Human Rights: A Reconceptualisation' (2017) 37 *Oxford Journal of Legal Studies* 862.

[35] Booth (n 22); C Brown, 'Universal Human Rights: A Critique' (1997) 1 *International Journal of Human Rights* 41.

[36] J Raz, *Morality of Freedom* (Oxford University Press, 1986); M Ignatieff, 'I. Human Rights as Politics; II. Human Rights as Idolatry', Tanner Lectures on Human Values, Princeton University (4–7 April 2000).

[37] J Finnis, *Natural Law and Natural Rights* (Oxford University Press, 1980); SP Marks, 'On Human Nature and Human Rights' in D Hanschel (ed), *Mensch und Recht: Liber Amicorum Eibe Riedel* (Duncker & Humblot, 2013).

[38] K Booth, 'Human Wrongs and International Relations' (1995) 71 *International Affairs* 103.

Take another example of the account of rights offered by Rawls in his theory of justice as based on the principle that 'each person is to have an equal right to the most extensive scheme of equal basic liberties compatible with a similar scheme of liberties for others'.[39] The universal application of this principle is based on the equality of all persons, which in turn is conceived on the basis of them being moral persons.[40] The idea of moral personality is explained as 'characterized by two capacities: one for a conception of the good, the other for a sense of justice'.[41] Universality is thus premised on this equal moral personality.[42] Any deviation in the principle of equality and application of universal basic rights is based on 'the difference principle' according to which inequalities may be sustained if they benefit the most disadvantaged members of the society.[43] Rawls explains that these inequalities may be based on 'fixed natural characteristics', such as sex, race, culture, caste and ethnicity, which cannot be changed.[44] They matter to human rights only to the extent that they create perceivable advantage gaps and not in any other general sense. In fact, if differences in human identity and condition do not create advantage gaps, they do not matter on their own. There is no primordial significance of difference in Rawls' account as there is in Arendt's.

Griffin's five-step account of human rights grounds human rights in the idea of personhood as embodied in a functioning human agent.[45] This, in turn, is grounded in notions of autonomy and freedom because, for Griffin, they explain the fundamental human interests from which rights can be derived.[46] According to him, there is something objective, factual and hence universal about these human interests. He explains thus:

> [T]here is a weighty case for thinking that basic human interests are features of the world, and that these interests' being met or not met are goings-on in the world. One of our basic interests is in avoiding pain. In fact, our concept of pain is made up both of how pains feel and how those feelings characteristically figure in human life – that we want to avoid them, to have them alleviated, and suchlike.[47]

For Griffin, the quality of pain and our interest in avoiding it seems to be universal. One may ask whether the quality of pain suffered by women in childbirth is actually universal, given that a section of the human species (men) or non-child-bearing women cannot know this quality of pain or would even have a way of characterising it as 'pain', other than in an evaluative rather than an objective sense.

---

[39] J Rawls, *A Theory of Justice*, revised edn (Belknap, 1999) 53.
[40] ibid 114.
[41] ibid 85. See also ibid 11, 17.
[42] ibid 85: 'The nature of the self as a free and equal moral person is the same for all.'
[43] ibid 5–6.
[44] ibid 84–85.
[45] J Griffin, *On Human Rights* (Oxford University Press, 2008) 35 ('by the word "human" in the phrase "human rights" we should mean, roughly, a functioning human agent').
[46] ibid.
[47] ibid 35–36.

The concept of pain of such kind may be distinctive, and that difference *may* matter in avoiding and alleviating such pain. In fact, we know that this is true following the discrete demand for the recognition of women's reproductive rights and reproductive justice. Difference in status, biological or otherwise, may matter in how human interests are understood and, in turn, ground the idea of human rights, but in Griffin's account there is no possibility to look past this very abstract idea of interests (say, in avoiding pain) inhering in a disembodied (genderless) human being. For him, neither biological nor social statuses determine why human rights are granted universally and equally; what matters is human status as captured by the idea of personhood.[48] Charles Beitz recognises this in his own account, clarifying that 'a right belongs to persons "as such" if the ground or justification of the right appeals to features that persons possess regardless of their contingent relationships or social setting'.[49] Similarly, Martha Nussbaum's capability-based justification of human rights describes a human right as a 'claim that a person has, simply by virtue of being a human adult, and independently of membership in a particular nation, or class, or sex, or ethnic or religious or sexual group'.[50] Sen follows both Rawls and Nussbaum in grounding his own theory of justice in the 'notion of human rights [that] builds on our shared humanity'.[51]

There is nothing too surprising about these formulations. Such is the classical liberal idea of human rights, one which runs through theories of human rights to date. Waldron acknowledges the problem with this liberal tradition as one of abstraction. In response to the complaint that theories of human rights pay insufficient attention to the concrete features of human condition, he remarks:

> We are not the abstract persona of liberal theory washed ashore on a desert island where we can design our society as we please; nor are we astronauts stumbling on a distant planet with the technology to implement whatever principles of justice and right we agree upon. A plausible morality and in particular a plausible political morality must come to terms with the fact that we are embodied albeit thinking animals, vulnerable to each other and our environment, with conflicting needs, desires and commitments, living both in a natural world that offers limited opportunities for satisfaction and in a social world that is largely not of our making.[52]

Yet Waldron does not have much of a concrete suggestion as to how this abstract universal ideal of human rights is to be suitably modified. How are we to come to terms with embodied humans in theories of human rights? In particular, how are we to materialise Arendt's kind of universality in human rights according to which human rights matter *because of* the difference and diversity in humans, *not in spite of* it: that the humans of human rights are all singularly diverse and also equal in that diversity. What it means for rights is that although rights apply equally to all,

---

[48] ibid 34, 40.
[49] CR Beitz, *The Idea of Human Rights* (Oxford University Press, 2009) 4.
[50] M Nussbaum, 'Capabilities and Human Rights' (1997) 66 *Fordham Law Review* 273, 292.
[51] A Sen, *The Idea of Justice* (Belknap, 2009) 143.
[52] Waldron (n 17) 141.

their ontological reality as lived through humans is rather diverse. But then it is not enough to simply acknowledge the latter because it changes the former; diversity changes the basis of universal human rights such that diversity becomes the reason for which they matter and ultimately how they are conceived. Thus, diversity feeds back into universal human rights and gives it a new meaning. However, this feedback loop seems to be absent in the mainstream theories of human rights. In fact, the main route through which difference has come to bear on the general discussion on universal human rights is via the right to equality and non-discrimination. How far does it take us? Does it help us crack the Grenfell kind of plurality in human rights? This is worth considering.

II. Non-discrimination

To recap, the Grenfell problem is one of violation of multiple rights of those who were multiply disadvantaged. That there seems to be a link between the violation of rights and multiple disadvantages does not appear to be a stretch. So how does the discourse on human rights actually conceive the link? From the preceding survey, it is clear that the universal basis of human rights does not quite help to crack the issue. Human rights theory explicitly rejects the notion that differences between people make a difference to their human rights. But, more importantly, few except Arendt take human rights to be fundamentally constituted by the recognition of differences and plurality. It is one thing to recognise difference, but quite another to centre it in human rights. That said, some of human rights theory, especially the positional[53] and cultural[54] politics of differences, did develop as a direct response to the difference blackout identified in the previous section. This discourse, commencing in the 1980s and continuing to date, mediates universality to an extent. However, as this section argues, the non-discrimination approach does not treat difference centrally and is rather limited in addressing the Grenfell kind of complexity.

The central theme of the politics of difference discourse has been the rejection of formal equality or equal treatment as the natural disposition of universal human rights. Recognising that these conceptions of equality did nothing to address structural inequality between social groups, the proposal has been to 'recognize group difference and either compensate for disadvantage, revalue some attributes, positions or actions, or take special steps to meet needs and empower members of disadvantaged groups'.[55] Simply put, differences are to be redressed rather than disregarded.

---

[53] I Marion Young, *Justice and the Politics of Difference* (Princeton University Press, 1990).

[54] C Taylor, 'The Politics of Recognition' in A Gutman (ed), *Multiculturalism: Examining the Politics of Recognition* (Princeton University Press, 1994); W Kymlicka, *Multicultural Citizenship: A Liberal Theory of Minority Rights* (Oxford University Press, 1995).

[55] I Marion Young, 'Structural Injustice and the Politics of Difference', paper for the AHRC Centre for Law, Gender and Sexuality Intersectionality Workshop, 21–22 May 2005, Keele University.

The appeal to politics of difference came not from human rights theory, but from praxis. It came with the realisation that the general commitment to universality did little to actually guarantee the universal or equal realisation of human rights to those who were bereft of them. The evolution of specific discourses of women's human rights, LGBTQIA+ rights, disabled rights, children's rights and refugee rights exposed the 'built-in selectivity of the [human rights] regime'.[56] For example, the women's movement poured scorn on the international human rights regime based on the male norm, which ignored the interests of women in (until then) unrecognised rights, such as the right to sexual and reproductive autonomy, and also ignored the interests of women in realising the rights already guaranteed, such as the rights to life, liberty and security, in responding to issues of gender-based violence. There were thus two routes established for addressing difference: (i) the recognition of specific rights of disadvantaged groups; and (ii) the application of existing human rights to disadvantaged groups without discrimination. Both these routes have been pursued in specific human rights treaties concerning women, children, disabled persons and migrants. In the course of the former route, the human rights movement recognises discrete issues, such as gender-based violence against women, legal capacity and reasonable accommodation for disabled persons, child sexual abuse and displacement of migrants, as matters of human rights of these groups. New rights are inscribed and old rights are re-inscribed to be stated specifically from the standpoint of disadvantaged groups. In the latter route, the norm of non-discrimination is meant to be interpreted expansively and as a matter of substantive rather than formal equality already embedded in universality, to ensure that human rights actually apply to all, including those belonging to disadvantaged groups.

What is of interest here is that both the routes have been explored not only in the context of first-order disadvantaged groups (ie, concerning a single category of analysis such as race, religion, sex, gender, disability, age or sexual orientation), but also in relation to those belonging to multiple disadvantaged groups at once. Thus, the CEDAW Convention speaks not only of women but also of rural women and women in marriage.[57] The CRPD, a state-of the-art human rights treaty, follows a twin-track approach that speaks of rights of disabled persons generally throughout, and also of those disadvantaged specifically as women with disabilities and children with disabilities.[58] Moreover, it expressly provides that the general non-discrimination guarantee applies across a range of disadvantages and not just disability. In one of the most advanced General Comments to date, and perhaps the most sophisticated rendering of non-discrimination in human rights law, the CRPD Committee in 2018 recognised that: 'Discrimination can be based

---

[56] G Ashworth, 'The Silencing of Women' in Dunne and Wheeler (n 20) 259.

[57] United Nations Convention on the Elimination of All Forms of Discrimination against Women (opened for signature 18 December 1979, entered into force 3 September 1981) 1249 UNTS 13, arts 8, 14, 16.

[58] United Nations Convention on the Rights of Persons with Disabilities (opened for signature 30 March 2007, entered into force 3 May 2008) 2515 UNTS 3.

on a single characteristic, such as disability or gender, or on multiple and/or intersecting characteristics. "Intersectional discrimination" occurs when a person with a disability or associated to disability suffers discrimination of any form on the basis of disability, combined with, colour, sex, language, religion, ethnic, gender or other status.'[59] Non-discrimination thus assumes a rather more complex character now than was initially imagined. Yet, the non-discrimination paradigm is still severely limited in realising the full potential of the 'intersectional' turn in politics of difference. Before we turn to consider how intersectionality can be imagined beyond non-discrimination and more centrally in the context of human rights, it is useful to see why non-discrimination needs to be transcended first. Three lines of critique may be pursued: first, that the model of non-discrimination is essentially one which treats difference as irrelevant and not central to human rights; second, that it is primarily concerned with identities and not necessarily with structures of disadvantage associated with difference; and, third, that it is, in any case, not one fit to address material inequality.

At the risk of repetition, let us restate the positioning of anti-discrimination norms in human rights. In one of the more fleshed-out accounts of universal human rights, Donnelly explains it thus:

> The history of struggles for human rights in the following three centuries can be seen as leading to a gradual expansion of recognised subjects of human rights, towards the ideal of full and equal inclusion of all members of the species. Gender, race, property and religion have been formally eliminated as legitimate grounds for denying the enjoyment of natural or human rights in almost all realms of public life in almost all Western countries (and most other countries as well).[60]

This is an account of difference as irrelevance. It treats differences between humans, on grounds such as gender, race, property and religion, to be essentially irrelevant to the enjoyment of human rights. It takes difference into account, but in a rather limited way. Donnelly accepts that:

> [I]ndividual human rights do not presume atomized individuals, they do not presume either identical or merely abstract individuals. They are fully compatible with – and in fact regularly used to protect – individual and group difference. They simply do so in a particular way, relying on two principal mechanisms: nondiscrimination and freedom of association and participation.

> Individual rights approaches to group difference rest on the idea that group affiliations – other than membership in the species Homo sapiens – ought to be irrelevant to the rights and opportunities available to human beings. Therefore, a central focus is protecting members of despised or disadvantaged groups against discrimination based on group membership.[61]

---

[59] CRPD Committee, General Comment No 6 on equality and non-discrimination (2018) UN Doc CRPD/C/GC/6, [19]. The CEDAW and the CRPD Committees have made similar pronouncements previously, but none quite so precise in the definition of intersectional discrimination.

[60] Donnelly (n 20) 82.

[61] Donnelly (n 14) 46. This chapter does not consider the freedom of association and participation component in Donnelly's accommodation of difference. However, note that non-discrimination

Difference – individual or group-based – is thus accounted, only to be discounted. The assertion is that while difference exists, it *should not* make a difference to the enjoyment of human rights. Non-discrimination in human rights law has thus developed as a 'but for' consequence in the application of universal human rights law – that 'but for' a certain characteristic which distinguishes someone from others, they would not have suffered a violation of their rights. This is distinct from the difference model, which treats difference as the reason for which human rights matter, in that difference not similarity becomes not only the justification for why human rights are guaranteed, but also the reason for which their enjoyment matters. In the non-discrimination model of difference, which may appear to recognise at least the latter, the connection with the former (ie, human rights) is suspect. In fact, non-discrimination is treated as a human right itself and thus a distinct wrong which is not necessarily about human rights broadly. In this version, discrimination is a specific kind of treatment of individuals or groups 'because of' certain characteristics. It is not necessarily discrimination *in respect of* human rights. It need not be so. In fact, human rights law recognises both the version of discrimination as a specific wrong and discrimination in human rights in principle. Take, for example, the ICCPR which recognises the first version in Article 26 and the second in Article 2(1):

> Article 26: All persons are equal before the law and are entitled without any discrimination to the equal protection of the law. In this respect, the law shall prohibit any discrimination and guarantee to all persons equal and effective protection against discrimination on any ground such as race, colour, sex, language, religion, political or other opinion, national or social origin, property, birth or other status.

> Article 2(1): Each State Party to the present Covenant undertakes to respect and to ensure to all individuals within its territory and subject to its jurisdiction the rights recognized in the present Covenant, without distinction of any kind, such as race, colour, sex, language, religion, political or other opinion, national or social origin, property, birth or other status.

The Article 2(1) formulation does seem to draw an explicit link between discrimination and the enjoyment of human rights. And yet, the link is one of irrelevance where human rights are guaranteed 'without distinction' rather than in recognition of distinctions between human beings.

On the other hand, in the difference-positive version like that of Arendt, human rights are essentially affirmed in full recognition of the many differences between human beings. Such a normative basis alludes to the significant differences in the experience of human rights, without banishing difference as undesirable or irrelevant. It thus grounds difference to be treated more fundamentally in how human rights actualise: how they are articulated – to whom (all or to specific groups or attributes) and under which terms (universal or specific); how they are realised

---

and freedom of association are not the only ways of recognising how human diversity bears on rights. There may be others: freedom of religion, sexual harassment law, indigenous peoples' rights, self-determination etc.

for people situated differently (in terms of race, sex, gender, class, neighbourhood etc); how they are violated (because of the many differences in terms of how people are situated); and, ultimately, how they are redressed (that there are no universal remedies, but that the violation of universal human rights requires diverse and creative solutions). I will say more about each of these in the final section. But for now, it is useful to note that the non-discrimination version of difference does not quite provide a foot in the door for the kind of analysis intended along these lines.

A second criticism which may be levelled is that the understanding of difference in the non-discrimination version is limited to what may be called 'status-identities'. Human rights treaties construe discrimination in both its versions as prohibition 'on any ground such as race, colour, sex, language, religion, political or other opinion, national or social origin, property, birth or other status'.[62] The practice does not indicate that difference has been seen as anything much broader and as extending to other attributes of difference across humans – neighbourhood, socio-economic status, class, income, employment status etc. The problem is not, as discrimination lawyers would argue, that the construct of 'status' is limited to what are immutable characteristics, like race and sex, or those associated with fundamental choices of religion and marriage.[63] It is that, but more importantly, the problem is that discrimination on the basis of these statuses has been understood in identarian terms rather than in structural terms. This is reflected in theory even more strongly. Take, for instance, Joseph Raz's assertion that:

> Discrimination on grounds of religion, nationality or race affects its victim in a more fundamental way. It distorts their ability to feel pride in membership in groups identification with which is an important element in their life ... the right [against discrimination] is meant to perpetuate the separateness of the group. The important point is that the right is meant to foster a public culture which enables people to take pride in their identity as members of such groups.[64]

Allen Buchanan makes a similar point:

> The public recognition of one's equal basic moral status is threatened when one is treated in ways that, given the historical context, put one at risk of being regarded as naturally inferior in certain respects, where being naturally inferior in those respects is thought to disqualify one from participation as an equal in important social practices or roles, and where natural inferiority is understood as the normal condition of individuals of the sort of human being one is (as opposed to cases of impairment of rationality due to illness or injury, for example). To be regarded as naturally inferior – inferior by virtue of one's nature as a woman, as a person of color, or as a homosexual – is especially threatening because the assumption is that the flaw goes as deep as possible and is irremediable.[65]

[62] UDHR, art 7; ICCPR, arts 2(1) and 26; ICESCR, art 2(2).
[63] S Fredman, *Discrimination Law*, 2nd edn (Oxford University Press, 2011) ch 3; J Sealy-Harrington, 'Assessing Analogous Grounds: The Doctrinal and Normative Superiority of a Multi-variable Approach' (2013) 10 *Journal of Law and Equality* 37.
[64] Raz (n 36) 254.
[65] A Buchanan, *The Heart of Human Rights* (Oxford University Press, 2013) 90–91.

Non-discrimination may have many aims.[66] But as construed by Raz and Buchanan, it is seemingly about real or perceived views of people's identities: of superiority-inferiority, shame-pride, attachment-detachment, complete-distorted, significant-insignificant, free-unfree etc. While there is nothing wrong with this per se, there is little or no analysis of structures of power around which such dichotomous views take hold. Difference is not a simple point-of-view question, but really a question of structures which sustain those differences in substantive terms. Thus, the point about identities is not one of viewpoints because they are not freestanding, but are embedded in the power relations which come to define identities of religion, nationality or race. The point is that there are socio-economic, cultural and political disadvantages attached to some identities which cannot simply be considered irrelevant or reversed by positively affirming them in some intangible sense. Non-discrimination as a norm does not render identities meaningless or meaningful just by saying so.[67]

A final point of critique is of material inequality. Non-discrimination does not quite speak of poverty, class, socio-economic disadvantage, income or material disadvantage in any significant terms.[68] It may regard conditions of material inequality *within* the statuses it recognises (race, colour, sex, language and so on), but it does not consider material inequality to be relevant independent of other statuses. In fact, human rights as a whole relegates material concerns to socio-economic rights exclusively. Again, the implication is that material inequality is something to be addressed via the entitlements of education, employment, housing, health etc, but does not quite matter in and of itself in terms of how we conceive human rights. The mandate of the UN Special Rapporteur on Extreme Poverty and Human Rights, first established in 1998, does seem to bridge this gap by studying the impact of poverty on the enjoyment of human rights, thus seeing poverty both as a cause and a consequence of the violation of human rights.[69] Furthermore, this mandate is carried out to reflect the impact of poverty on disadvantaged groups, such as women, children, disabled persons, older persons, ethnic minorities and asylum seekers, seeing the complexity of and interaction between differences based on poverty as well as other grounds.[70] But beyond conditions of poverty or

---

[66] B Hepple, 'The Aims of Equality Law' (2008) 61 *Current Legal Problems* 1.

[67] Donnelly (n 14) 53–54: 'Almost all adults have multiple identities. It is for such real, and realistically complex, human beings to balance the varied roles and histories that shape their life. Such choices are, of course, conditioned, and thus in some (relatively uninteresting) sense not "free", but if equal treatment and freedom of association are effectively realized, those choices can appropriately be seen as autonomous exercises of internationally recognized human rights.'

[68] M Langford, 'Critiques of Human Rights' (2018) 14 *Annual Review of Law and Social Science* 69, 80; S Atrey, 'The Intersectional Case of Poverty in Discrimination Law' (2018) 18 *Human Rights Law Review* 411.

[69] See the mandate of the Special Rapporteur on Extreme Poverty and Human Rights, https://www.ohchr.org/en/issues/poverty.

[70] See the latest Report of the Special Rapporteur on Extreme Poverty and Human Rights of the Visit to the United Kingdom of Great Britain and Northern Ireland, Human Rights Council, 41st session (24 June–12 July 2019) UN Doc No A/HRC/41/39/Add.1.

extreme poverty, inequality itself has not been studied as a kind of difference that human rights should worry about. Both the theory and praxis of human rights show little engagement with concerns of material inequality per se and the difference such inequality makes to human rights in a Grenfell kind of situation. In Samuel Moyn's strong words, 'human rights have become prisoners of the contemporary age of inequality'[71] and it seems that the norm of non-discrimination, couched in formalistic identarian terms, is ill-equipped to address this charge in any way.

Non-discrimination as a human rights norm may thus be a rather limited site for addressing difference centrally – as fundamentally constitutive of the basis of human rights; comprehensively – going beyond an identarian view of difference and towards structures of power; and materially – in terms of the material or class-based inequalities. The question that arises now is whether the 'intersectional' turn in human rights conceives of difference any differently. The next section reflects on this.

III. Intersectionality

Somewhat paradoxically, much of the development in intersectionality theory can be viewed as a direct response to, or even a critique of, the politics of difference and identity politics. This is paradoxical, given that it too is part of these discourses and that both identity and difference are so central to intersectionality. It is useful to appreciate where the difference lies then. This is the aim of this section. However, it does not devolve into either providing a definition or an overview of intersectionality theory. Elements of the discussion below will resonate with the account I have previously offered elsewhere.[72] What follows is a more abstract inquiry both at the level of intersectionality theory as well as its connection with human rights.

For over 200 years, but more recently in the last four decades, Black women in the US, the first intersectionalists so to speak, have shown that the difference discourse has been too narrowly constructed to appreciate the full complexity of differences.[73] This theme unfolds in several ways. The main contention is that the way in which categories, such as race and sex, are constructed means that they include those solely disadvantaged by them, while excluding those who were disadvantaged by both at the same time. Thus, anti-racist discourse has concentrated on the position of Black men, while the feminist discourse has focussed on white women.[74] Neither discourse has considered Black women as

[71] S Moyn, *Not Enough* (Belknap, 2018) 6.
[72] Atrey (n 8) ch 2.
[73] Hancock (n 8).
[74] KW Crenshaw, 'Demarginalizing the Intersection of Race and Sex: A Black Feminist Critique of Antidiscrimination Doctrine, Feminist Theory and Antiracist Politics' (1989) *University of Chicago Law Forum* 139.

central to its movement. Intersectionality points out that difference in identity politics is seen all too narrowly – as unidimensional rather than one which appreciates how diverse differences based on race, sex and class come to intersect and combine for groups like Black women. This process of intersection and combination is described as 'the dynamics of sameness and difference',[75] which insists on seeing structures of disadvantage both in terms of their similarities and also, importantly, in terms of their uniqueness. Black women's position is thus to be construed in relation to both Black men and white women not only in terms of what they share with them as disadvantage based on race and sex, respectively, but also in terms of their unique position in relation to Black men and white women, as defined by their race, sex and class taken together. Accordingly, there is no essential core of the positions of difference (of Black men, white women, Black women etc); instead, the core is of complexity in the relationships of power between people.[76] Seen this way, there are no pure categories of difference, but only patterns of relationships defined both in terms of privilege and dis-privilege.[77] Furthermore, these patterns are seen not in identarian terms alone, as a form of positive or negative attribution of qualities or characteristics, but also in structural terms. Identity politics in the intersectional frame is thus 'interested in individual experience because it tells something useful about how people experience the systemic nature of racism etc'.[78] This systematic nature is comprehensive in terms of social, economic, political and cultural power differentials which inhabit the categories of difference. These categories of differences naturally transcend popular status-identities in politics and law, and reveal the blind spots in our analysis of difference, including those concealing poverty, class and material inequality.[79] Identities, broadly defined, are no longer mere signifiers *of* difference, but are constituted *by* difference, as a combination of racism, patriarchy, ableism, homophobia, transphobia, capitalism, imperialism etc.[80] They are broader still, and properly understood in terms of 'contexts of structural inequality, affective economies, ideological forces, history, social location, material structures, philosophical norms and more'.[81] They thus include the full breadth of identities, conditions and contexts which make up human lives. In fact, in her seminal work on intersectionality, Kimberlé Crenshaw uses references to 'identities', 'dimensions', 'grounds' and 'factors' interchangeably,

---

[75] Cho et al (n 9) 787.

[76] Collins and Bilge (n 8) ch 1; May (n 8) 27.

[77] T Grillo, 'Anti-essentialism and Intersectionality: Tools to Dismantle the Master's House' (2013) 10 *Berkeley Women's Law Journal* 16.

[78] Collins and Bilge (n 8) 75.

[79] G de Beco, 'Protecting the Invisible: An Intersectional Approach to International Human Rights Law' (2017) 17 *Human Rights Law Review* 633, 644. *cf* J Conaghan, 'Intersectionality and the Feminist Project in Law' in D Cooper et al (eds), *Intersectionality and Beyond: Law, Power and the Politics of Location* (Routledge-Cavendish, 2009).

[80] V Patil, 'From Patriarchy to Intersectionality: A Transnational Feminist Assessment of How Far We've Really Come' 38 (2013) *Signs* 847.

[81] May (n 8) 99.

all with the purpose of revealing how the 'social world is constructed'.[82] It is this purpose that guides how we see things, rather than *qua* the non-discrimination paradigm, setting blinkers of status-identities in viewing how the social world is constructed.

One can immediately appreciate that this rendition of intersectionality is in contrast to both the universality as commonality and non-discrimination as irrelevance paradigms. First of all, its framing of difference is central to our view of the world and our disposition towards how it is constructed, including our view of rights. In a state-of-the-field review, Cho et al explained intersectionality both in terms of being 'an analytic sensibility'[83] and 'part of a larger critique of rights and legal institutions'.[84] Both the disposition and the critique of rights are centrally premised on the treatment of difference as something multi-dimensional and all-pervasive. May describes this as a kind of 'insistence on recognizing ontological plurality in ways that do not slip into primary and secondary identities, or primary and second forms of subordination'.[85] It is not that humans are human first in an abstract sense and then, secondly, men-women, straight-gay, rich-poor, Black-white etc, and then intersectional in the third sense when two or more of the second-order identities collide as straight middle-class white men, poor Black gay women etc. Instead, people are only (but fully) seen in all their complexity in terms of their location and relationships with others. Much like Arendt, the only universality that emerges then is this complexity of difference revealed by intersectionality. We may call it intersectional universality. It is distinct from universality as commonality based on sameness in the status of human persons which runs through much of the traditional human rights theory. It is also distinct from the non-discrimination paradigm which admits difference as relevant, only to declare that it should not be so normatively or practically. Intersectionality's starting point is on the ground, here and now, like Arendt, taking off from ontological plurality and treating it as significant rather than flattening it out. It does not treat difference as merely one that needs to be addressed via non-discrimination, ie, as a prohibition on serving as a basis of distinction. Difference is not merely one which can (should) be declared away. If we recognise that difference is complex (intersectional) and embedded in the world, and in fact constitutes the world, then such recognition furnishes a different basis in normative terms. Human rights thus come to matter from this normative standpoint. The fact that this position is ontologically inspired should make it no less compelling as a basis for theorisation. In fact, it is based on the recognition of ontological plurality as much as it is based on the appreciation of ontological similarities. In any case, it does not deny that there *are* similarities across individuals and groups, especially in their *humanness*.

---

[82] KW Crenshaw, 'Mapping the Margins: Intersectionality, Identity Politics, and Violence against Women of Color' (1991) 43 *Stanford Law Review* 1241, 1245.
[83] Cho et al (n 9) 795.
[84] ibid 791.
[85] May (n 8) 40.

All it asks for is that the social world be understood both in terms of sameness and difference simultaneously and comprehensively. Universality rests on the appreciation of this dynamic.[86]

What are the implications of this rendering on human rights? In other words, what difference does the modification of universality into intersectional universality make to human rights in concrete terms?

It appears that intersectional universality has some very obvious and direct implications on human rights. First and foremost, a different (intersectional) basis of why human rights matter changes the basis for which rights are realised or violated. If the human in human rights refers to the complex ways in which humans are constituted socially in terms of their many identities, conditions and contexts, then it becomes important to see how rights transpire as a matter of this intersectional reality – ie, how does intersectionality affect the realisation or violation of rights? It makes us ask when rights are realised or violated, if that depends on the relative privilege or dis-privilege attached to identities of race, sex, sexual orientation, religion, disability, age etc, or the conditions in which people live (of poverty, material inequality, climate crisis, civil war, asylum seeking, etc) and the different contexts in which they find themselves, of the laws that apply, the social norms which bind them, the neighbourhoods in which they live etc. It makes us look for the totality of intersectional reality of human life rather than just one characteristic of people's lives or just one status-identity as non-discrimination would have it. This totality explicates a much more complex understanding of the causality of realisation or violation of human rights. For example, in the case of Grenfell, intersectionality would find any of the many avowed 'causes' of the Grenfell fire unsatisfactory – austerity, indifference, incompetence or negligence. It would instead have us look within these phenomena and ask what conditions of austerity, indifference or incompetence of the state, or the downright negligence of authorities in respecting human rights, such as the right to life, liberty and security and the right to private and family life or the right to housing, have to do with *whose* rights are at stake. It would thus have us appreciate the difference between Grenfell residents and those in similar housing conditions, and others who escape such conditions in terms of their poverty, race, religion, gender, age, disability, nationality, employment status and neighbourhood. Rights thus come to reflect reality in a far more real and grounded way, not only when they are realised, but especially when they are violated. To know more about either is a particularly important thing for human rights practice. Causation has always been a weak point in human

---

[86] A similar argument about 'qualified universalism' is offered by Johanna Bond in the context of women's human rights; see J Bond, 'International Intersectionality: A Theoretical and Pragmatic Exploration of Women's International Human Rights Violations' (2003) 52 *Emory Law Journal* 71; JE Bond, 'Intersecting Identities and Human Rights: The Example of Romani Women's Reproductive Rights' (2004) 5 *Georgetown Journal of Gender and the Law* 897. See also another version of qualified universalism in the context of cultural relativism in D Otto, 'Rethinking the Universality of Human Rights Law' (1997) 29 *Columbia Human Rights Law Review* 1.

rights.[87] The investigation of the reason(s) why human rights violations occur is often terminated at the level of liability, ie, whether an action or omission which leads to a violation can be attributed to the state. The 'root causes' inquiry in the mandates of many UN special procedures goes a little further in connecting violations to poverty and discrimination.[88] However, in Susan Marks' estimation, this too falls short because the:

> [A]ttention is directed at abuses, but not at the vulnerabilities that expose people to those abuses. Or there is discussion of vulnerabilities, but not of the conditions that engender and sustain those vulnerabilities. Or the focus is turned to the conditions that engender and sustain vulnerabilities, but not to the larger framework within which those conditions are systematically reproduced.[89]

The shortcoming can be attributed to the non-discrimination paradigm, which sees identities distinctly, unidimensionally and often formally. Even if the root causes literature seeks to transcend these limitations with a substantive version of non-discrimination, the paradigm is still of non-discrimination, of distinct abuses which take the form of treatment meted out *because of* certain characteristics. The paradigm is hardly one which interrogates structures per se and their impact on the enjoyment of human rights generally. Marks' suggestion is to move to a 'planned misery' inquiry on causation which interrogates the logic of particular socio-economic arrangements that give rise to human rights violations.[90] Intersectionality may allow for the logic to be comprehensively interrogated in terms of the full complexity of particular socio-economic arrangements between individuals and groups and across a range of variables.

This may matter significantly to the idea of indivisibility of human rights. Seeing human rights as a function of intersectionality allows us to see human rights as a whole.[91] This is because in intersectional terms, when humans experience rights through the full complexity of their identities, conditions and contexts, they experience rights as a whole and not as discrete packets of entitlements of life, liberty, security, privacy, education, employment, housing, healthcare etc. The experience of an individual right is mediated through other rights. For instance, in the case of Grenfell, intersectionality would have us appreciate that there is no point in delineating interests in safe housing or the enjoyment of family and private life from interests in the right to life per se; the realisation of one involves the simultaneous realisation of all and the violation of one cannot be disconnected from others. The reason for this is that it is the same intersectional dynamics which matter for each

---

[87] S Marks, 'Human Rights and Root Causes' (2011) 74 *Modern Law Review* 57.

[88] See, eg, Working Group on Women and Women's Rights, Background Briefing on Intersectionality (2001), https://www.cwgl.rutgers.edu/about-110/staff/70-policy-a-advocacy/cwgl-activities-at-the-un/197-commission-on-the-status-of-women-csw-march-2001.

[89] ibid 71.

[90] ibid 18–22.

[91] LA Crooms, 'Indivisible Rights and Intersectional Identities or, "What Do Women's Human Rights Have to Do with the Race Convention?"' (1996) 40 *Howard Law Journal* 619, 625–32.

right, even if differently, based on the particular interest in the right(s) involved. Thus, the intersectional position of Grenfell residents may have mattered equally in terms of securing a safe home as well as securing their life, including private and family life. But then the lack of secure housing could and did lead to the violation of the right to life, and the violation of the right to life led to the denial of the right to private and family life and home. The point is that intersectional dynamics cannot be disentangled and that they matter to all human rights equally and simultaneously. This can be especially helpful in bringing together rights, which are not explicitly recognised or are expressly denied, such as, in the case of Grenfell, the right to housing, which is absent in the particular context of the UK.

Insistence on intersectionality also means that the interest in each right is embedded in other rights and that the absence of one from the framework of rights does not quite exclude that interest from being considered as part of another right. Margaret Satterthwaite explains this as a kind of process where the whole gamut of protections is seen together at once in order to make sense of the obligations with respect to groups like migrant women.[92] The upside of this process is that rights which may seem to be excluded from one system of protection may be included in another and hence protected in totality. Practically speaking, given that every UN member state is party to at least one of the six major human rights treaties – the ICCPR, the ICESCR, CEDAW, CERD, the CRPD and the CRC – each treaty may be interpreted as situated in the recognition of intersectional universality and hence the relatedness or indivisibility of human rights.[93] Thus, the ratification of CERD in the absence of ratification of CEDAW or vice versa may not matter in terms of protecting the rights of Black women who may be considered subjects of both race and women's conventions, but also either of them. Slippage of the kind witnessed in Grenfell, of both intersectional positions (poverty, class, migrant status, employment status etc) as well as rights (housing) being left unrecognised, may thus become impossible in practice. Human rights become a single concentrated point of analysis for a good life, however defined, rather than a scattered collection of entitlements.

While the conception of a good life may be broad-based, intersectionality influences its meaning in at least one significant way. Intersectionality ultimately aspires to transformation or social change by dismantling the complex structures of disadvantage it reveals.[94] It does not necessarily imply that this would erase all difference in the world, but that such difference would no longer stand for disadvantage. People may still have different sexes, genders, sexual orientations, housing situations, living conditions, incomes, abilities, ages etc, and these

---

[92] M Satterthwaite, 'Women Migrants' Rights under International Human Rights Law' (2004) 77 *Feminist Review* 167.

[93] By the same token, it means that every single one of the eight billion persons in the world is protected under the international human rights regime. See AF Bayefsky, 'The UN Human Rights Treaty System: Universality at the Crossroads' (2001), www.bayefsky.com/report/finalreport.pdf.

[94] Cho et al (n 9) 786.

identities, conditions and contexts would define people's position in relation to human rights. But the point of intersectionality is to subvert at least those structures that impinge on the enjoyment of human rights based on these. These structures cannot be subverted until they are known. Therefore, intersectionality both provides the cognitive framework for understanding the complexity of these structures and insists on transforming them. This emphasis on transformation is one shared with the broader project of human rights, such that transformation, social change and global justice are considered to be endpoints or highpoints of human rights. Intersectionality helps track closely with them by showing that the achievement of transformation, change or justice is the opposite of intersectional dynamics which impinge on human rights negatively. This does not quite tell us *what* it takes to subvert those dynamics, but it sets the goal as the absence of intersectional dynamics which leads to the violation of human rights, while at the same time showing the kind of intersectional dynamics which do not impede human rights. This revelation may help in the crafting of considered and creative solutions to achieving transformation. This is because once we know the workings of human rights, ie, on what basis they matter (intersectional universality) and on what basis they transpire (how they are realised or violated in intersectional terms), we can work backwards in designing interventions to respect, protect and fulfil human rights. But without an understanding of the inner workings of intersectionality, we would not know the workings of human rights or how to steer them.

Conclusion

This chapter casts doubt on the accepted version of universality as commonality as the basis of human rights. It takes Arendt's distinctive version of difference as universality as a possible alternative and argues that it resonates with the kind of universality imagined in intersectionality. This rendition is called intersectional universality. It is argued that it modifies the basis on which human rights are guaranteed; not on the basis of commonality alone, but on the basis of having equally complex and intersectional lives which make humans *human*. Intersectionality views humans not only in terms of their sameness but also of the differences in the structures of power that define them, and both of them at the same time. It is suggested that the recognition of these dynamics may have a significant impact not just on understanding why rights matter, but also practically in terms of understanding how they transpire (ie, how they are realised or violated).

2

Harnessing the Full Potential of Intersectionality Theory in International Human Rights Law

Lessons from Disabled Children's Right to Education

GAUTHIER DE BECO*

Introduction

Despite recent efforts to capitalise on intersectionality, the field of international human rights law has not been able to harness the full potential of intersectionality theory. Intersectionality has often been interpreted in the field, *qua* norms of equality and antidiscrimination, as a theory of identities. It is thus divorced from the structural analysis of identity-categories that is at the heart of intersectionality's theoretical and methodological framework. This misreading of intersectionality plays into the way in which it is invoked in international human rights law as simply focusing on identity-categories instead of the structures of disadvantage associated with one or several of them simultaneously. This chapter aims to refocus on a systems-based understanding of intersectionality, with the aim of illuminating the lived reality and experience of human rights between different groups of people. This systems-based understanding of intersectionality involves balancing the attention to identities with an inquiry into the relationships of power that underpin those identities. The chapter thereby excavates what may be the actual significance of intersectionality theory for the purposes of human rights, especially beyond the equality and anti-discrimination model, which is often limited to focusing on identity-categories.

* The author would like to thank Shreya Atrey and Peter Dunne, the editors of the volume, for their comments and advice throughout the writing of this chapter. He also benefited from the opportunity to present an earlier version at the Workshop on Intersectionality and Human Rights Law organised by them at the University of Bristol School of Law on 14 November 2018.

With this, the chapter offers a way to unlock intersectionality theory's full potential, which is subsequently illustrated with the right of disabled children to education. It not only analyses disability in its various expressions but also considers its intersection with other characteristics in order to explicate the wide range of issues that result in disabled children's exclusion from education. Drawing upon the various provisions of human rights treaties and the recommendations of the United Nations (UN) treaty bodies, it shows how international human rights law's greater alignment with intersectionality theory could be conducive to strengthening human rights protection. It argues that the UN treaty bodies would then be in a position to address those human rights violations that are often left concealed and hence unaddressed.

I. Retracing Intersectionality in International Human Rights Law

This section retraces how the consideration of intersectionality has evolved in the field of international human rights law. It first explores how the field has engaged with intersectionality and then critiques its present engagement as too focused on identity-categories. It suggests that a correct reading of intersectionality – which has more to do with relationships of power than with identity-categories – may not only be preferable in international human rights law, but also be a more accurate rendering of intersectionality at all. It thus pleads for a systems-based understanding of intersectionality which could help realise the actual significance of intersectionality theory for the purposes of human rights.

A. International Human Rights Law

The concept of intersectionality stems from the recognition that discrimination on the basis of multiple grounds can lead to a unique and specific kind of discrimination, termed intersectional discrimination, which is different from discrimination based on a single ground. The term 'intersectionality' was coined by Kimberlé Crenshaw to explain the discrimination suffered by Black women, which was based neither on race nor on sex, but on both of them at the same time.[1] Intersectionality has since been commonly considered in the context of equality and anti-discrimination norms enshrined in domestic legislation. In international human rights law, these norms take the form of general anti-discrimination clauses,

---

[1] K Crenshaw, 'Demarginalising the Intersection of Race and Sex: A Black Feminist Critique of Antidiscrimination Doctrine, Feminist Theory and Antiracist Politics' (1989) 4 *University of Chicago Legal Forum* 139; K Crenshaw, 'Mapping the Margins: Intersectionality, Identity Politics, and Violence against Women of Color' (1991) 43 *Stanford Law Review* 1241.

such as in the International Covenant on Civil and Political Rights (ICCPR) and the International Covenant on Economic, Social and Cultural Rights (ICESCR). These general anti-discrimination clauses guarantee the exercise of human rights free from discrimination on the basis of a non-exhaustive list of grounds, including race, colour, sex, language, religion, political or other opinion, national or social origin, property, birth or other status.[2] The bulk of research on intersectionality has therefore been concentrated in the field of anti-discrimination law.[3] This research has identified both the theoretical and the practical problems of combining several grounds of discrimination into one intersectional claim. On the one hand, there are theoretical problems like the question of finding an appropriate comparator (ie, a similarly situated group that does not possess the relevant characteristics as those invoked by the plaintiff).[4] Black women, for instance, differ not only from white men, but also from Black men and white women. Who then should be the relevant comparator on a principled basis in an intersectional claim brought by a Black woman? On the other hand, there are practical questions like a closed list of grounds available to a victim. Victims will pick a ground that is available and has the greatest chances of success.[5] Scholars have offered possibilities to resolve these problems, which include the use of hypothetical comparators and the role of positive duties in redressing intersectional claims.[6]

Intersectionality has also been considered in international human rights law beyond the prohibition of discrimination that has defined intersectional debates in the domestic context. Here, instead of concentrating on particular grounds, the focus is on specific groups that have a particular human rights treaty devoted to their rights, such as women, children and disabled people. The so-called group-specific human rights treaties not only prohibit discrimination against

[2] International Covenant on Civil and Political Rights, 1966, 999 UNTS 171, art 2(1); International Covenant on Economic, Social and Cultural Rights, 1966, 993 UNTS 3, art 2(2). The ICCPR also has a provision prohibiting discrimination beyond the enjoyment of the rights protected by the Covenant (art 26).

[3] D Schiek and A Lawson (eds), *European Union Non-discrimination Law and Intersectionality: Investigating the Triangle of Racial, Gender and Disability Discrimination* (Ashgate, 2011); D Schiek and V Chege (eds), *European Union Non-discrimination Law: Comparative Perspectives on Multidimensional Equality Law* (Routledge-Cavendish, 2009).

[4] E Ellis and P Watson, *EU Anti-discrimination law* (Oxford University Press, 2012) 156.

[5] J Milner, 'EU Equality Law: From Protecting "Groups" to Protection of All' in JE Wetzel (ed), *The EU as a Global Player in the Field of Human Rights Law* (Routledge, 2014) 213, 222; R Kahn Best et al, 'Multiple Disadvantages: An Empirical Test of Intersectionality Theory in EEO Litigation' (2011) 45 *Law & Society Review* 991, 1019; European Commission, *Tackling Multiple Discrimination: Practices, Policies and Laws* (Luxembourg, Office for Official Publications of the European Communities, 2007) 21.

[6] D Schiek, L Waddington and M Bell, *Cases, Materials and Text on National, Supranational and International Non-discrimination Law: Ius Commune Casebooks for the Common Law of Europe* (Hart Publishing, 2007) 218–22; M Jonker and S Halrynjo, 'Multidimensional Discrimination in Judicial Practice: A Legal Comparison between Denmark, Norway, Sweden and the Netherlands' (2014) 34 *Netherlands Quarterly of Human Rights* 408, 422–28; V Chege, 'The European Union Anti-discrimination Directives and European Union Equality Law: The Case of Multi-dimensional Discrimination' (2012) 13 *ERA Forum* 275, 288; K Koldinska, 'EU Non-discrimination Law and Policies in Reaction to Intersectional Discrimination against Roma Women in Central and Eastern Europe' in Schiek and Lawson (n 3) 241, 253–54.

such groups, but also provide both general and specific human rights to those groups. These human rights treaties include the Convention on the Elimination of All Forms of Discrimination against Women (CEDAW), the Convention on the Rights of the Child (CRC) and the Convention on the Rights of Persons with Disabilities (CRPD).[7] There are thus separate human rights regimes put in place for women, children and disabled people. However, this has contributed to a fragmentation of norms across the range of human rights treaties; no norm across these treaties seems to indicate forthrightly the obligations that states have towards those who fall within the remit of several of these treaties. The question spurred by intersectionality is how does international human rights law work for those who belong to two or more of these (and other) groups?

Research on this question in the field of international human rights law initially concentrated on the intersection of gender and race.[8] More recently, it has expanded to the consideration of difficulties faced by the UN treaty bodies in handling intra-group differences and inter-group similarities.[9] However, individual treaty bodies have had to work primarily with the specific group protected by the corresponding human rights treaty. This approach is still too limiting in terms of realising intersectionality theory[10] and, in practice, not expanding beyond the grounds of gender and race.[11] In order to pay attention to intra-group differences and inter-group similarities, it is nonetheless possible to apply human rights treaties in combination for protecting those belonging to more than one group at once.[12] This is particularly possible with a systems-based understanding of intersectionality as it was originally conceived in intersectionality theory and will be highlighted throughout this chapter. But before we consider this possibility, it is important to first justify the need for such a move – ie, in what way does this reading of intersectionality go beyond or improve the current group-based practice of the UN treaty bodies?

---

[7] Convention on the Rights of the Child, 1989, 1577 UNTS 3; Convention on the Rights of Persons with Disabilities, 2006, 46 ILM 443.

[8] C Ida Ravnbøl, 'The Human Rights of Minority Women: Romani Women's Rights from a Perspective on International Human Rights Law and Politics' (2010) 17 *International Journal on Minority and Group Rights* 1; A Vakulenko, 'Gender and International Human Rights Law: The Intersectionality Agenda' in S Joseph and A McBeth (eds), *Research Handbook on International Human Rights Law* (Edward Elgar, 2010) 97; N Yuval-Davis, 'Intersectionality and Feminist Politics' (2006) 13 *European Journal of Women's Studies* 193; J Bond, 'International Intersectionality: A Theoretical and Pragmatic Exploration of Women's International Human Rights Violations' (2003) 52 *Emory Law Journal* 71; M Satterthwaite, 'Crossing Borders, Claiming Rights: Using Human Rights Law to Empower Women Migrant Workers' (2005) 8 *Yale Human Rights & Development Law Journal* 1.

[9] PY Chow, 'Has Intersectionality Reached its Limits? Intersectionality in the UN Human Rights Treaty Body Practice and the Issue of Ambivalence' (2006) 19 *Human Rights Law Review* 453.

[10] I Truscan and J Bourke-Martignoni, 'International Human Rights Law and Intersectional Discrimination' (2016) 16 *Equal Rights Review* 103, 107–08.

[11] B Smith, 'Intersectional Discrimination and Substantive Equality: A Comparative and Theoretical Perspective' (2016) 16 *Equal Rights Review* 73, 73–74.

[12] G de Beco, 'Protecting the Invisible: An Intersectional Approach to International Human Rights Law' (2017) 4 *Human Rights Law Review* 633, 644–45.

B. From Identity-Categories to Systems

Intersectionality rejects the unidimensional analysis of identity-categories constructed along single identities.[13] Instead, it draws attention to power relationships that emerge from the social context in which those identities operate together.[14] To be sure, intersectionality does not reject the importance of identity politics in understanding how identities intersect; however, it goes further by highlighting how such intersecting identities may bring about disadvantages that transcend those identities.

UN treaty bodies have tried to overcome the logic of separate human rights regimes embodied in CEDAW, the CRC and the CRPD. They have done so from within the ambit of their corresponding human rights treaty, albeit also broadening this ambit in order to deal with categories otherwise protected by other human rights treaties.[15] The way in which the UN treaty bodies have approached intersectionality has therefore been to bring together those identities that straddle the main category along which they operate.

For instance, the UN Committee on the Elimination of All Forms of Discrimination against Women (hereinafter the CEDAW Committee) ruled that the absence of emergency healthcare for a pregnant woman of African descent was a violation of CEDAW in the case of *Da Silva Pimental Teixeira v Brazil*.[16] While the Committee noted that the pregnant woman had been discriminated 'not only on the basis of her sex, but also on the basis of her status as a woman of African descent and her socio-economic background',[17] it did not assess how the various identities through their interaction eventually led to her death.[18] In the case of *RPB v The Philippines*, concerning the rape of a deaf (minor) girl, the CEDAW Committee considered that the failure to provide sign language in court proceedings amounted to discrimination within the meaning of CEDAW.[19] However, the isolated consideration of disability, alongside the CEDAW Committee's complete neglect of the age dimension, prevented it from looking into the mutually enforcing oppressions at play. What has been missing is an integration of the theoretical framework of intersectionality into international human rights law going further than the current equality and anti-discrimination model where all the attention is given to identity-categories themselves.

---

[13] See in particular the critique of single-axis discrimination initially set out by Crenshaw in 'demarginalising' (n 1) and 'Mapping the Margins' (n 1).

[14] V May, *Pursuing Intersectionality, Unsettling Dominant Imaginaries* (Routledge, 2015) 112–18; P Hill Collins and S Bilge, *Intersectionality* (Polity Press, 2016) 95–97.

[15] de Beco (n 12) 657.

[16] CEDAW Committee, *Da Silva Pimental Teixeira v Brazil*, 2011, CEDAW/C/49/D/17/2008 [7.5].

[17] ibid [7.7].

[18] M Campbell, 'CEDAW and Women's Intersecting. Identities: A Pioneering Approach to Intersectional Discrimination' (2015) *Revista Diretio GV* 479, 488.

[19] CEDAW Committee, *RPB v The Philippines*, 2014, CEDAW/C/57/D/34/2011 [8.7].

This does not mean that the UN treaty bodies have entirely overlooked cases of intersectional discrimination. To their credit, they have both acknowledged that individuals may be discriminated on the basis of various grounds and responded to intersectional claims in light of these various grounds. Nonetheless, the focus has been on identity-categories which, when added up, may exacerbate prejudice against certain groups. The CEDAW Committee declared that discrimination on the basis of sex 'is inextricably linked with other factors that affect women, such as race, ethnicity, religion or belief, health, status, age, class, caste, and sexual orientation and gender identity' in the *Kell v Canada* case,[20] and again that gender stereotypes had been magnified through 'disregard for the individual circumstances of the case, such as the author's disability and age' in the *RPB v The Philippines* case.[21] While considering multiple identities, it has still neglected to investigate how these multiple identities are situated in interlocking relationships of power that result in infringements of human rights in a way that is different from just a matter of discrimination on the basis of the different grounds.

In addressing intersectionality, international human rights law has therefore essentially proceeded by identifying subgroups in need of protection through the aggregation of identities. Although critics have claimed that intersectionality theory encourages such aggregation, this theory does not simply seek to add up identity-categories or the disadvantages faced (or not faced) by the different groups to which these identity-categories relate.[22] By adopting a purely identarian understanding of intersectionality, the field of international human rights law has overlooked an important aspect of intersectionality theory (thereby replicating the misreading of intersectionality by its critics). It has failed to determine how the identities are connected to specific forms of oppression as these identities interact and intersect in multiple permutations and combinations.

Intersectionality theory points to the pitfalls of simply adding up identity-categories alongside the individual structures of disadvantage associated with race, gender, age, disability and so on. Such a reading of intersectionality misconstrues the structures of disadvantage as existing independently and thus capable of merely being brought together to reveal intersectional disadvantage. In fact, forms of oppression co-exist and intersect with one another, thereby forming a 'matrix of domination' which varies in time and space.[23] Intersectionality theory is a reaction against any approach that provides no more than a comparison between a number of categories and separates the different structures of disadvantage or simply assembles them together.[24] What is needed, with a view to replacing this approach with a proper reading of intersectionality, is an approach that better

---

[20] CEDAW Committee, *Kell v Canada*, 2012, CEDAW/C/ 51 /D/19/2008 [10.2].

[21] CEDAW Committee (n 19) [8.9].

[22] S Atrey, *Intersectional Discrimination* (Oxford University Press, 2019) 57–58; A Carastathis, *Intersectionality. Origins, Contestations, Horizons* (University of Nebraska Press, 2016) 140–42.

[23] P Hill Collins, *Black Feminist Thought: Knowledge, Consciousness, and the Politics of Empowerment* (Routledge, 2000) 228.

[24] L McCall, 'The Complexity of Intersectionality' (2005) 30 *Signs* 1771, 1787.

accounts for the lived reality and experience of human rights between different groups of people. Such an approach, it is argued here, should draw upon a wider systems-based understanding of intersectionality that exceeds the identarian understanding of intersectionality that has so far prevailed in the field of international human rights law.

This systems-based understanding of intersectionality should make it possible to get to grips with the forms of oppression that harm some groups disproportionally. These forms of oppression can again be due to disadvantages associated with a distinct identity-category or group, but they may also relate to aspects that appertain to different identities or that are unrelated to identities at all, such as poverty. Intersectionality takes all these forms of oppression on board. The human rights discourse, *qua* this understanding of intersectionality, would no longer revolve only around identities strictly covered by particular group-specific human rights treaties, but look for forms of oppression associated with identities that intersect with those already recognised in and across treaties. Intersectionality theory shows that the disadvantage suffered at the intersection of multiple forms of oppression is both similar to and different from individual forms of oppression.[25] It calls for an inquiry into the 'ideological structures in which subjects, problems, and solutions [are] framed'.[26] Instead of dwelling more deeply into categories themselves, it is social institutions that become the central point of analysis. These social institutions spread across a range of domains, from family, healthcare, employment and education to political participation and community life, from which individuals can be excluded as they possess certain characteristics in a given social context. In order to seek to capitalise on intersectionality, the field of international human rights law must move away from a preoccupation with the characteristics that are enlisted in human rights instruments and move towards efforts to see these characteristics as fundamentally infused with structures of disadvantage that shape the experience of human rights. The focus on identity-categories has impeded the consideration of human rights issues that affect those belonging to several groups at once. It misses the fact that the various structures of disadvantage are themselves a product of how identities are enmeshed and integrated to begin with.[27]

While the UN treaty bodies have been aware of the need to interpret human rights more consistently across the range of human rights treaties, there is yet 'the lack of cross-referencing among [them]', which hinders the actual pursuit of intersectionality theory.[28] However, this method of 'cross-referring' will not be enough by itself for intersectionality to be duly accounted for. If the field of international human rights law is to consider intersectionality in its true sense, there must be an interrogation of what this cross-referencing entails and what it is aimed at.

---

[25] Atrey (n 22) 38–41.
[26] S Cho, K Crenshaw and L McCall, 'Toward a Field of Intersectionality Studies: Theory, Applications and Praxis' (2013) 38 *Signs* 785, 791.
[27] Yuval-Davis (n 8) 193.
[28] Truscan and Bourke-Martignoni (n 10) 107.

This cross-referencing can only be meaningful if it helps raise issues which span across treaties and concern identity-categories relating to more than just one group falling within the remit of a particular treaty. Only such cross-referencing may permit intersectionality to be accounted for in terms of understanding and addressing multiple and crosscutting structures of disadvantage.

C. Operation

Some of the UN treaty bodies have spelled out how their corresponding human rights treaties relate to intersectionality. The Committee on Economic, Social and Cultural Rights (hereinafter the CESCR Committee) has declared that individuals 'face discrimination on more than one of the prohibited grounds ... [which] has a unique and specific impact on individuals'.[29] By contrast, the Human Rights Committee has not gone further than recognising that different grounds can be intertwined,[30] while its approach, especially under its individual communications procedure, remains embedded in the unidimensional analysis of identity-categories.[31] The CEDAW Committee has issued several general recommendations on specific groups of women, recognising that women face intersectional discrimination.[32] It has also examined how gender issues intersect with other systemic issues of migration and family relations, amongst others.[33] In relation to disabled women, the Committee on the Rights of Persons with Disabilities (hereinafter the CRPD Committee) went a step further by recognising that individuals 'do not experience discrimination as members of a homogenous group but rather, as individuals with multidimensional layers of identities, statuses and life circumstances'.[34] It further defined intersectional discrimination, adding that it 'can appear as direct or indirect discrimination, denial of reasonable accommodation or harassment'.[35]

---

[29] CESCR Committee, *General Comment No 20. Non-discrimination in Economic, Social and Cultural Rights*, 2009, E/C.12/GC/20 [17].

[30] Human Rights Committee, *General Comment No 28: Article 3 (The Equality of Rights between Men and Women)*, 2000, HRI/GEN/1/Rev.9 [30].

[31] S Atrey, 'Fifty Years on: The Curious Case of Intersectional Discrimination in the ICCPR' (2017) 35 *Nordic Journal of Human Rights* 220, 221–22.

[32] CEDAW Committee, *General Recommendation No 26 on Women Migrant Workers*, 2008, CEDAW/C/2009/WP.1/R; CEDAW Committee, *General Recommendation No 27 on Older Women and Protection of Their Human Rights*, 2010, CEDAW/C/GC/27; CEDAW Committee, *General Recommendation No 18 on Disabled Women*, 1991, A/46/38; CEDAW Committee, *General Recommendation No 28 on the Core Obligations of States Parties under Article 2*, 2010, CEDAW/C/GC/28 [18]; CEDAW Committee, *General Recommendation No 25 on Article 4, Paragraph 1, on Temporary Special Measures*, 2004, A/59/38 at 78 [12].

[33] Campbell (n 18) 489–90.

[34] CRPD Committee, *General Comment No 3 on Article 6: Women and Girls with Disabilities*, 2016, CRPD/C/GC/3 [16].

[35] CRPD Committee, *General Comment No 6 on Equality and Non-discrimination*, 2018, CRPD/C/GC/6 [19].

The UN treaty bodies have also drawn attention to a number of intra-group differences and inter-group similarities. This attention has varied according to their willingness to consider identity-categories that relate to more than one group at once. These treaty bodies thus assume that the intersectional characteristics by themselves lead to further disadvantages, which they undertake to address through some irregular exercise of addition or multiplication.[36] While stating that discrimination is potentially more severe for people who possess such intersectional characteristics, they have stopped short of setting forth what that severity means or does to the experience of human rights; instead, they have relied on identities to embark on a repeated exercise of recategorisation. Although this approach attests to their commitment to take into account intra-group differences and inter-group similarities, it does not encapsulate that intersectional characteristics can generate co-constituted structures of disadvantage that are associated with two or more identity-categories at the same time.

What is needed is a more comprehensive approach that avoids groups of people being left out, rather than one that makes partial use of intersectionality's theoretical framework leaning excessively on identity politics. The CRPD has taken a step in this direction by declaring that different grounds can 'interact with each other at the same time in such a way that they are inseparable and thereby expose relevant individuals to unique types of disadvantage and discrimination.'[37] It thereby brought home the fact that any disadvantages regarding human rights may be intersectional and the structures of disadvantage be constituted by one another. In order to offer specific groups of people more adequate human rights protection, the UN treaty bodies should inquire into how intersectional disadvantage produces forms of oppression that an exclusive focus on identity-categories does not allow them to detect. The question is not only about the possible consequences of belonging to one or more groups, as these treaty bodies have envisaged so far, but also about shortcomings in social institutions that have the effect of ignoring the complexity of human diversity and difference.

The way to unlock intersectionality theory's potential in the field of international human rights law is therefore to relate human rights to whatever forms of oppression that can harm a particular group of people. The approach may translate differently depending on how social arrangements are designed to cope with these forms of oppression. Rather than revolving around a number of identities, the UN treaty bodies could lay out the obligations imposed on states to make society more sensitive to intersectional characteristics. The CEDAW Committee indicated that 'the convergence or association of the set of elements described may have contributed to the failure to provide necessary and emergency care', causing the plaintiff to pass away in the *Da Silva Pimental Teixeira v Brazil* case.[38]

---

[36] Chow (n 9) 473.
[37] CRPD Committee (n 35) [19].
[38] CEDAW Committee (n 16) [4.11].

However, while it concluded that she has been discriminated against on the basis of different grounds, it did not explain that this was the *result* of the interaction of identities and, additionally, it did not mention 'intersectional discrimination'.[39] While the Committee recommended that judicial proceedings be 'conducted in an impartial and fair manner and free from prejudices or stereotypical notions regarding the victim's gender, age and disability' in the *RPB v The Philippines* case,[40] it similarly limited itself to considering separately the individual structures of disadvantage and ended up over-emphasising some of them at the expense of others.[41]

A proper reading of intersectionality does not call for the simple acceptance of intra-group differences and inter-group similarities; it requires highlighting the steps to be taken in order to mitigate the disadvantages that intersecting identities may intensify. Thus, it is about reflecting upon a range of identities that correlate to co-constituted structures of disadvantage associated with them. States must be urged to both break down the relationships of power and cater for specific forms of oppression that are due to the sharing of these intersecting identities. How this could be done is shown below through an examination of disabled children's right to education.

II. Disabled Children in Education

This section examines the intersectional issues raised in the context of the education of disabled children. After considering the intersectional position of disabled children in the field of international human rights law, it discusses how it bears on their right to education in terms, specifically, of the different kinds of impairments as well as the intersection of disability and other characteristics, like age and gender, which can exacerbate exclusion from education. It suggests that international human rights law could redress such exclusion from education through better alignment with intersectionality theory. The examination foremost draws on the two group-specific human rights treaties, which mark the boundaries of human rights protection in this context: the CRC and the CRPD. The section thereby aims to explore how far is it possible to look beyond the logic of separate human rights regimes established in international human rights law and, from there, to reach conclusions as to the real added value of intersectionality theory in the field.

A. Disabled Children

Disabled children are especially disadvantaged in society. While vulnerability due to young age is aggravated by another layer of prejudice for being disabled,

---

[39] Campbell (n 18) 498.
[40] CEDAW Committee (n 19) [8.9].
[41] Truscan and Bourke-Martignoni (n 10) 119.

age leads to an exacerbation of the image of disabled people as dependent and inferior. As a result, disabled children are surrounded by extremely negative stereotypes and are amongst the most vulnerable groups.[42] Their families also face challenges, as these children are particularly dependent on them.[43] As disabled children are defined both by their age and their disability, they are an apt example of how intersectionality has an impact on the experience of human rights.

Disability has its own specificity. It refers to a diverse reality and experience informed by the interaction of various kinds of impairments with barriers in society. There is even considerable variation within the different types of disabilities.[44] Disabled people therefore represent a very heterogeneous group.[45] Whatever is done in order to distinguish them, it is impossible to capture the phenomenon as a whole. This heterogeneity must then be put into further perspective, as disabled people (as any group of people) might simultaneously belong to other groups, such as racial minorities, women and children. Any additional characteristic will result in someone's disability intersecting with their race, gender, age or other identity in a particular way.

Disabled children fall within the remit of two group-specific human right treaties: the CRC and the CRPD. Adopted in 1989, the CRC provides for a whole series of rights attached to children. Adopted in 2006, the CRPD's purpose likewise is to 'promote, protect and ensure the full and equal enjoyment of all human rights and fundamental freedoms by all persons with disabilities'.[46] As the CRPD largely borrowed from, and expanded upon, the CRC (which chronologically precedes it), both conventions have some similarities. It is also worth noting the fact that the former has been ratified at an extremely rapid pace, with 182 parties at the time of writing,[47] while the latter has achieved almost universal ratification, that is, all countries except one.[48]

However, the two conventions approach disabled children from two different perspectives. The CRPD and the CRC each regard such children mainly from *their own* viewpoint of a single identity, which dominates the way in which they provide human rights protection to them, either as disabled persons first or as children first.

---

[42] UNICEF, *The State of the World's Children. Children with Disabilities* (UNICEF, 2013) 2, https://www.unicef.org/sowc2013/files/SWCR2013_ENG_Lo_res_24_Apr_2013.pdf.

[43] A Rimmerman, *Family Policy and Disability* (Cambridge University Press, 2015) 38.

[44] R Garland Thomson, 'Disability, Identity, and Representation' in T Titchkosky and R Michalko (eds), *Rethinking Normalcy* (Canadian Scholar's Press, 2009) 63, 69.

[45] T Siebers, *Disability Theory* (University of Michigan Press, 2008) 71.

[46] CRPD, art 1.

[47] See https://treaties.un.org/Pages/ViewDetails.aspx?src=TREATY&mtdsg_no=IV-15&chapter=4&clang=_en.

[48] See https://treaties.un.org/Pages/ViewDetails.aspx?src=IND&mtdsg_no=IV-11&chapter=4&clang=_en.

On the one hand, the CRPD is a human rights treaty that is concerned with disability. Recalling that disabled people are rights-holders, it focuses on inclusion into society and the promotion of independence. Its sweeping scope can be seen in its affirmation that disabled people 'include those who have long-term physical, mental, intellectual or sensory impairments',[49] while its Preamble recognises that disability is 'an evolving concept'.[50] Underscoring the point that such impairments 'in interaction with various barriers may hinder their full and effective participation in society',[51] the CRPD is viewed as inspired by the social model of disability.[52] While this view has been criticised,[53] as is the social model itself,[54] the social model remains a powerful tool to call for the removal of obstacles created by society.

The CRPD's particular attention to disabled children is evident from its provisions. While it contains a separate article on disabled children,[55] it also has a number of provisions highlighting issues related to age.[56] It further prohibits 'discrimination on all grounds'.[57] Yet, the CRPD does not recalibrate each provision with respect to disabled children. So, for example, although it protects disabled children against separation from their parents,[58] it does not consider the situation of families as such.[59] Similarly, while autonomy is one of the general principles of the CRPD,[60] it may be somewhat at odds with early childhood and does not entirely square with the relevance of age for disabled children.

On the other hand, the CRC is a human rights treaty that is concerned with childhood. It promotes children's wellbeing while stressing the role of families and communities in upholding their rights. It covers both civil and political as well as economic, social and cultural rights, thereby bridging the two sets of rights for the first time in a human rights instrument,[61] a move also repeated in the CRPD.[62]

---

[49] CRPD, art 1.

[50] ibid preamble.

[51] ibid art 1.

[52] R Kayess and P French, 'Out of Darkness into Light? Introducing the Convention on the Rights of Persons with Disabilities' (2008) 8 *Human Rights Law Review* 1, 21; P Bartlett, 'The United Nations Convention on the Rights of Persons with Disabilities and Mental Health Law' (2012) 75 *Modern Law Review* 752, 758–61; P Harpur, 'Embracing the New Disability Rights Paradigm: The Importance of the Convention on the Rights of Persons with Disabilities' (2012) 27 *Disability & Society* 1, 3–4.

[53] T Degener, 'A Human Rights Model of Disability' in P Blanck and E Flynn (eds), *Routledge Handbook of Disability Law and Human Rights* (Routledge, 2016) 31, 34–48.

[54] T Shakespeare, *Disability Rights and Wrongs Revisited* (Routledge, 2014) 21–23, 77; L Terzi, 'The Social Model of Disability: A Philosophical Critique' (2004) 21 *Journal of Applied Philosophy* 141, 152; J Morris, 'Impairment and Disability: Constructing an Ethics of Care that Promotes Human Rights' (2001) 16 *Hypatia* 1, 14; L Barclay, 'Natural Deficiency or Social Oppression? The Capabilities Approach to Justice for People with Disabilities' (2012) 9 *Journal of Moral Philosophy* 500, 520.

[55] CRPD, art 7.

[56] ibid arts 8, 13, 16, 23.

[57] ibid art 5(2).

[58] ibid art 23(4).

[59] Rimmerman (n 43) 85.

[60] CRC, art 3(a).

[61] R Brett, 'Rights of the Child' in C Krause and M Scheinin (eds), *International Protection of Human Rights: A Textbook* (Åbo Akademi University, 2009) 227, 229.

[62] G de Beco, 'The Indivisibility of Human Rights and the Convention on the Rights of Persons with Disabilities' (2019) 68 *International & Comparative Law Quarterly* 141, 149–52.

The CRC is the first human rights treaty to mention disability explicitly in its general anti-discrimination clause,[63] and, like the CRPD, it devotes an entire article to disabled children.[64]

However, the CRC has a number of drawbacks in relation to disability. It aims more at *protecting* disabled children against discrimination than guaranteeing their *inclusion*, which is often evaded on account of their human difference.[65] This then allows for a kind of separate-but-equal type of human rights protection. And even though it is more detailed than its equivalent in the CRPD, the CRC's separate article on disabled children refers to 'special care' and 'assistance ... provided free of charge, whenever possible', which implies that disability is only a matter of welfare and not of rights.[66] At the same time, some of its provisions follow a rights-based approach that may compensate for such weakness (although they do not mention disability),[67] including the requirement to 'provide material assistance and support programmes' in order to protect children's right to an adequate standard of living.[68]

Both the CRPD and the CRC together can help resolve some of the inconsistencies in considering the intersectional position of disabled children in the field of international human rights law. The CRPD upholds the view that disabled children are rights-holders, guaranteeing the enforcement of their rights via access to justice 'through the provision of procedural and *age*-appropriate accommodations' (emphasis added).[69] The CRC, in turn, pays attention to parental involvement in the realisation of children's rights. This includes 'appropriate assistance to parents ... and services for the care of children',[70] which speaks to the reality that families of disabled children often experience poverty.[71] Nonetheless, the CRC does not recognise inclusion for its own sake, whereas inclusion is one of the CRPD's general principles.[72] The CRC's definition of the child as being 'every human being below the age of eighteen' also contrasts with the more dynamic approach to defining disability in the CRPD.[73] In view of this, it has been suggested that the social model of disability could enrich the CRC's understanding of childhood and contribute to discerning disability's intersection with age in more than just medicalised or

---

[63] CRC, art 2(1).

[64] ibid art 23.

[65] M Sabatello, 'Children with Disabilities: A Critical Appraisal' (2013) 21 *International Journal of Children's Rights* 464, 469–70.

[66] CRC, art 23(2)–(3).

[67] G Quinn and T Degener, *The Current Use and Future Potential of United Nations Human Rights Instruments in the Context of Disability* (UN, 2002) 196–97.

[68] CRC, art 27(3).

[69] CRPD, art 13(2).

[70] CRC, art 18(2).

[71] UNICEF (n 42) 13–14; World Health Organization (WHO), *World Report on Disability* (WHO, 2011) 39.

[72] CRPD, art 3(c).

[73] CRC, art 1.

biological terms.[74] In any case, neither the CRPD nor the CRC seems to provide complete protection for disabled children whose interests may be well served by both – but only in parts. A joint, intersectional reading of the CRPD and the CRC may cover this gap in protection and in fact provide for more protection than is currently afforded under each independently. The right to education helps explore how this could be done.

B. Exclusion from Education

The right to education is recognised by several human rights treaties in addition to the UDHR.[75] While it is generally protected by both the CRC and the ICESCR,[76] the CRPD specifically focuses on disabled people's right to education. Article 24 stipulates that: 'With a view to realizing this right without discrimination … States Parties shall ensure an inclusive education system at all levels and life long learning.'[77] Despite initial disagreement on the matter, the CRPD's drafters endorsed the goal of inclusive education for all disabled people.[78] Even though the CRC does not explicitly consider disability in relation to education, the Committee on the Rights of the Child (hereinafter the CRC Committee) also recognised that '[i]nclusive education should be the goal of educating [disabled children]'.[79] In order to achieve inclusive education, the CRPD further provides that states parties must ensure that disabled children can 'access an inclusive, quality and free primary education and secondary education … [and] … receive the support required, within the general education system, to facilitate their effective education'.[80] Besides provisions that specifically consider age-related issues, Article 24 of the Convention is probably the most relevant provision for disabled children in the entire Convention.[81] As a result, an examination of the right to education of disabled children may shed light on what a correct reading of intersectionality could offer in terms of enhanced human rights protection.

Disabled children's right to education provides an example of how a particular domain – that is, in this case, education – perpetuates marginalisation and

---

[74] R Sandland, 'A Clash of Conventions? Participation, Power and the Rights of Disabled Children' (2017) 5 *Social Inclusion* 93, 97.
[75] UN General Assembly, *Universal Declaration of Human Rights*, 1948, 217 A (III), art 26.
[76] ICESCR, arts 13 and 14; CRC, arts 28 and 29.
[77] CRPD, art 24(1).
[78] G de Beco, 'Comprehensive Legal Analysis of Article 24 of the Convention on the Rights of Persons with Disabilities' in G de Beco, J Lord and S Quinlivan (eds), *The Right to Inclusive Education in International Human Rights Law* (Cambridge University Press, 2019) 58, 64–66.
[79] CRC Committee, *General Comment No 9: The Rights of Children with Disabilities*, 2007, CRC/C/GC/9 [66] (footnote omitted).
[80] CRPD, art 24(2)(b)–(d).
[81] R McCallum and H Martin, 'Comment: The CRPD and Children with Disabilities' (2013) 20 *Australian International Law Journal* 17, 21.

disempowerment. It highlights the inadequacy of education systems in meeting the varied needs of disabled children, which results in their exclusion from education. This inadequacy is usually attributed to these children's lack of capacity, as well as the difficulty of offering them the support they require in regular schools or simply the costs involved in having more convenient settings and facilities for them.[82] For this reason, many children are referred to special schools where their needs can be met,[83] if they are educated at all. Thus, rather than removing obstacles to inclusive education, states opt for the segregation of disabled children. The question is why regular schools are unable to cope with such needs in the first place.

An inquiry into the way in which regular schools are letting disabled children down does not lie in dealing with the issue in the same way for all disabled children; it requires understanding how disability frames the life experience of disabled children and how their intersectional position creates structures of disadvantage that are unique to them. This involves examining both particular kinds of impairments and disability's intersection with other identities as well as other crosscutting issues. Such examination means appreciating disability both from the inside and from the outside. On the one hand, disability should be seen in its full diversity, given its multifarious manifestations, so as to acknowledge disabled children's varied life experience. On the other hand, its understanding should factor in a range of other issues associated with age, ethnicity, gender and socioeconomic background, which concern children generally but will affect those who are disabled in very specific ways in terms of how these children actually experience human rights. Although this examination takes a particular characteristic as the point of departure, it moves outwards from it to enlarge the perspective taken in the application of human rights treaties and sheds light on the structures of disadvantage associated with that characteristic and in relation to all others it intersects with. In the words of Joanna Bond, it explores 'all of the relevant human rights that are violated in a given situation along multiple axes of oppression'.[84]

Take, for example, autism and deafness, two kinds of impairments that pose very specific practical challenges to education systems. First, autism calls for strategies to avoid disturbing routines and drawing special attention to things that may

---

[82] D Anastasiou and J Kauffman, 'Disability as Cultural Difference: Implications for Special Education' (2012) 33 *Remedial and Special Education* 139, 143–44; D Anastasiou and J Kauffman, 'A Social Constructionist Approach to Disability: Implications for Special Education' (2011) 77 *Exceptional Children* 367, 380.

[83] Inclusion Europe, *Children's Rights for All! Implementation of the United Nations Convention on the Rights of the Child for Children with Intellectual Disabilities* (Inclusion Europe, 2011) 18–19, http://www.eenet.org.uk/resources/docs/6130.pdf; S Ebersold, *Inclusive Education for Young Disabled People in Europe: Trends, Issues and Challenges: A Synthesis of Evidence from ANED Country Reports and Additional Sources*, April 2011, 7, http://www.includ-ed.eu/sites/default/files/documents/aned_2010_task_5_education_final_report_-_final_2_0.pdf.

[84] Bond (n 8) 155.

be unsettling for autistic children.[85] Making an education system autism-friendly entails fostering a feeling of safety as well as offering children spaces to recharge. It also means adopting different approaches to education in order to facilitate communication with them.[86] Although certain forms of traditional communication will remain difficult for some of those who are autistic, complete ignorance of different communication skills will actually diminish any chance of inclusion. Second, deafness necessitates not only a mix of sign language as well as speech, fingerspelling, gestures and lip-reading training and provision for deaf children, but also the facilitation of all of these mixed methods with the purpose of enabling social interaction in general. This entails supporting both deaf and non-deaf children in creating an atmosphere conducive to social interaction.[87] Since those who are deaf often self-identify as members of a linguistic community, they view sign language as more than a tool of communication.[88] It is therefore imperative not to impose assimilation on them, but to favour communication in their preferred language more widely. As all these measures involve a balancing exercise that takes into account the entire school population, they pertain to questions that point to careful adjustments to be made across the whole of the education system.

Ethnic background, culture and linguistic particularities too may increase the level of prejudice against disabled children.[89] Consideration of these particularities requires building good relationships with families, who may themselves experience their children's disability differently.[90] Another relevant aspect is the mistaken attribution of disability to racial minorities, as testified in the over-representation of racial minorities in special schools. Alternatively, the under-identification of disability can deprive racial minorities of access to services.[91] The misconception of the cultural and linguistic particularities thus culminates in further exclusion from education. Gender comes into play as well, as boys suffer more often from such misconceptions than girls, especially regarding emotional and behavioural difficulties.[92] This lack of understanding shows how insufficient attention to the

[85] N Humphrey and S Lewis, 'What Does "Inclusion" Mean for Pupils on the Autistic Spectrum in Mainstream Secondary Schools?' (2008) 8 *Journal of Research in Special Educational Needs* 132, 137–38; S Lindsay et al, 'Exploring Teachers' Strategies for Including Children with Autism Spectrum Disorder in Mainstream Classrooms' (2014) 18 *International Journal of Inclusive Education* 101, 110.

[86] J Ravet, 'Inclusive/Exclusive? Contradictory Perspectives on Autism and Inclusion: The Case for an Integrative Position' (2011) 15 *International Journal of Inclusive Education* 667, 674–76.

[87] Y-H Xie, M Potměšil and B Peters, 'Children Who are Deaf or Hard of Hearing in Inclusive Educational Settings: A Literature Review on Interactions with Peers' (2014) 19 *Journal of Deaf Studies and Deaf Education* 423, 434–35.

[88] S Batterbury, 'Language Justice for Sign Language Peoples: the UN Convention on the Rights of Persons with Disabilities' (2012) 11 *Language Policy* 253, 256–58.

[89] A Liasidou, 'Inclusive Education and Critical Pedagogy at the Intersections of Disability, Race, Gender and Class' (2012) 10 *Journal for Critical Education Policy Studies* 168, 173–74.

[90] R Caldin, 'Inclusive Social Networks and Inclusive Schools for Disabled Children of Migrant Families' (2014) 8 *European Journal of Disability Research* 105, 107–08.

[91] J Travers and M Krezmien, 'Racial Disparities in Autism Identification in the United States during 2014' (2018) 84 *Exceptional Children* 403, 416.

[92] S Tomlinson, 'Special Education and Minority Ethnic Young People in England: Continuing Issues' (2015) 37 *Discourse: Studies in the Culture and Politics of Education* 1, 2 and 9; S Strand and G Lindsay,

various structures of disadvantage associated with race, gender, age and disability may exacerbate the position of those defined by more than one of them simultaneously. Education systems should respond to such differences acutely and comprehensively rather than by targeting some groups of people based on common tropes surrounding particular types of disabilities alone.

States must realise disabled children's right to education by reconciling the applicable human rights treaties that protect that right. The CRPD provides that education systems should aim at '[t]he development by persons with disabilities of their personality, talents and creativity, as well as their mental and physical abilities'.[93] In order to do so, states parties 'must support the creation of opportunities to build on the unique strengths and talents of each [of them]'.[94] They should also ensure that 'everyone feels safe, supported, stimulated and able to express themselves'.[95] In the UK, the Upper Tribunal has ruled that inappropriate behaviour may not be invoked as a motive for expulsion due to autism, notwithstanding an exemption from the protection of the Equality Act 2010 in the case of 'tendency to physical abuse' (an exemption that was considered contrary to the European Convention on Human Rights as regards autistic children).[96] The CRC Committee has also recommended that 'teaching methods should be tailored to the different needs of different children',[97] which is crucial so that these methods can work for all those who are disabled. The CRC further stresses the responsibilities of parents to whom 'States Parties shall render appropriate assistance ... in the performance of their child-rearing responsibilities'.[98] This confirms the importance of enabling these parents to ensure the education of their children, regardless of disability.

Moreover, the CRPD provides that states parties must facilitate 'the learning of Braille, alternative script, augmentative and alternative modes, means and formats of communication'.[99] While such 'modes, means and formats of communication' are especially important for those who are blind, the obligation may be equally relevant, mutatis mutandis, for other disabled children. Education systems must again recognise that children have diverse ways of communicating. According to the CRPD, states parties must therefore ensure that education 'is delivered in the most appropriate languages and modes and means of communication for the individual, and in environments which maximize academic and social development'.[100]

'Ethnic Disproportionality in Special Education: Evidence from an English Population Study' (2009) 43 *Journal of Special Education* 174, 175.

[93] CRPD, art 24(1)(b).

[94] CRPD Committee, *General Comment No 4 on Article 24: Right to Inclusive Education*, 2016, CRPD/C/GC/4 [16].

[95] ibid [12(f)].

[96] *C & C v Governing Body* [2018] UKUT 269 (AAC).

[97] CRC Committee, *General Comment No 1: The Aims of Education (Art 29(1))*, 2001, CRC/GC/2001/1 [9].

[98] CRC, art 18(2).

[99] CRPD, art 24(3)(a).

[100] ibid art 24(3)(c).

As indicated by the CRPD Committee, 'for such inclusive environments to occur, the States Parties should provide the required support, including by way of resources, assisted technology, and provision of orientation and mobility skills'.[101] In order to include those with different communication skills, this obligation means more than just translation into particular forms of language, such as sign language. Education systems must be rethought, not by viewing disabled children as a unified category to be protected, but by accepting, once again, that inclusion entails different approaches to education itself. By appreciating disability both discretely on its own varied terms and as a whole with respect to other characteristics, states might be in a better position to tackle intersectional disadvantage suffered by disabled children in enjoying their right to education.

Further, the International Convention on the Elimination of All Forms of Racial Discrimination (ICERD)[102] forbids racial discrimination in the enjoyment of the right to education,[103] and the CRC too explicitly refers to 'race' (as well as 'disability') in its general anti-discrimination clause.[104] Although these conventions do not consider cultural and linguistic particularities, they point to the necessity to do so with regard to education. Lack of consideration for such particularities has led to a number of cases, especially before the European Court of Human Rights, where states have been condemned for the segregation of Roma children, allegedly for reasons concerning disability, but in fact because of race.[105] This is also the view expressed by the Special Rapporteur on the Right to Education, who believes that inclusive education concerns any type of pupil, including 'students with different cultural and linguistic backgrounds or, in general, any student who requires additional support to succeed in the education system'.[106] The CRPD itself provides for the 'recognition ... of ... specific cultural and linguistic identity, including sign languages and deaf culture',[107] which could pertain to any racial minority. In the same vein, the CRPD Committee considers that all children must be 'welcomed equally, with respect for diversity according to, inter alia, disability, race, colour, sex, language, linguistic culture ... or other status'.[108] All of this makes clear that it is the education systems that need transforming and that transformation is only possible when those education systems grapple with the full wherewithal of intersectionality.

In sum, if the field of international human rights law is to harness the full potential of intersectionality theory, its unidimensional analysis of identity-categories must

---

[101] CRPD Committee (n 94) [34(c)].

[102] International Convention on the Elimination of All Forms of Racial Discrimination 1965, 660 UNTS 195.

[103] ICERD, art 5(c).

[104] CRPD, art 2(1).

[105] *DH and Others v Czech Republic* (ECtHR, 13 November 2007); *Sampanis and Others v Greece* (ECtHR, 5 June 2008); *Oršuš and Others v Croatia* (ECtHR, 17 July 2008); *Horváth and Kiss v Hungary* (ECtHR, 29 January 2013).

[106] K Boly Barry, *Report of the Special Rapporteur on the Right to Education*, 2017, A/72/469 [26].

[107] CRPD, art 30(d).

[108] CRPD Committee (n 94) [12(e)].

give way to a structural analysis of identity-categories that transcends identities and instead focuses on the various structures of disadvantage that feed those identities. UN treaty bodies should investigate whether and how social institutions themselves, and not simply group membership, restrict the reach of human rights protection. The question does not relate to any distinct identity-category or group; rather, it concerns all those whose disadvantages are particularly exacerbated by multiple forms of oppression that make the realisation of their human rights a distant reality. While intersectionality may raise issues related to a specific group of people, those issues are in fact a manifestation of concerns that are interconnected to those related to other groups. Addressing such interconnected concerns involves directing attention towards those factors that are shown to affect all disadvantaged groups. For the field of international human rights law, this means working both within and across separate human rights regimes for women, children and disabled people – as per CEDAW, the CRC and, finally, the CRPD. The way of putting intersectionality to work would be seeing how the disadvantages attached to each of the categories (race, gender, age, disability and so on) intersect to produce co-constituted structures of disadvantage associated with two or more of them at the same time. In such a way, international human rights law would not only commit itself to the pursuit of intersectionality, but would also advance intersectionality theory itself by giving effect to its structural analysis of identity-categories that forms its very essence.

Conclusion

International human rights law has adopted an interpretation of intersectionality that, in many ways, replicates a theory of identities. In order to embrace the theoretical and methodological framework of intersectionality, this chapter has proposed replacing this identarian understanding of intersectionality with a wider systems-based understanding of intersectionality. Instead of a narrow focus on identity-categories, the attention would go to the co-constituted structures of disadvantage that are associated with two or more identity-categories at the same time. UN treaty bodies would in such a way be able to determine why those defined by intersecting identities are systematically excluded from various domains. Rather than treating intersectionality as an aggregation of identities, international human rights law would set out to inquire into the intersectional disadvantage that results from the interaction of these identities.

This chapter has also illustrated the proposed way to harness the full potential of intersectionality theory through the example of disabled children's right to education. This example shows how it is possible to bridge the separate human rights regimes for women, children and disabled people, and to interpret human rights across the whole range of human rights treaties. An approach has been developed through which the UN treaty bodies could look into a certain characteristic as a stepping stone towards drawing attention to the various structures of disadvantage associated with that characteristic and in relation to other character-istics and to the impact that they have on the lived reality and experience of human rights between different groups of people.

Finally, intersectionality theory has so far been used to improve human rights protection by distinguishing specific groups amongst well-established categories. It could also be used to cast a critical eye on the different ways in which social arrangements increase disadvantages as they fail to acknowledge the real complex-ity of human diversity. The field of international human rights law could mobilise intersectionality theory in actually delivering its own promises by remedying those human rights violations that are beyond sight with a single-minded focus on a distinct identity-category or group. Such an invocation of intersectionality theory would avoid intersectionality being interpreted as simply cutting between (as per its original meaning in Latin, ie, 'intersecare') groups and into ever-smaller subgroups, an interpretation it precisely opposes. Intersectionality would then furnish a renewed basis of solidarity within and between groups in international human rights law.

3

The Potential and Pitfalls of Intersectionality in the Context of Social Rights Adjudication

COLM O'CINNEIDE*

Introduction

Over the last 30 years, the concept of intersectionality has generated an impressive, extensive and steadily growing body of scholarship. Within the legal domain, intersectionality analysis is now routinely applied by academics and activists to critique the shortcomings of established anti-discrimination law and policy – in particular, its limited capacity to engage with the interlocking and mutually constitutive nature of structural inequalities.[1] However, despite the conceptual ambition of such critique and the enthusiasm with which it has been applied, it has generated relatively little in the way of tangible law reform. Intersectionality remains more talked about than implemented.

Having said that, interesting developments are afoot within human rights law. Doctrinal developments have opened up room for courts and other adjudicatory bodies to take account of intersectionality when reviewing state action for compliance with fundamental rights norms. This is particularly the case within an embryonic but growing area of human rights law, namely social rights adjudication.

Elements of this chapter derive from reflection on my experience as a member of the European Committee on Social Rights, the monitoring body for the European Social Charter, between 2006 and 2016. However, none of the views expressed here should be taken to reflect the views of the Committee in the past or at present. I am also grateful to the editors of this volume for their patient forbearance while this chapter took shape.

[1] For a cross-jurisdictional sample of some recent legal research on this point, see S Atrey, *Intersectional Discrimination* (Oxford University Press, 2019); D Schiek, 'On the Use, Mis-uses and Non-uses of Intersectionality before the Court of Justice of the EU' (2018) 18(2) *International Journal of Discrimination and the Law* 82; B Goldblatt and L Steele, 'Bloody Unfair: Inequality Related to Menstruation: Considering the Role of Discrimination Law' (2019) 41(3) *Sydney Law Review* 293; DW Carbado and KW Crenshaw, 'An Intersectional Critique of Tiers of Scrutiny: Beyond "Either/or" Approaches to Equal Protection' (2019) 129 *Yale Law Journal Forum* 108.

For now, the relevant case law is limited and patchy. It nevertheless high-lights how intersectionality analysis can enhance human rights law and deepen its capacity to engage with the dignity-corroding impact of poverty and material inequality. More generally, it also serves to emphasise how any serious attempt to give substance to social rights must grapple with issues of intersectionality, while also spotlighting the need for intersectional analysis to engage properly with the primary role played by poverty and material inequality in generating structural inequalities within contemporary society. However, there are also certain concep-tual traps that need to be avoided if the development of this essential intersectional dimension to social rights adjudication is not to undermine the wider project of constructing a genuinely substantive and universally applicable framework of legal social rights protection.

Section I of this chapter outlines the scope and ambition of intersectionality as a conceptual framework. Section II analyses how human rights law has developed in a way that opens up some limited room for the application of intersectionality analysis, principally through the related doctrinal concept of 'group vulnerability'. Section III examines how these developments are playing out in the specific and newly emerging field of social rights adjudication. Section IV examines the rich potential of intersectionality in this context. Section V concludes by analysing some of the conceptual traps that complicate the application of intersectionality analysis within social rights adjudication. Reference is primarily made to European legal standards, but the arguments made here are intended to be of general application.

I. The Ambitions of Intersectionality

Virtually all academic discussion of intersectionality begins by genuflecting to Kimberlé Crenshaw's famous 1989 paper on the topic. As is well known, Crenshaw argued that both feminist theory and anti-racist politics were limited by a failure to recognise the distinct forms of disadvantage inflicted by the overlap of different forms of discrimination:

> With Black women as the starting point, it becomes more apparent how dominant conceptions of discrimination condition us to think about subordination as disad-vantage occurring along a single categorical axis. I want to suggest further that this single-axis framework erases Black women in the conceptualization, identification and remediation of race and sex discrimination by limiting inquiry to the experiences of otherwise privileged members [white women/Black men] of the group.[2]

Crenshaw's analysis of the impact of such 'intersectional discrimination' harked back to the earlier insights of Audre Lorde, Barbara Smith and others involved

---

[2] K Crenshaw, 'Demarginalizing the Intersection of Race and Sex: A Black Feminist Critique of Antidiscrimination Doctrine, Feminist Theory and Antiracist Politics' (1989) 140 *University of Chicago Legal Forum* 139, 154.

in the Combahee River Collective, whose 1977 Statement had affirmed that 'the major systems of oppression are interlocking ... [t]he synthesis of these oppressions creates the conditions of our lives'.[3] This was itself subsequently further developed by Crenshaw, as well as by other critical race feminists such as Patricia Hill Collins. Over time, Crenshaw's original insights – focused primarily on the intersection of race and sex discrimination within the specific US context – have morphed into a cross-disciplinary conceptual/analytical framework, used by scholars and activists across the world to critique the reproduction of social inequalities.

This critique emphasises: (i) the porous and mutually constituting nature of social identities such as gender, class, race, age, disability and sexual orientation; (ii) the intersecting impact of the various forms of discrimination that play out across this complex web of identities; (iii) the way in which such 'intersectional discrimination' reinforces existing structural power hierarchies; and (iv) the limitations of anti-discrimination strategies structured around a single-axis approach, in particular those which adopt a particular 'baseline' identity as their de facto 'central case' and thus constrain their capacity to engage in any meaningful way with intersectional discrimination (eg, Crenshaw's examples of white women/ Black men for sex/race discrimination respectively).[4] More generally, it calls into question the traditional 'siloed' approach to combating oppressive power dynamics that play out along the different axes of gender, race, poverty/class and so forth, and encourages instead a turn towards a 'multi-dimensional' understanding of discrimination and the forms of critical praxis needed to combat it.[5]

In an era where individual and group identities have become more multi-faceted,[6] and discrimination is increasingly conceptualised in more wide-ranging and variegated ways than was the case hitherto, this critique has resonated.[7]

---

[3] 'The Combahee River Collective Statement' (April 1977) published, inter alia, in JS Ritchie and K Ronald (eds), *Available Means: An Anthology of Women's Rhetoric(s)* (University of Pittsburgh Press, 2001) 292–300. For an intellectual genealogy of intersectionality, see AM Hancock, *An Intellectual History of Intersectionality* (Oxford University Press, 2016).

[4] Collins argues that intersectionality is based upon the insight that 'cultural patterns of oppression ... are bound together and influenced by the intersectional systems of society, such as race, gender, class, and ethnicity': PH Collins, 'Gender, Black Feminism, and Black Political Economy' (2000) 568 (1) *Annals of the American Academy of Political and Social Science* 41, 42.

[5] Collins suggests that intersectionality can function as a form of 'critical praxis', challenging the manner in which interlocking 'vectors of oppression' serve to perpetuate established inequalities: PH Collins, 'Intersectionality's Definitional Dilemmas' (2015) 41 (1) *Annual Review of Sociology* 1.

[6] Malleson notes that there has been a 'shift in identity configurations', marked by the 'emergence of a much wider range of identity characteristics' and 'the increasing tendency to reconstruct identity characteristics along a spectrum'; see K Malleson, 'Equality Law and the Protected Characteristics' (2018) 81(4) *Modern Law Review* 598.

[7] Intersectionality critique has both reflected and contributed to that process by increasing awareness of the multi-dimensional nature of personal identity and the negative essentialising impact of overlapping forms of discrimination: see ibid. Note, however, the recent significant argument made by Carbado and Harris that intersectionality should not be viewed as incompatible with essentialist perspectives on group disadvantage: see DW Carbado and CI Harris, 'Intersectionality at 30: Mapping the Margins of Anti-essentialism, Intersectionality, and Dominance Theory' (2019) 132 *Harvard Law Review* 2193.

Furthermore, intersectionality chimes with other critical approaches to equality, in particular those which aim to reconfigure social structures in line with the ambitions of 'substantive' or 'transformative' equality, as outlined by MacKinnon, Fredman, Anderson, Albertyn and others.[8] Intersectionality shares with such perspectives an ambition to move beyond the ground-specific, formalist, de-contextualised approach of much existing equality law and policy, and towards a more substantive engagement with the multi-faceted and structural nature of discrimination in contemporary societies. Its impact on contemporary debates about equality has both fuelled and been fuelled by the growing influence of this wider 'substantive' turn, with intersectionality critique being particularly influential in spotlighting how the interlocking impact of structural inequalities plays a distinctive role in reinforcing patterns of group subordination.

In general, intersectionality has come to exert a significant influence over how inequality is conceptualised across multiple academic disciplines, as well as in public debate. Intersectionality has even seeped into wider public discourse and gone 'viral'.[9] However, in so doing, it has become somewhat caricatured and a victim of the occasional political attack on so-called 'identity politics'.[10] Furthermore, its impact on public discourse has not translated into much in the way of tangible policy outcomes. Confusion exists about what combating 'intersectional discrimination' actually entails.[11] Scepticism also exists in policy-making circles about the potentially disruptive consequences of departing from the deeply embedded 'single-axis' approach to non-discrimination.

As a result, intersectionality remains more talked about than implemented, especially when it comes to legislative protection against discrimination.[12] However, recent developments in human rights law have seen courts and other adjudicatory bodies begin to engage with the structural impact of intersectional inequalities, with the embryonic field of social rights law being at the fore in this regard.

---

[8] See eg, CA MacKinnon, 'Substantive Equality Revisited: A Reply to Sandra Fredman' (2016) 14(3) *International Journal of Constitutional Law* 739; S Fredman, 'Substantive Equality Revisited' (2016) 14(3) *International Journal of Constitutional Law* 712; E Anderson, 'What is the Point of Equality?' (1999) 109(2) *Ethics* 287; C Albertyn, 'Contested Substantive Equality in the South African Constitution: Beyond Social Inclusion towards Systemic Justice' (2018) 34(3) *South African Journal on Human Rights* 441.

[9] J Coaston, 'The Intersectionality Wars', *Vox*, 28 May 2019, https://www.vox.com/the-highlight/2019/5/20/18542843/intersectionality-conservatism-law-race-gender-discrimination.

[10] See eg, M Continetti, 'The Battle of Woke Island', *National Review*, 7 April 2018, https://www.nationalreview.com/2018/04/the-battle-of-woke-island. Continetti refers to 'the post-modern dogma of "intersectionality" that promotes solipsism at the personal level and division at the social level'. Crenshaw has responded with understandable bemusement to this bowlderisation of her original concept: see Coaston (n 9).

[11] A Christofferson, 'Are We All "Baskets of Characteristics"? Intersectional Slippages and the Displacement of Race in English and Scottish Equality Policy' in JS Jordan-Zachery and O Hankivsky (eds), *The Palgrave Handbook of Intersectionality in Public Policy* (Palgrave Macmillan, 2019) 705.

[12] This is particularly true of legislative non-discrimination frameworks, which remain generally wedded to a 'single-axis' approach despite sustained criticism on this point from academics and activists.

This generates some interesting and complex issues. However, before these are discussed, it is necessary to set out exactly how human rights law has begun to gradually acquire an intersectional dimension, and the particular importance of this in respect of social rights.

II. The Emerging Intersectional Dimension to Human Rights Jurisprudence

Following Crenshaw's lead in her 1989 paper, intersectionality critique has repeatedly highlighted the limitations of how legal systems conceptualise discrimination and inequality more generally. Historically, legal systems have defined discrimination by reference to the 'single-axis' approach critiqued by Crenshaw (ie, the assumption that discriminatory treatment plays out along neat vectors that align with the traditional protected grounds, such as race, sex and disability). Furthermore, it has tended to adopt a largely formal approach to defining what qualifies as discrimination, which focuses on the rationale for less favourable treatment rather than on its substantive impact on disadvantaged groups within a specific context. Taken together, these characteristics have limited the capacity of law to address more complex and substantive forms of discrimination, including intersectional discrimination.

However, the old assumptions, which underpinned the traditional 'siloed' approach of law to such issues are breaking down, in part thanks to the prodding of intersectionality critique.[13] The single-axis approach to defining discrimination no longer tallies with contemporary views about the multi-faceted nature of personal identity and the overlapping impact of structural inequalities. In addition, formal conceptions of equality are giving way to more substantive understandings of the concept, with discrimination increasingly viewed in terms of its systemic and structural impact rather than as the product of individual decisions motivated by specific ground-based prejudicial attitudes.[14]

Thus, it is no surprise that intersectionality looms large in debates about the future development of law in this area. In the eyes of many expert commentators, an embrace of intersectionality should form part of the next stage of the evolutionary development of equality as part of a wider upgrade to a fully fleshed-out commitment to substantive equality.

Such intersectionality critique has particularly featured in debates about the future of anti-discrimination legislation, such as the UK's Equality Act 2010 or the EU equality directives. As already noted, in this context, intersectionality has generated considerable heat, but little in the way of substantive legal reform.[15]

---

[13] Malleson (n 6).

[14] See the authors cited at n 8 above.

[15] Note, for example, that the 'combined discrimination' provisions of s 14 of the UK Equality Act 2010 have not come into force, as the necessary ministerial authorisation has not been forthcoming.

However, such critique can also be applied to other aspects of law, in particular to human rights law – both as regards its specific equality and non-discrimination provisions, and also its wider package of substantive rights guarantees.

Human rights instruments, whether they be national constitutional charters or international treaties, invariably contain provisions requiring respect for the right to equality and non-discrimination. Such 'equality clauses', like Article 15 of the Canadian Charter of Fundamental Rights and Freedoms and Article 14 of the European Convention on Human Rights (ECHR), are often 'open-ended' in scope (ie, the protection they offer against discrimination is not necessarily confined to a specific set of equality grounds, unlike most forms of national anti-discrimination legislation). However, they are generally interpreted and applied by courts and other adjudicative bodies in line with the standard single-axis approach. Furthermore, such clauses are usually interpreted in a formalistic, de-contextualised manner, which often reflects the 'baseline' identity assumptions critiqued by Crenshaw.

But attitudes are beginning to change on both fronts, reflecting in part the influence of intersectionality critique and also the wider influence of the substantive turn in equality law.[16] A range of national courts, along with the European and Inter-American Courts of Human Rights and other international human rights adjudicatory bodies, have in recent years begun to adopt what Atrey has described as a 'flexible' and context-sensitive approach to comparator analysis.[17] They have also shown greater willingness to review state action that discriminates on a combination of status grounds, in particular when it impacts upon groups deemed to be 'vulnerable' on account of their disadvantaged social status. This amplifies the ability of such courts to engage with multiple discrimination broadly defined, including intersectional discrimination.

For example, the Strasbourg Court has begun to take account of the vulnerable status of particular groups in determining the scope of state obligations under Article 14 ECHR.[18] State action which subjects such groups to particular disadvantage can be subject to more intensive review than when it is applied in other contexts, while states may also be subject to positive obligations to take special measures to secure equality of treatment for such groups. Crucially, the Court has been willing to extend this protection to groups whose vulnerability is generated by the overlapping impact defined by two or more structural patterns of social exclusions, thereby opening the door to intersectional concerns.

The stand-out case in this regard thus far is *BS v Spain*,[19] where the Strasbourg Court found a violation of Article 14 ECHR, taken in conjunction with Article 3 ECHR, in respect of a failure to investigate allegations of police harassment

---

[16] See, in general, S Fredman, *Human Rights Transformed: Positive Rights and Positive Duties* (Oxford University Press, 2008).

[17] S Atrey, 'Comparison in Intersectional Discrimination' (2018) 38(3) *Legal Studies* 379.

[18] L Peroni and A Timmer, 'Vulnerable Groups: The Promise of an Emerging Concept in European Human Rights Convention Law' (2013) 11(4) *International Journal of Constitutional Law* 1056.

[19] *BS v Spain* App No 47159/08 (ECtHR, 24 July 2012).

directed towards an African woman working as a prostitute. The Court recognised the applicant's 'particular vulnerability' arising from the intersection of her gender and ethnic origin, taken together with the nature of her work.[20] Also, more recently, in the case of *JD and A v UK*,[21] the Court concluded that the UK had breached Article 14 ECHR in deducting housing benefits from mothers who had been the victims of domestic violence but were nevertheless deemed to be occupying accommodation with more space than their families required, notwithstanding the fact that the accommodation in question had been specially modified to ensure their personal safety.

In both of these cases, the Court recognised that states parties owed particular obligations to specific groups of women defined by overlapping forms of disadvantage: in *BS*, the structural inequalities arising by virtue of the intersection of the claimant's ethnicity and profession, and in *JD*, arising by virtue of the claimant's dependence on social welfare support taken together with her status as a survivor of serious domestic violence. Respect for the right to equality under Article 14 ECHR was thus deemed to require special state action to take account of the particular vulnerability of the claimants generated by the impact of intersecting forms of structural inequalities, showing how this developing strand of the Court's case law is potentially able to accommodate intersectionality, in situations of clear 'group vulnerability' at least.

This vulnerability approach has been only partially integrated into the Strasbourg jurisprudence.[22] It is not always applied in a consistent or rigorous manner. Furthermore, the Court's case law in this context has sometimes been criticised for reinforcing negative stereotyping about the alleged inherent powerlessness of such 'vulnerable' groups.[23] Nevertheless, the relevant ECHR case law recognises that the overlapping impact of various structural power imbalances may have a particularly negative impact upon specific groups in ways that do not readily qualify as straightforward instances of single-axis, ground-specific discrimination. It thus reflects aspects of intersectionality critique: even though the framing concept of 'vulnerability' – which perhaps reflects the influence of Martha Fineman's theorising[24] – is wider in scope and has a different genealogy and definitional logic, it shares with intersectionality a common focus on the specific contextual impact, and can serve as a vector for judicial recognition of the interlocking impact of structural inequalities.

---

[20] See MC La Barbera and MC López, 'Toward the Implementation of Intersectionality in the European Multilevel Legal Praxis: *B.S. v Spain*' (2019) 53(4) *Law and Society Review* 1167.

[21] *JD and A v UK* App Nos 32949/17 and 34614/17 (ECtHR, 24 October 2019).

[22] O Arnardóttir, 'Vulnerability under Article 14 of the European Convention on Human Rights: Innovation or Business as Usual?' (2017) 4(3) *Oslo Law Review* 150.

[23] Peroni and Timmer (n 18). See also K Nieminen, 'Eroding the Protection against Discrimination: The Procedural and De-contextualized Approach to *S.A.S. v France*' (2019) 19(2) *International Journal of Discrimination and the Law* 69.

[24] MA Fineman, 'The Vulnerable Subject: Anchoring Equality in the Human Condition' (2008) 20(1) *Yale Journal of Law and Feminism* 1.

A similar approach as adopted by the ECtHR has been adopted by a range of UN and other Council of Europe bodies in determining the scope of state obligations arising by virtue of the various equality rights guaranteed in human rights treaty instruments. Indeed, certain international human rights bodies have explicitly recognised intersectional discrimination as constituting a breach of such equality rights. For example, the Committee on the Elimination of Discrimination against Women has stated that intersectionality is a 'basic concept for understanding the scope of the general obligations of States parties' under the UN Convention on the Elimination of All Forms of Discrimination Against Women (CEDAW).[25] National courts have also shown some openness in this regard, albeit while generally moving with baby steps.[26]

Analogous case law developments are also under way in other areas of human rights law beyond the specific scope of application of 'equality clauses'. Courts and other adjudicatory bodies are increasingly recognising that the scope and substance of state human rights obligations in general may vary according to the contextual status of groups. Specific obligations may arise in respect of certain vulnerable groups across a range of fundamental rights, just as happens in relation to equality rights narrowly defined.[27] Furthermore, such vulnerability is increasingly defined by reference to overlapping identities. This again opens the door to intersectionality considerations.

Thus, in *Yordanova v Bulgaria*,[28] the ECtHR held that eviction notices issued against a socio-economically disadvantaged Roma community constituted a disproportionate interference with Article 8 ECHR on the basis that the 'underprivileged status' of this community and their need for alternative housing arrangements were not adequately taken into account. This represents a development of the Court's vulnerability approach, extended beyond the specific framework of Article 14 ECHR. And, again, it opens the door to intersectionality concerns – as neatly illustrated in *Yordanova* by how the Court implicitly acknowledged that patterns of social exclusion rooted in the overlap of socio-economic disadvantage and ethnicity had generated the uniquely vulnerable status of the particular Roma community affected by eviction in this case.

Similar case law developments can be identified elsewhere in national, regional and international human rights jurisprudence.[29] In such decisions, the specific

---

[25] CEDAW, General Recommendation No 28: *The Core Obligations of State Parties under Article 2 of the Convention on the Elimination of All Forms of Discrimination against Women*, 16 December 2010 [18]. For the situation in respect of the UN Convention on the Rights of Persons with Disabilities, see G de Beco, 'Intersectionality and Disability in International Human Rights Law' (2019) *International Journal of Human Rights*, DOI: 10.1080/13642987.2019.1661241.

[26] S Atrey, *Intersectional Discrimination* (Oxford University Press, 2019) ch 1.

[27] See Peroni and Timmer (n 18).

[28] *Yordanova v Bulgaria* App No 25446/06 (ECtHR, 24 April 2012) [133]. The Court took the view that the art 14 ECHR claim brought by the applicant was subsumed within the art 8 ECHR complaint (at [145]–[149]). See also *Connors v UK* (2005) 40 EHRR 9.

[29] See Peroni and Timmer (n 18).

characteristics of vulnerable or targeted groups are increasingly taken into account in determining both (i) the scope of the right at issue and the obligations it imposes upon states, and (ii) the adequacy of any justification offered for state interference with this right. Again, this has opened the way for intersectional factors to be taken into account across a spectrum of human rights.

It is important not to exaggerate the extent of these case law developments. At present, intersectionality critique occupies at best a marginal place in debates about the scope and substance of human rights law taken as a whole.[30] However, avenues have opened up within human rights law for the application of intersectionality analysis. This in turn highlights the potential of intersectionality critique to 'bite' in the field of human rights in general. Patterns of social exclusion often overlap, generating intersectional forms of inequality, which can impact profoundly on the enjoyment of an assortment of human rights. Intersectionality critique can help to diagnose these potential blind spots and thus offers a way of deepening the substantive turn in equality law and within human rights jurisprudence at large.[31]

III. Intersectionality and Social Rights

So, given all the above, how do social rights fit into the picture? What does intersectionality have to say to law and policy approaches that engage with social rights considerations or have some link to their interpretation and development?

A. The Emergence of Social Rights Jurisprudence

Some context is necessary here. Social rights, such as the right to education or the right to social security, have for a long time been a missing piece in the puzzle of human rights law. Their importance as political concepts has been acknowledged from the inception of the modern human rights era, as reflected in the extensive list of such rights acknowledged in the text of the Universal Declaration of Human Rights in 1948. They receive plenty of lip service as important guarantors against the worst excesses of poverty and material inequality. However, at both the national and international levels, deep scepticism has persisted about the desirability of protecting them through law. Until recently, national legal systems made very little provision – if any – for such rights to be enforceable in law. The international mechanisms for monitoring state compliance with such rights were also

---

[30] PYS Chow, 'Has Intersectionality Reached its Limits? Intersectionality in the UN Human Rights Treaty Body Practice and the Issue of Ambivalence' (2016) 16(3) *Human Rights Law Review* 453.
[31] G de Beco, 'Protecting the Invisible: An Intersectional Approach to International Human Rights Law' (2017) 17(4) *Human Rights Law Review* 633.

very limited. Indeed, if anything, social rights constituted something of a legal 'exclusion zone': they were widely viewed as not fit subjects for legal enforcement.[32]

However, things have begun to change. As Leitjen puts it, using a neat German phrase, social rights are increasingly acknowledged to be *salonfähig* (ie, presentable in good legal company).[33] The absence of a social dimension to national and international human rights law is now increasingly regarded as a defect, which limits its capacity to protect essential aspects of human dignity.[34] This has generated greater willingness on the part of judges and law-makers to extend the scope of human rights law into socio-economic terrain. As a result, two methods of protecting social rights through law have emerged.

First, there is the 'indirect' route, whereby established legal guarantees covering 'core' civil and political rights – including equality and non-discrimination rights – are interpreted in a way that protects individual access to certain social entitlements. Thus, in *R (Adam and Limbuela) v Secretary of State for the Home Department*,[35] the UK House of Lords held that denying welfare benefits to asylum seekers who were prohibited from seeking work risked exposing them to a level of destitution that qualified as inhuman and degrading treatment, and thus would qualify as a breach of Article 3 ECHR. Similarly, in *MSS v Belgium and Greece*, the ECtHR[36] ruled that the conditions in which refugees were living in Greece constituted a breach of Article 3 ECHR. The *JD* and *Yordanova* judgments cited above are further examples of civil and political rights being interpreted in a way that protects individuals and groups against unjustified deprivation of welfare support and public housing, respectively. This indirect approach is inherently limited, as it only protects those aspects of social rights that can be shoehorned into the framework of a civil and political rights claim. However, it protects individuals against egregious breaches of their social rights in situations where such 'shoehorning' is possible and where state responsibility is clearly engaged.[37]

The 'direct' approach sets out to protect social rights through the establishment of national or international legal mechanisms which directly review state compliance with such rights. Examples include the Optional Protocol mechanism to the International Covenant on Economic, Social and Cultural Rights (ICESCR), whereby individuals can bring claims alleging a breach of the ICESCR to the UN Committee on Economic, Social and Cultural Rights (CESCR); the 'collective complaint' mechanism provided for under the European Social Charter (ESC), which allows certain types of non-governmental organisations (NGOs) and

---

[32] C O'Cinneide, 'The Problematic of Social Rights: Uniformity and Diversity in the Development of Social Rights Review' in L Lazarus, C McCrudden and N Bowles (eds), *Reasoning Rights: Comparative Judicial Engagement* (Hart Publishing, 2014) 297–315.

[33] I Leitjen, 'Book Review – *The Future of Economic and Social Rights*' (2019) 17(4) *International Journal of Constitutional Law* 1354, 1354.

[34] See, in general, J King, *Judging Social Rights* (Cambridge University Press, 2012).

[35] *R (Adam and Limbuela) v Secretary of State for the Home Department* [2005] UKHL 66.

[36] *MSS v Belgium and Greece* (2011) 53 EHRR 2.

[37] O'Cinneide (n 32).

'representative bodies' to bring complaints of a Charter violation to the European Committee on Social Rights (ECSR); and the constitutional mechanisms for reviewing the adequacy of state measures to give effect to social rights established in states, such as South Africa, Colombia and Portugal.[38] Such mechanisms obviously give more comprehensive protection to social rights than is available via the indirect route, and permit closer legal engagement with their substance. They also complement the normative approach to social rights that has been developed by various UN Special Rapporteurs in relation to issues such as access to housing, water and food, and the fight against extreme poverty. However, the trade-off is that the impact of international social rights mechanisms is often muted and scepticism persists about the desirability or workability of such direct enforcement of social rights standards.[39]

Neither indirect nor direct approaches can yet be said to have become an integral part of the mainstream of human rights law. But their emergence is a clear sign that social rights are now squarely on the human rights law agenda. There is growing support for human rights law to acquire a meaningful 'social dimension' and to acquire the capacity to address dignity-eroding measures, which generate poverty and material inequality. This again reflects the existence of the above-mentioned dynamic of reform and reinvigoration, and the desire to make human rights law more responsive to existing patterns of social exclusion.[40] Given this ambition, intersectionality critique offers some important lessons for how social rights protection should develop. Its emphasis on the specific and contextual nature of intersectional discrimination – and the need for this to be taken into account across the full spectrum of human rights standards – has particular relevance for this developing area of law.

B. Intersectionality as a Necessary Ingredient for Social Rights Adjudication

The impact of poverty and material inequality may play out in different registers across different social contexts and may impact differently on different groups. In particular, inadequate protection for social rights or cuts to existing levels of protection may overlap with other forms of discriminatory or exclusionary treatment in a way that imposes particular disadvantages on specific groups.[41]

[38] See, in general, J Dugard et al (eds), *Research Handbook on Economic, Social and Cultural Rights as Human Rights* (Edward Elgar, 2020).

[39] O'Cinneide (n 32).

[40] King (n 34); C O'Cinneide, 'The Constitutionalisation of Socio-economic Rights' in H Alviar García, K Klare and L Williams (eds), *Socio-economic Rights in Theory and Practice: Critical Inquiries* (Routledge 2014) 258–76.

[41] S Atrey, 'The Intersectional Case of Poverty in Discrimination Law' (2018) 18 *Human Rights Law Review* 411.

Structural deficiencies, blind spots or other limitations in social rights protection will often have a disproportionate impact on groups already subject to structural disadvantages in the labour market or other forms of discriminatory treatment. Furthermore, the intersection of poverty/material inequality with ascribed identity grounds, such as race, disability and gender, has historically been a major generator of specific disadvantage and continues to be so today.[42]

As such, a single-axis, 'one-size-fits-all' approach to social rights, which fails to take factors such as gender, race and disability into account when assessing the legitimacy of state action impacting upon such rights, risks being too reductionist. Particular limitations on the enjoyment of social rights might be defensible in terms of their general impact, but not as regards their disproportionate impact upon a specific subgroup delineated by two or more characteristics (including the socio-economic vulnerability generated by the social rights restriction in question). If a form of social rights review – whether indirect or direct in nature – confines itself to assessing the general impact of the restriction under review, then such group-specific disproportionate impacts will be left out of the picture. This would replicate the 'baseline' problem identified by Crenshaw, gloss over particular contexts where overlapping forms of social exclusion have especially concentrated effect, and generate the type of narrow, formalist analysis that is increasingly depreciated across the spectrum of human rights law. In other words, it would be wide open to the intersectionality critique and would deviate from the contextual, substantive approach increasingly adopted in other areas of human rights adjudication, especially equality law.

C. The Embrace of Intersectionality in Social Rights Adjudication

Given this, it is not surprising that both indirect and direct forms of social rights adjudication have grappled with intersectional issues. The concept of 'vulnerability' has again played an important role in this regard, serving as the vector for the type of contextual and group-focused analysis that opens the door to intersectionality considerations.

For example, in the 'indirect' *JD* and *Yordanova* cases cited above, the ECtHR engaged in close analysis of the specific context in which the claimants found themselves and concluded that the state parties in question had failed to take adequate account of claimants' particular vulnerabilities, as generated by the intersection

---

[42] B Goldblatt, 'Intersectionality in International Anti-discrimination Law: Addressing Poverty in its Complexity' (2015) 21(1) *Australian Journal of Human Rights* 47; B Goldblatt, *Developing the Right to Social Security: A Gender Perspective* (Routledge, 2016); M Maroto, D Pettinicchio and AC Patterson, 'Hierarchies of Categorical Disadvantage: Economic Insecurity at the Intersection of Disability, Gender, and Race' (2019) 33 *Gender and Society* 64.

of socio-economic status and gender (*JD*) and socio-economic status and race (*Yordanova*), respectively.

Direct forms of social rights adjudication have also engaged with intersectional forms of discrimination and social exclusion. For example, in its collective complaints case law, the ECSR has repeatedly engaged with intersectional issues, albeit generally again through the specific lens of 'vulnerability'. Indeed, complaints concerning the situation of specific minority groups subject to overlapping forms of social exclusion have made up a substantial part of the Committee's case law. This is striking, given that the ECSR's case law is perhaps one of the best-developed sets of legal social rights norms that currently exist at the international level: it illustrates how intersectionality concerns are directly relevant to the business of social rights adjudication.

In *ERRC v Greece*, the Committee stated that one of the underlying purposes of the social rights protected by the Charter is to express solidarity and promote social inclusion, and that state parties must take the particular needs of minority groups into account when taking measures to address social exclusion.[43] It went on to conclude that the available evidence clearly indicated that local authorities in Greece were failing to take proportionate steps to address the specific housing needs of the Roma minority, which arose by virtue of their particular status as a social group that had been historically marginalised by the intersection of ethnicity and socio-economic status.

Subsequently, in *ERRC v Italy*, the Committee concluded that the inadequate supply of housing for Roma communities in Italy, the failure to take into account their specific accommodation needs and a failure by the local authorities to implement administrative decrees requiring the provision of adequate shelter and support for these communities constituted a violation of Article 31 of the revised ESC (right to housing), taken together with the right to equality and non-discrimination set out in Article E.[44] In later cases, the Committee affirmed the need for state parties to take the special situation of Roma and Traveller communities into account in implementing eviction procedures,[45] and to take protective action where required to defend Roma housing sites against xenophobic attacks and other forms of discriminatory action.[46] In *ERRC v Bulgaria*, the Committee extended this logic into the area of healthcare, concluding that Bulgarian healthcare

---

[43] Complaint No 15/2003, *ERRC v Greece* (Decision on the merits of 7 February 2005). In this respect, the ECSR cross-referred to the judgment of the European Court of Human Rights in *Connors v UK* (2005) 40 EHRR 9. The Committee subsequently reiterated its findings in this regard in Complaint No 49/2008, *INTERIGHTS v Greece* (Decision on the merits of 25 January 2010).

[44] Complaint No 27/2004, *ERRC v Italy* (Decision on the merits of 21 December 2005); see in particular §§ 18–19. See also Complaint No 49/2008, *ERRC v Portugal* (Decision on the merits of 1 July 2011).

[45] Complaint No 31/2005, *ERRC v Bulgaria* (Decision on the merits of 1 July 2011).

[46] Complaint No 58/2009, *Centre on Housing Rights and Evictions (COHRE) v Italy* (Decision on the merits of 6 July 2010); Complaint 63/2010, *COHRE v France* (Decision on the merits of 13 July 2011).

provision policies did not adequately address the specific health risks affecting Romani communities.[47]

Beyond the specific context of the Roma, the Committee has also applied similar logic in concluding that Belgium had breached the Social Charter's requirements by failing to take adequate measures to secure the fundamental social rights of distinct groups of persons with disabilities;[48] Italy had failed to provide pregnant women living in particular geographical regions with secured access to abortion services (classified in that specific national context as constituting an aspect of the right to healthcare);[49] Finland had failed to take account of the specific socio-economic situation of particular groups of older persons in receipt of social care;[50] and the Netherlands had failed to give due regard to the specific situation of irregular child refugees in denying them secured access to emergency shelter.[51] In all of these cases, the Committee recognised the vulnerabilities of specific social groups defined by the intersecting impact of two or more 'logics' of social exclusion and took this vulnerability into account in evaluating whether the state parties in question had failed to take adequate steps to discharge their positive obligations under the ESC.[52]

At the UN level, the CESCR has also taken account of the specific situation of vulnerable groups defined by the intersecting impact of overlapping forms of social exclusion in reviewing state compliance with their ICESCR obligations.[53] For example, in its merits decision in the individual complaint of *Djazia and Bellili v Spain*,[54] brought under the Optional Protocol to the ICESCR that permits such complaints, the Committee concluded that Spain had failed to take adequate steps to secure the right to housing of families in deprived socio-economic circumstances who faced a threat of eviction. Similarly, in *Calero v Ecuador*,[55] the

---

[47] Complaint No 46/2007, *ERRC v Bulgaria* (Decision on the merits of 3 December 2008); Complaint No 67/2011, *Médecins du Monde v France* (Decision on the merits of 20 September 2012).
[48] Complaint No 41/2007, *Mental Disability Advocacy Center (MDAC) v Bulgaria*, (Decision on the merits of 10 June 2008); Complaint No 75/2011, *International Federation of Human Rights (FIDH) v Belgium* (Decision on the merits of 26 March 2013).
[49] Complaint No 87/2012, *International Planned Parenthood Federation – European Network (IPPF EN) v Italy* (Decision on the merits of 10 September 2013).
[50] Complaint No 70/2011, *The Central Association of Carers in Finland v Finland* (Decision on the merits of 4 December 2012).
[51] Complaint No 47/2008, *Defence of Children International v The Netherlands* (Decision on the merits of 20 October 2009).
[52] The Committee thus primarily uses group vulnerability as an evaluative tool in assessing the adequacy of state measures to give effect to social rights rather than as a 'status' ground for the purpose of non-discrimination analysis; see the discussion below in section V of this chapter of the Committee's decision in Collective Complaint No 48/2008, *ERRC v Italy* (Decision on the merits of 31 March 2009).
[53] See, in general, S Liebenberg, 'Between Sovereignty and Accountability: The Emerging Jurisprudence of the United Nations Committee on Economic, Social and Cultural Rights under the Optional Protocol' (2020) 42(1) *Human Rights Quarterly* 48.
[54] *Djazia and Bellili v Spain*, Views Adopted by the Committee under the Optional Protocol to the International Covenant on Economic, Social and Cultural Rights with Regard to Communication No 5/2015, UN ESCOR, Comm on Econ, Soc & Cult Rts, 61st Sess, ¶ 11.5, UN Doc E/C.12/61/D/5/2015 (2017).
[55] *Calero v Ecuador*, Views Adopted by the Committee under the Optional Protocol to the Covenant Concerning Communication No 10/2015, UN ESCOR, Comm on Econ, Soc & Cult Rts,

Committee decided that Ecuador had failed to take adequate measures to secure the right to social security for older female domestic workers.

In its General Comment No 20, the CESCR has expressly recognised that individuals or groups may face 'cumulative discrimination' on two or more grounds, which merits 'particular consideration and remedying' by state parties.[56] It also indicates that a violation of the ICESCR may be generated by 'the intersection of two prohibited grounds of discrimination, e.g. where access to a social service is denied on the basis of sex and disability'.[57] UN Special Rapporteurs have adopted a similar stance with, for example, successive Special Rapporteurs on the right to housing, emphasising how the impact of lack of security of tenure is often amplified by the intersecting impact of factors, such as gender, race and disability.[58] As Atrey has argued, some traces of a willingness to engage with the intersecting impact of poverty and other discrimination grounds is even detectable in the social rights jurisprudence of certain national courts.[59]

In general, a similar dynamic is thus playing out in the context of social rights adjudication as it is for equality law and human rights law more generally. Courts and other adjudicatory bodies are recognising that the scope of social rights obligations may vary according to the contextual status of the affected groups, and, in particular, the extent of their vulnerability, increasingly defined by reference to the intersecting impact of different forms of social exclusion.

IV. What Intersectionality Contributes to Social Rights Adjudication: The Complex Interface between Poverty, Material Inequality and Identity Discrimination

For now, this vulnerability approach is at an embryonic stage of development (as is true for social rights jurisprudence more generally). However, the salience of intersectional issues thus far in its development is striking. It confirms the relevance of intersectionality critique to social rights adjudication and its

---

63rd Sess ¶¶ 9.4–9.5, UN Doc E/C.12/63/D/10/2015 (2018). As Liebenberg notes, the complainant had 'experienced intersectional discrimination on the grounds of gender and age', in addition to suffering a deprivation of social security protection: Liebenberg (n 53) 80.

[56] General Comment No 20, *Non-discrimination in Economic, Social and Cultural Rights*, UN ESCOR, Comm on Econ, Soc & Cult Rts, 42nd Sess, Agenda Item 3, ¶ 5, UN Doc E/C.12/GC/20 (2009), [17].

[57] ibid [27].

[58] See eg, UNHRC, *Report of the Special Rapporteur on Adequate Housing as a Component of the Right to an Adequate Standard of Living, and on the Right to Non-discrimination in This Context*, Miloon Kothari, 13 February 2008, UN Doc A/HRC/7/16 [40]; UNHRC, *Report of the Special Rapporteur on Adequate Housing as a Component of the Right to an Adequate Standard of Living, and on the Right to Non-discrimination in This Context*, Raquel Rolnik, 26 December 2011, UN Doc A/HRC/19/153 [1]–[3].

[59] Atrey (n 41).

potential to add depth to its development. Discourse about material inequality and social rights has sometimes glossed over the role played by discrimination based on ascribed identity grounds, such as gender, race or disability, in reinforcing patterns of poverty and social exclusion.[60] However, the accommodation of intersectionality within social rights jurisprudence has the potential to bring these two dimensions of equality together. It lays down foundations for the development of a multi-dimensional understanding of social rights, which would be capable of engaging with the multiplicity of factors that generate social exclusion – and, in particular, the complex ways in which material inequality can intersect with other modes of discriminatory treatment. It also underscores that, as Conaghan puts it, 'all inequalities are intersectional': the inequalities generated by poverty and material inequality are co-constituted by, and inherently bound up with, multiple other interlocking forms of structural disadvantage.[61]

In this regard, it is also worth highlighting that the emergence of social rights jurisprudence is, in itself, significant from an intersectionality perspective. For, by enlarging the scope and substance of human rights law, it also enlarges its capacity to engage with the greatest generator of social inequality – namely, poverty and the consequences of material inequality.[62] And, by extension, this also extends its capacity to address the intersectional impact of poverty and material inequality taken in combination with other discriminatory factors. As Atrey has noted:

> The vast canon on intersectionality, which spans far beyond discrimination law and its notion of grounds, has thus centred on unravelling and addressing the complexity of intersectional disadvantage and discrimination suffered by people. Seen from this perspective, poverty or poverty discrimination appears to be a paradigmatic intersectional case. It is intersectional not only in terms of its complex structural disadvantage which goes beyond the level of income or wealth towards a broader conception of harms including loss of dignity and autonomy, social exclusion and so on, but also because it cuts across other systems of subordination associated with status groups like Blacks, women, Roma, Dalits, gays, disabled, the aged and so on.[63]

However, human rights law in general – and equality law in particular – has historically provided little or no meaningful legal protection against the socially exclusionary impact of poverty and material inequality.[64] This has been viewed as

---

[60] See Stuart Hall's penetrating comments on this topic: the critique 'that [political correctness] concerns itself with irrelevant and trivial issues as compared with the "real" questions of poverty, unemployment and economic disadvantage … is the product of an archaic view, a sort of crass, low-flying materialism, that "class" is both more real and more simple to address than, say, gender; that "class", because it is linked to the economic, is somehow more materially determining, and that the economic … factors work as it were on their own, outside of their social and ideological, their gendered and "raced" conditions of existence'; S Hall, 'Some "Politically Incorrect" Pathways through PC' in S Dunant (ed), *The War of the Words: The Political Correctness Debate* (Virago, 1994) 164–84.

[61] J Conaghan, 'Intersectionality and the Feminist Project in Law' in D Cooper et al (eds), *Law, Power and the Politics of Subjectivity: Intersectionality and Beyond* (Routledge, 2008) 21–48, 42.

[62] Malleson (n 6).

[63] Atrey (n 41).

[64] In part, this has reflected the divide famously identified by Nancy Fraser between scholars and activists primarily concerned with social redistribution and those focused on 'recognition' issues

a problem beyond the concerns of law: something for the political branches of the state to address, but a 'zone of exclusion' for court-focused remedies.[65] As a result, as Atrey has noted, courts have been very slow to extend existing parameters of equality law or rights jurisprudence to engage with the impact of poverty-related discrimination.[66] In turn, this has hampered the already constrained ability of the law to engage with intersectional discrimination: legal systems generally lack the capacity to respond in any meaningful way to how poverty and material inequality amplify the impact of other forms of inequality.

Furthermore, this lack of legal protection has arguably also helped to obscure the intersectional impact of poverty and material inequality more generally within both public policy debates and conceptual discussions about intersectional discrimination. To quote Atrey again:

> [P]overty in discrimination law has been understood not in intersectional terms ... but as a fragmented or simplistic case of economic redistribution which has nothing to do with other forms of disadvantage and discrimination of status groups ... [T]his omission appears neither calculated nor well-meaning but based on an unquestioning assumption of the dominant framework in discrimination law which is too removed from complex disadvantages associated with poverty, and too fixated on grounds or status groups considered independently and in isolation of the poverty which exists within them.[67]

In other words, much work on intersectionality has focused on the overlapping and reinforcing impact of the standard forms of discrimination recognised in equality law (ie, the ascribed identity grounds of race, sex, disability and so on). In contrast, the impact of poverty and material inequality has often been left out of the picture, in part because of the lack of legal recognition of this key aspect of inequality. This has arguably impoverished intersectionality discourse and blunted its critique of the traditional 'single-axis' ascribed identity approach: a major limitation of this approach – namely, its lack of a 'poverty dimension' and the intersectional consequences that flow from that – has been glossed over.[68]

But the emergence of social rights adjudication, in both its direct and indirect forms, has opened up a new front for intersectionality critique. While still embryonic in form (a qualifier that deserves repeated emphasis), it offers a set of legal tools which can engage with the intersectional effects of poverty and material inequality, as demonstrated by the use of 'group vulnerability' as an evaluative tool for assessing the adequacy of state action in the case law of the ECtHR, the ECSR

---

relating to the ascribed identity grounds; N Fraser, 'Social Justice in the Age of Identity Politics: Redistribution, Recognition, Participation' in N Fraser and A Honneth, *Redistribution or Recognition?: A Political-Philosophical Exchange* (Verso, 2003) 7–109.

[65] O'Cinneide (n 32).

[66] Atrey (n 41).

[67] ibid.

[68] See ibid 411: 'this way, grounds serve as the gatekeepers of discrimination law and seldom admit poverty or its attendant deprivations like homelessness, unemployment, starvation, malnutrition or illiteracy in the inner circle of protected characteristics'. See also Malleson (n 6).

and the CESCR discussed above. Furthermore, by establishing new legal avenues for challenging unequal treatment linked to poverty, social rights jurisprudence has the potential to focus attention on how such inequality contributes to individual and group subordination, and, by extension, on its intersectional impact. In essence, it puts a legal spotlight on poverty and material inequality that has hitherto not been much in evidence, and, as a result, has the potential to add the missing 'poverty dimension' that is often glossed over in intersectionality critique.

In general, social rights discourse needs an intersectional dimension extending beyond the specific impact of poverty and material inequality, just as existing intersectionality discourse relating to ascribed identity discrimination needs a material inequality/socio-economic rights dimension. The new emerging social rights jurisprudence – and in particular the use of 'group vulnerability' as an evaluative tool by the ECtHR, the ECSR and the CESCR – attempts to merge these two parallel tracks. In so doing, this case law highlights the oft-neglected poverty/ material inequality dimension to intersectionality, while also demonstrating the importance of intersectional analysis to the development of any serious social rights jurisprudence.[69] There is a possibility here of a virtuous feedback loop opening up: the evolution of social rights adjudication may draw more attention in general to the poverty/material inequality dimension to intersectionality, while itself being enriched and deepened by the multi-faceted perspectives on inequality generated by intersectional critique.

Also, it is clear that the intersectional dimension to social rights jurisprudence is capable of being widely applied. The adequacy of state delivery of social goods, such as education, welfare and health, often varies significantly in terms of its impact on groups caught at the intersection of different modes of social exclusion.[70] As such, vulnerability analysis informed by intersectional perspectives has plenty of issues on which to 'bite'.

For example, in the UK, austerity cuts introduced in the early 2010s have been subject to repeated legal challenges under Article 14 ECHR on the basis that they had a disproportionate impact on a variety of different groups defined by the intersection of vulnerable socio-economic status and standard identity grounds, such as domestic carers, certain categories of persons with disabilities, and victims of domestic violence[71] (*JD and A v UK* is a Strasbourg continuation of one of these domestic challenges). Some have been successful and some have not. But, taken together, they illustrate the fertile ground that has been opened up even within indirect forms of social rights jurisprudence for intersectional inequalities to form the basis of legal challenges.

---

[69] Indeed, it is likely that social rights jurisprudence will draw heavily upon legal and conceptual developments in other areas of law concerned with equality: see M Stein, 'Disability Human Rights' (2007) 95 *California Law Review* 75.

[70] Goldblatt, 'Intersectionality in International Anti-discrimination Law' (n 42).

[71] *R (Rutherford) v Secretary of State for Work and Pensions* [2016] UKSC 58; *Hurley v Secretary of State for Work and Pensions* [2015] EWHC 3382 (Admin).

Thus, intersectionality has much to contribute to the emergence of social rights jurisprudence – just as social rights jurisprudence does for intersectional critique. Furthermore, the emerging intersectional dimension to social rights protection is already proving to be a highly significant component part of this case law. As channelled in particular via the evaluative concept of 'group vulnerability', intersectionality is being used to add more depth and substance to the review of state action impacting on the enjoyment of social rights, and as an analytical tool for coming to grips with the complex ways in which social inequalities are generated and sustained. This reflects the wider ambitions of intersectionality critique more generally and shows that it has the capacity to be applied beyond the narrow limits of anti-discrimination law. Indeed, it demonstrates that intersectionality is relevant across the full spectrum of human rights law and discourse on account of how it helps to sharpen comprehension of how overlapping forms of disadvantage may generate rights violations, and also because of how it helps to dissolve artificial conceptual boundaries between different categories of fundamental rights and, in particular, between social rights and equality/non-discrimination entitlements.[72]

However, before acclaiming all this as a straightforward 'win' for the ambitions of intersectionality, a cautionary note must be added. The emerging intersectional dimension to social rights jurisprudence is also bringing to the fore some conceptual tensions that are immanent to intersectionality critique in general. These tensions complicate the attempt to develop this intersectional dimension to social rights adjudication and also raise interesting questions about the extent to which intersectionality can be given effect through law more generally.

V. The Risks of Intersectionality When Applied in the Context of Social Rights Adjudication

The progenitors of intersectionality have always emphasised that it can and should be applied across all the major overlapping forms of structural inequality in contemporary society, including poverty and material inequality.[73] However, as already discussed, intersectionality critique has been primarily developed and applied with reference to established non-discrimination grounds, such as race and gender, while the overlapping impact of poverty and material inequality has often been ignored.

This situation may, as this chapter has argued, change with the emergence of social rights jurisprudence. However, it remains the case that intersectionality is widely viewed as predominantly concerned with the overlapping impact of identity grounds, such as race, gender and disability. Furthermore, discrimination law, as it relates to these identity grounds, is much better developed than social

---

[72] I am grateful to Shreya Atrey for this point.
[73] See, eg, 'The Combahee River Collective Statement' (n 3).

rights jurisprudence and it will often have greater credibility within domestic legal systems in particular, while the NGO/activist infrastructure that has been built around issues such as race and sex discrimination is often much more developed than is the case for poverty/material inequality.

As a result, there is a risk that the development of an intersectional dimension to social rights jurisprudence will generate case law and a set of associated legal outcomes and standards that focus predominantly on the impact of discrimination based on these established identity grounds, while neglecting or downplaying the exclusionary impact of poverty/material inequality, taken together with identity grounds. Litigants may be happier to focus their arguments on the former set of norms rather than develop arguments around the latter.[74] A similar temptation may apply to courts and other adjudicatory bodies applying direct or indirect modes of social rights adjudication.[75] This is understandable: existing legal standards relating to grounds-based discrimination are more evolved than those applying to the poverty/material inequality side of the equation and thus are easier to rely upon. But this may result in a lopsided growth of intersectional social rights jurisprudence, with the overlapping impact of inequalities linked to income or class giving way to the impact of more familiar and legally established forms of discrimination. This, in turn, risks limiting the development of social rights jurisprudence, and contributing to the elision of poverty and material inequality as key determinants of inequality.

Furthermore, intersectional critique tends to place considerable emphasis on the need to take account of how overlapping patterns of social exclusion can have a particular impact on specific groups, with a view to adding more groups to the list of 'who or what counts for purposes of equality protection in law'.[76] In other words, it aims to expand legal cognisance of intersectional forms of discrimination and how they impact upon specific social groups. However, when applied in the context of social rights adjudication, this focus on highlighting intersectional group disadvantage risks obscuring the prior question of what constitutes the minimum baseline floor of treatment which all individuals and groups must enjoy

---

[74] This is illustrated by many of the collective complaints relating to the European Social Charter litigated before the ECSR. In many of the intersectional cases mentioned above, such as Complaint 48/2008, *ERRC v Bulgaria* (Decision on the merits 31 March 2009), the pleadings of the NGOs initiating the complaints were often much more developed in respect of the overlapping impact of identity discrimination than they were in respect of the impact of poverty/material inequality.

[75] For example, CESCR General Comment No 20 on non-discrimination in economic, social and cultural rights only devotes six lines to outlining when discrimination on the basis of socio-economic status may breach the requirements of the Covenant, with a few more lines devoted to acknowledging the possibility of multiple and intersectional discrimination, while the rest of the Comment focuses on standard identity grounds, such as race and sex discrimination. See UN Committee on Economic, Social and Cultural Rights (CESCR), General Comment No 20: Non-discrimination in economic, social and cultural rights (art 2, para 2, of the International Covenant on Economic, Social and Cultural Rights), 2 July 2009, E/C.12/GC/20 [35].

[76] Conaghan (n 61); J Conaghan, 'Intersectionality and UK Equality Initiatives' (2007) 23(2) *South African Journal of Human Rights* 317.

as of right. In other words, a concern with securing equality of treatment across a spectrum of different social groups, reflecting the origins of intersectionality as a critique of the specific limits of anti-discrimination law, might divert attention away from the core ambition of social rights adjudication – namely, to set out the dignitarian substance of such rights that should be universally enjoyed by all members of a given society.[77]

These concerns can be exaggerated. Indeed, the evaluative 'group vulnerability' approach discussed above, as applied by the ECSR in particular, is primarily concerned with identifying what constitutes the minimum level of support that a state should provide to a specific social group: it integrates dignitarian and equal treatment concerns into a contextual analysis of what respect for social rights entails in relation to the specific needs of a specific group of individuals defined by reference to shared vulnerabilities.[78] However, as Conaghan has argued, the legal imagination as it relates to intersectionality is often narrowed by its tendency to refer back to its original starting point – ie, a focus on the intersecting impact of ascribed identity grounds such as race and sex.[79] As a consequence, there is a risk that a hypertrophic growth of intersectionality within social rights jurisprudence may stunt the development of its universalist dimension by encouraging a focus on group disadvantage when wider issues of general baseline provision are at stake.[80]

Arguably, these concerns need to be factored into the application of intersectional approaches in the context of social rights jurisprudence. The ECSR confronted them directly in its decision on *European Roma Rights Centre v Bulgaria*.[81] This case concerned the adoption by Bulgaria of US-style 'welfare roll' reforms, whereby individuals receiving unemployment insurance for an extended period of time would lose entitlement to that benefit. The complainant NGO argued that this measure would have a disproportionate impact on Bulgaria's vulnerable Roma minority, who suffered from high degrees of unemployment, and therefore argued that the reforms constituted indirect discrimination on the grounds of race. However, the majority of the Committee concluded that the reforms would impact, with equal seriousness, all individuals deprived of unemployment benefit, and that a total deprivation of welfare support in this way would breach the universal guarantee of access to social assistance set out in Article 13§1 of the Social Charter. The majority thus treated the specific disadvantage faced by Roma

---

[77] Similar concerns have been expressed at the political level about the potential for intersectionality critique to divert focus away from arguments in support of universal social provision or to disaggregate general issues of social justice into a disparate set of identity group-focused claims. See, eg, A Haider, *Mistaken Identity: Race and Class in the Age of Trump* (Verso, 2018).

[78] See eg, the decision of the ECSR in *ERRC v Bulgaria* (n 47).

[79] Conaghan (n 61).

[80] This risk is amplified by how indirect forms of social rights adjudication will often involve the application of non-discrimination analysis, as happens in ECHR cases where art 14 of the Convention is invoked to challenge cuts in welfare benefit rather than direct engagement with substantive social rights guarantees.

[81] *ERRC v Bulgaria* (n 74).

in receipt of unemployment assistance (an intersectional category) as subsumed within the wider breach of the right to social assistance (a universal category), conscious of how the disadvantage in question would impact equally on everyone denied access to welfare. In so doing, they framed their conclusion in terms of a breach of universal minimum standards rather than as an intersectional violation or 'single-axis' discrimination, which arguably better reflected the 'essence' of the rights violation at issue.[82]

Another potential concern is that intersectionality analysis places heavy reliance on the 'relative disadvantage' paradigm adopted by equality and non-discrimination law taken as a whole – ie, it generally defines wrongful behaviour by reference to groups suffering less favourable treatment based on a combination of grounds, as compared to the treatment of other such groups. However, establishing whether such 'relative disadvantage' exists can be a challenging exercise, which is amplified in the context of social rights adjudication, given how state measures affecting entitlement to education, healthcare, welfare and other forms of social rights may impact on different groups in a variety of different ways.

In the academic literature on intersectionality, it is generally recognised that the traditional rigid comparator approach applied in 'single-axis' discrimination case law is very difficult (if not impossible) to apply to intersectional discrimination. Instead, a more 'contextual' approach is required, which zeroes on the concrete disadvantages generated by intersectional discrimination in respect of a particular group within a particular field of activity, while abandoning the usual requirement to point to a comparator in a directly analogous situation.[83]

As already noted, this approach chimes with the 'substantive turn' in equality and human rights law, and is reflected in the development of group vulnerability analysis. It has particular appeal in the social rights field, given the wide variety of circumstances in which vulnerable groups can be caught up in the overlap of poverty-based exclusion and other forms of structural discrimination, and how such groups may be affected in very distinct ways by the complex and often Byzantine structure of state systems of social welfare provision.

However, there is inevitably going to be some scepticism about the appropriateness of adopting such a 'contextual' approach. The very thing about this approach that attracts proponents of intersectionality – its focus on the specific situation of a vulnerable group – may repel supporters of a more formal, cautious understanding of equality. From this latter perspective, the singling out of a particular group for special protection may beg the question as to why this group should be treated any differently from other groups who find themselves in a similar state of disadvantage. Questions may also arise about how homogeneous the group is and

---

[82] The author was a member of this majority. Three members of the Committee dissented on this point, taking the view that a separate violation of the Charter was made out on the grounds of indirect race discrimination.

[83] S Atrey, 'Comparison in Intersectional Discrimination' (2018) 38(3) *Legal Studies* 379; I Solanke, 'Putting Race and Gender Together: A New Approach to Intersectionality' (2009) 72(5) *Modern Law Review* 723.

whether an 'over-broad concept of vulnerability and dependence' is being applied in a given situation.[84]

Furthermore, sceptics can argue that the complexity of such systems of social provision and the multiplicity of different groups that are affected in different ways by the intersectional impact of poverty/material inequality and other grounds are actually arguments that speak in favour of judicial non-intervention. In general, social rights are viewed as an area where courts and other adjudicatory bodies should tread with great caution: they are often viewed as lacking the expertise and democratic legitimacy to assess the legitimacy of the various trade-offs that states make in giving effect to such rights. As such, the multi-faceted nature of inter-sectional disadvantage when poverty/material inequality is taken into account, and the sheer number of different groups that could be classed as 'vulnerable' in contemporary socio-economic conditions, could be cited as an additional reason for human rights law to be reined in and not extended in this context.[85]

These sceptical arguments can be answered. The impact of intersectional discrimination is real, with the overlapping impact of poverty and material inequality often amplifying its consequences in unfair ways. Furthermore, the 'group vulnerability' approach offers a way of identifying particularly exposed groups without disappearing down a comparative 'rabbit hole' involving endless and indeterminate group comparison. It takes account of historical context and contemporary socio-economic reality in evaluating the adequacy of state action as it impacts upon social groups at particular risk of destitution or socio-economic marginalisation, and it focuses on identifying the minimum baseline of provision that such groups should receive rather than assessing the comparative favourable-ness of their treatment as opposed to others.[86]

Having said that, the potential objections of sceptics signal the need for the group vulnerability approach to be applied with rigour.[87] Assumptions of group vulnerability should be backed up by compelling argumentation and objective justification analysis should be applied with due regard for the complexity of decision-making relating to social rights.[88]

---

[84] See the partially dissenting opinion of Judge Sajó in *MSS v Belgium and Greece* (2011) EHRR 108, who raised these points of concern about the majority's assumption that asylum seekers were a particu-larly vulnerable group (as opposed to other persons dependent upon state welfare support) for the purpose of assessing whether the basic level of welfare support given to them by the Greek government satisfied the requirements of art 3 ECHR. See also Peroni and Timmer (n 18) 1083.

[85] For an example of this line of argument, see the dissenting opinions of Judges Pejchal and Wojtyczek in the ECHR case of *JD and A v UK* (n 21). They concluded that there were insufficient grounds for treating female victims of domestic violence as a uniquely vulnerable group when compared to other groups also affected by the housing benefit cuts at issue in that case, and emphasised that courts should be slow to second-guess how governments handle the difficult classification decisions that inevitably have to be made in allocating welfare resources.

[86] For more on this point, see Peroni and Timmer (n 18).

[87] ibid 1083–85.

[88] Thus, in *JD and A v UK* (n 21), in concluding that the UK had discriminated against female victims of domestic violence by not exempting them from benefit cuts designed to encourage families living in oversized public housing to downsize to smaller accommodation, the majority of the Court highlighted

Taken together, these concerns suggest that an intersectional approach to social rights adjudication needs to be applied with one eye on its potential down-sides. This does not mean abandoning the ambitions of intersectionality. However, its limits need to be recognised, along with the importance of universal minimum standard-setting to this new and embryonic area of law.

Conclusion

The ambition of intersectionality to reconfigure 'single-axis' concept of discrimination is gradually being extended to encompass the overlapping impact of poverty and material inequality. This ambition is reflected in the development of social rights adjudication, where intersectional concerns – often refracted through 'group vulnerability' analysis – loom increasingly large in the existing case law. This is a healthy development, reflecting the need for an intersectional approach in this context which engages with the interlocking impact of poverty, material inequality and other forms of identity ground discrimination. There are risks involved in developing such an intersectional approach and plenty of potential wrong turns. However, these can be contained, especially if the 'group vulnerability' approach is applied with due caution and rigour, and due attention is paid to what should be the core ambition of social rights adjudication, namely to set out minimum baseline standards capable of being applied across the whole of society.

how the UK government had recognised the symbolic and emotional importance of ensuring that victims of domestic violence were to remain in their homes – a goal which the benefit cuts undermined. In so doing, the Court distinguished the treatment of this group with the treatment afforded to another group of claimants, namely disabled persons living in accommodation, which had been adjusted to meet their needs: discretionary funds were available to limit any negative impact on this second group, and there was no similar policy imperative to maintain a continuous residence in one place.

4

The Right to Education and Substantive Equality

An Intersectional Reading

SANDRA FREDMAN

Introduction

Despite the apparent universality of human rights, it has long been clear that having a right does not mean that it is equally enjoyed. Instead, access to the full range of human rights is still patterned by race, gender, disability and poverty. Nowhere is this clearer than in relation to the right to education. Education is an accelerator right, a crucial pathway out of poverty. It is also a multiplier right, enabling the full enjoyment of other rights, such as freedom of speech.[1] Yet it is still the case, both globally and in national contexts, that women, minorities, persons with disabilities and, above all, people living in poverty face considerable obstacles in accessing education. Most affected are those at the intersection of all of these, consigning those at this dangerous juncture to ongoing poverty.

I have previously argued that in order to play a role in addressing gendered poverty, human rights themselves need to be engendered.[2] In particular, I have argued that human rights need to be fashioned to take account of the interlocking factors which operate synergistically to cause and maintain gendered poverty. This in turn requires an approach to human rights which incorporates the insights of substantive equality. In this chapter, I take this further and suggest that only through an intersectional understanding of human rights can we make any progress towards the ideal of a right to education to which everyone is equally entitled.

[1] See further S Fredman, *Comparative Human Rights Law* (Oxford University Press, 2018) ch 11.
[2] S Fredman, 'Engendering Social Welfare Rights' in B Goldblatt and L Lamarache (eds), *Women's Rights to Social Security and Social Protection* (Hart Publishing, 2015); S Fredman, 'Engendering Socio-economic Rights' [2009] 25 *South African Journal of Human Rights* 1; S Fredman, 'Women and Poverty: A Human Rights Approach' (2016) 24 *African Journal of International and Comparative Law* 494.

Section I of this chapter examines the extent to which discrimination on the grounds of race, gender and poverty, and particularly the synergism between them, causes and perpetuates barriers to the right to education. This in turn creates a vicious cycle of intergenerational transmission of inequality in access to human rights. Section II develops the principles of substantive equality which need to be used to refashion the right to education in an intersectional sense. Sections III, IV and V apply this analysis by comparing and contrasting the ways in which these issues have been dealt with in the jurisprudence of the US and South Africa, respectively. Thus, *Brown v Board of Education*[3] focused on race but ignored poverty, leaving racialised poverty in access to education untouched. By contrast, later cases consciously focused on disadvantage, which meant that the crucial role of race went unaddressed. In South Africa, jurisprudence on the right to education has similarly failed to take an intersectional approach. Racially inferior education under apartheid left a legacy of racialised poverty which has proved challenging to shift. Nevertheless, the robust right to education in the South African Constitution has primarily been used to address poverty and disadvantage rather than race. Even less attention has been paid to gender and its intersection with race and poverty. This is particularly acute in relation to pregnancy at school, which is dealt with in section V.

I. Education: An Unequal Right

The disproportionate representation of women, minorities and poor people among those denied full enjoyment of their right to education is clear from even a snapshot of global statistics. Recent figures show that as many as 750 million adults globally remain illiterate. Of these, a staggering two-thirds are women. Nor is this likely to change for the next generation. About one-third of countries in developing regions have not achieved gender parity in primary education. In Central Asia, for example, 27 per cent more girls than boys of primary school age are not attending school. The barriers faced by girls in entering primary and secondary education inevitably limit their access to opportunities in the labour market. This in turn perpetuates poverty.

The correlation between lack of access to education and poverty is not limited to women. More than half of children who have not enrolled in school live in Sub-Saharan Africa. Even if children do attend school, the quality of education they achieve is highly dependent on their social position. In 2015, more than 55 per cent of the global total of children and adolescents of primary and lower secondary school age lacked minimum proficiency in reading and mathematics. Correspondingly, more than half the schools in Sub-Saharan Africa do not have

---

[3] *Brown v Board of Education* 347 US 483 (1954) (US Supreme Court).

access to basic drinking water and handwashing facilities, or crucial modern resources, such as the internet and computers.[4]

The intersectionality of violations of the right to education is similarly stark in the two countries examined in this chapter. In the US, in 2018, Blacks had the highest poverty rate at 20.8 per cent, contrasting starkly with the rate of 8.1 per cent among non-Hispanic whites. Poverty is also gendered. Families headed by a single woman have a poverty rate of 24.9 per cent, accounting for half of all families in poverty. The intersectionality of race and poverty in relation to education is dramatic. Nearly one-quarter (24.9 per cent) of adults over 25 years of age who do not have a high school diploma live in poverty. This contrasts with 4.4 per cent poverty in adults of the same age group with a college degree.[5] The key factor is racialised poverty rather than race per se. According to a recent study: 'The association of racial segregation with achievement gaps is completely accounted for by racial differences in school poverty: racial segregation appears to be harmful because it concentrates minority students in high-poverty schools, which are, on average, less effective than lower-poverty schools.'[6] This is not a coincidence. According to this research: 'Racial segregation tends to concentrate black and Hispanic children in schools where most of the students come from poor families because of the persistent connection between race and income in the United States. And those high-poverty schools provide fewer opportunities than schools that are more affluent.'[7]

In South Africa, the apartheid system deliberately created racialised poverty. However, the end of apartheid has not brought with it an end to this intersectional inequality. Although poverty has declined since 1994, inequality has risen, making South Africa the world's most unequal country according to World Bank Group data.[8] In 2015, as many as 64.1 per cent of Black South Africans and 41.3 per cent of coloured South Africans were poor. This compares strikingly with the corresponding figure of 1 per cent for white South Africans.[9] The World Bank identifies insufficient skills and the legacy of apartheid education as the key constraints to reducing poverty and inequality. Completing secondary school and, ideally,

---

[4] Sustainable Development Goals, 'Quality Education: Why it Matters', https://www.un.org/sustainabledevelopment/wp-content/uploads/2017/02/4.pdf; Sustainable Development Goals Infographic, 'Quality Education', https://www.un.org/sustainabledevelopment/wp-content/uploads/2019/07/E_Infographic_04.pdf.

[5] US Census Bureau, 'Income and Poverty in the United States: 2018' (September 2019), https://www.census.gov/library/publications/2019/demo/p60-266.html. For a summary, see 'US Poverty Statistics', *Federal Safety Net*, http://federalsafetynet.com/us-poverty-statistics.html.

[6] SF Reardon et al, 'Is Separate Still Unequal? New Evidence on School Segregation and Racial Academic Achievement Gaps' (CEPA Working Paper No 19-06, 2019), Stanford Center for Education Policy Analysis, https://cepa.stanford.edu/content/separate-still-unequal-new-evidence-school-segregation-and-racial-academic-achievement-gaps.

[7] C Samuels, 'Poverty, Not Race, Fuels the Achievement Gap' (*Education Week*, 1 October 2019), https://www.edweek.org/ew/articles/2019/10/02/poverty-not-race-fuels-the-achievement-gap.html.

[8] 'An Incomplete Transition: Overcoming the Legacy of Exclusion in South Africa' (Wold Bank Group Report No 125838-ZA, 2018).

[9] ibid 22.

a university degree is therefore crucial to reducing poverty. There is a clear correlation: 93 per cent of those who had not experienced poverty in the past 10 years had at least some secondary education, whereas of the heads of household who were chronically poor, only 5 per cent had completed secondary education.[10] Gradin concludes that despite important progress since the end of apartheid and the end of formal race segregation in schools, the literature points to an increasing role of the racial gap in the quality of education, and the intergenerational transmission of poverty in households where heads of households have low educational achievement.[11] Importantly, however, this is not only an issue of race. The World Bank Group report shows that class is an increasing driver of inequality, but while more Blacks are entering the middle class, the poorest classes remain overwhelmingly Black. A recognition of the intersectionality between race, gender, class and poverty is therefore crucial in ensuring that the right to education is enjoyed equally by all.

II. Substantive Equality and the Right to Education: An Intersectional Analysis

What then does an intersectional analysis of the right to education entail? The first step is to probe more deeply into the promise that 'everyone has a right'. The above analysis shows vividly that formally equal access to a right is a far cry from the reality. A more substantive understanding of equality is required in order to fully illuminate this foundational intersectionality. Substantive equality remains a contested concept, but I have previously argued that the right to substantive equality resists reduction to a single conception.[12] Instead, I have argued for a four-dimensional approach to the right to equality, which requires attention to be paid to the need to redress disadvantage (the redistributive dimension), to address prejudice, stereotyping stigma and violence (the recognition dimension), to facilitate voice and participation (the participative dimension), and to celebrate difference and achieve structural change (the transformative dimension). These dimensions require simultaneous attention rather than falling into any type of lexical priority. In Alexy's terms, all four require optimisation to the fullest possible extent, both legally and factually.[13] I suggest here that this four-dimensional approach best illuminates how the right to education should be reshaped to fully

---

[10] ibid 23.

[11] C Gradin, 'Race, Poverty and Deprivation in South Africa' (2012) 22 *Journal of African Economies* 187, 220.

[12] S Fredman, 'Beyond the Dichotomy of Formal and Substantive Equality: Towards a New Definition of Equal Rights' in I Boerefijn et al (eds), *Temporary Special Measures* (Intersentia, 2003); S Fredman, 'Substantive Equality Revisited' (2016) 14 *International Journal of Constitutional Law* 712.

[13] R Alexy, *A Theory of Constitutional Rights* (Oxford University Press, 2004).

take into account the intersectional concerns set out above. These dimensions are briefly outlined below.

First, substantive equality should concentrate on remedying disadvantage rather than aiming at race or gender-neutrality. Where there is antecedent poverty and racism, an approach to the right to equality which assumes that race, poverty or gender should be treated as irrelevant simply reinforces existing inequality.[14] Substantive equality should therefore be deliberately asymmetric, focusing on the disadvantaged group. Intersectionality is crucial to the understanding of disadvantage. It makes it possible to depart from the comparative requirements of formal equality, which narrow the perspective to the difference between one identity group and another. Instead, the prism of disadvantage takes in the synergism of race, gender, poverty and any other identity in order to focus on the reality of the experience of deprivation of the right. For example, if a pregnant learner at a poor, racialised school is excluded from schooling, the nature of her synergistic disadvantage is in focus, without the need to find an equivalent comparator. In the context of education, this asymmetry means, crucially, that affirmative action in favour of the disadvantaged group may be required to achieve the right to education. It also means that an equal right to education cannot be achieved by 'levelling down' or lowering the quality of education for all.

The second dimension of the right to substantive equality aims to redress stigma, stereotyping, humiliation and violence in the experience of the right to education. This makes it possible to distinguish between forced segregation and the right to choose separate education to maintain minority language, religion or culture. Many of the obstacles to poor people enjoying their rights come from the stigma and stereotyping that accompany poverty. As the Committee on Economic, Social and Cultural Rights has recognised, living in poverty or being homeless can be a source of stigmatisation and negative stereotyping, leading to unequal access to the same quality of health or education as others.[15]

The third dimension of substantive equality aims to facilitate voice and participation. As has been recognised in several jurisdictions, equality should specifically compensate for the absence of political power of groups 'to whose needs and wishes elected officials have no apparent interest in attending'.[16] The intersectional perspective makes it essential to pay close attention to the diversity of voices within the group, to the possible disjuncture between those who speak and those who are affected, and to the need to ensure that the least vocal are nevertheless heard. Moreover, just as voice and participation are crucial to ensuring that the right to education is equally enjoyed, so the right to education gives those at the intersection of many disadvantages the capability to articulate their perspectives.

---

[14] A Sen, *Inequality Re-examined* (Oxford University Press, 1992).

[15] CESCR General Comment No 20 on non-discrimination in economic, social and cultural rights (E/C.12/GC/20, 2 July 2009) [36].

[16] JH Ely, *Democracy and Distrust: A Theory of Judicial Review* (Harvard University Press, 1980) 46.

The fourth dimension goes beyond formal equality's demand that outgroups conform to existing structures as a condition of inclusion. Instead, substantive equality requires a recognition and celebration of difference and a transformation of existing social structures to incorporate diverse identities. In the context of education, a focus on improving disadvantaged schools will not succeed unless placed in the context of tackling the structures of racialised poverty, which include residential segregation, parental disadvantage, fewer avenues to better-paid jobs and lack of political influence. Conversely, the right to education, reshaped to incorporate an intersectional perspective, is the pathway to transforming structures.

Having set out an intersectional approach to the right to education based on a four-dimensional understanding of substantive equality, I now turn to an analysis of some of the case law in the US and South Africa, respectively.

III. Separate Trajectories: The US Approach

In the US, it was racial discrimination which initially drove the agenda in relation to education.[17] The social reality of racialised poverty was conspicuous, but the remedy was considered to consist in racial integration rather than in directly redressing the disadvantage. This was perhaps inevitable given the absence of a constitutional right to education at the federal level, and the history of racism that institutionalised race discrimination in education. Thus, in the seminal case of *Brown v Board of Education*,[18] both the litigants and the Supreme Court deliberately suppressed the role of poverty and socio-economic disadvantage. Instead, the Court expressly based its finding on an assumption of equal educational facilities. This was crucial to the finding that segregated education was itself a breach of the right to equality. As Warren CJ famously held: 'In the field of public education, separate but equal has no place. Separate educational facilities are inherently unequal.'[19] Even if 'tangible factors' such as building, curricula and teachers were asserted to be equal, the effect of segregation itself meant that the result could never be equal.

The Supreme Court's finding is a ringing endorsement of the recognition dimension of substantive equality: 'To separate [African-American] children from others of similar age and qualifications solely because of their race generates a feeling of inferiority in their status in the community that may affect their hearts and minds in a way unlikely ever to be undone.'[20] However, the lack of attention to the other dimensions, which would have highlighted the inter-relationship of poverty and race and its multiplier effect for Black pupils, had a lasting limiting effect on the jurisprudence. It is well known that in reality, the facilities available to Black

---

[17] This section is taken from Fredman (n 1) ch 11.
[18] *Brown* (n 3).
[19] ibid 495.
[20] ibid 494.

learners were inevitably inferior. Had the Court paid attention to the redistributive dimension of substantive equality, this would have been obvious.

Nor did the case pay sufficient attention to the third or fourth dimensions, or the role of voice and participation and the need for underlying structural change. As Minow puts it: 'Because of *Brown*, schools stopped explicitly assigning students to schools that separate them by race, but parents and communities can produce similar results indirectly through housing patterns, district lines, and even some forms of school choice.'[21] This lack of ability to recognise both the lack of voice and the structural issues was epitomised by *Rodriguez v San Antonio*.[22] This case arose out of the extreme inequities in the state system of funding schools, due to the fact that public education was funded by local taxes. Schools in poor districts, with low property values, would inevitably be vastly worse off than schools in well-off districts. San Antonio was a school district in Texas, in which 90 per cent of students were Mexican American and 6 per cent were African American. Property values were so low that even though local rates were substantially higher than in the neighbouring, largely white, district, the per capita spending on education was only just over half of the neighbouring school district. The claimants, Mexican-American parents of children attending school in San Antonio, argued that this breached their rights under the Equal Protection Clause. To sustain their claim, they had to establish either that education was a fundamental right or that poverty was a 'suspect class' attracting strict scrutiny by the courts when treated less favourably than others.

The US Supreme Court, by a narrow majority of 5:4, rejected both claims. As well as refusing to regard education as a fundamental right, it also rejected the claim that poverty could itself be a ground for discrimination. It was unable to see the close connection between poverty, race and inequality in all its dimensions, including not just disadvantage, but also prejudice, lack of voice and structural inequality. Particularly salient was the Court's refusal to see the link between poverty and lack of voice or participation. According to the majority, the disadvantaged class was not a 'discrete and insular minority' similar to racial or ethnic minority groups: 'The system of alleged discrimination and the class it defines have none of the traditional indicia of suspectness: the class is not saddled with such disabilities, or subjected to such a history of purposeful unequal treatment, or relegated to such a position of political powerlessness as to command extraordinary protection from the majoritarian political process.'[23]

Taking these dimensions into account yields a very different outcome, as evidenced by Marshall J's dissent:

> The majority's holding can only be seen as a retreat from our historic commitment to equality of educational opportunity and as unsupportable acquiescence in a system which deprives children in their earliest years of the chance to reach their full potential

---

[21] M Minow, *In Brown's Wake* (Oxford University Press, 2010) 8.
[22] *San Antonio Independent School District v Rodriguez* 411 US 959 (1973) (US Supreme Court).
[23] ibid 28.

as citizens. The Court does this despite the absence of any substantial justification for a scheme which arbitrarily channels educational resources in accordance with the fortuity of the amount of taxable wealth within each district. In my judgment, the right of every American to an equal start in life, so far as the provision of a state service as important as education is concerned, is far too vital to permit state discrimination on grounds as tenuous as those presented by this record.[24]

The political process had 'proved singularly unsuited to the task of providing a remedy for this discrimination'.[25]

This inability to acknowledge the intersection of poverty and race through the prism of multi-dimensional inequality has been reinforced in recent cases. In particular, the US Supreme Court has insisted that there is a significant difference between officially mandated segregation and socially produced patterns,[26] thus making it difficult to address structural causes of enduring disadvantage in education. This culminated in the 2007 decision in *Parents Involved v Seattle*.[27] The Seattle School District had never operated legally segregated schools and had never been subject to court-ordered desegregation orders. However, responding to the effect of racially identifiable housing patterns on access to better-quality schools, it adopted a 'racial tiebreaker' for assigning pupils to oversubscribed schools to achieve a better racial balance. In this way, it recognised the intersection between race and poverty, using a substantive equality approach to redress disadvantage, facilitate voice and participation, and achieve structural change. However, parents of students who had not been assigned to particular schools solely on the basis of their race claimed that the policy violated the Equal Protection Clause. By a 5:4 majority, the Supreme Court held that, unless mandated by courts as a remedy for proven race discrimination, policies to promote racial integration by school boards through classifying students by race were themselves racially discriminatory.

The respondent attempted to bring in the intersectional angle, arguing that it was legitimate to assign students by race to ensure that, despite residential segregation, African-American children from disadvantaged areas could access better schools. Rejecting this argument, Roberts CJ took a strictly symmetric view of *Brown*, regarding assignment on the basis of race as invidious, even if its aim was to correct past disadvantage. 'Before *Brown*', he declared, 'schoolchildren were told where they could and could not go to school based on the colour of their skin … The way to stop discrimination on the basis of race is to stop discriminating on the basis of race.'[28] Justice Breyer, dissenting, saw the legacy of *Brown* from the opposite direction: 'All of those plans represent local efforts to bring about the kind of

---

[24] ibid 71.

[25] ibid.

[26] M Rebell, 'Ensuring Adequate Funding: The Role of Courts' in W Mathis and T Trujillo (eds), *Learning from the Federal Test-Based Reforms: Lessons for ESSA* (Information Age Publishing, 2016) 509.

[27] *Parents Involved in Community Schools v Seattle School District* 127 S Ct 2738 (2007) (US Supreme Court).

[28] ibid 2768.

racially integrated education that *Brown v Board of Education* long ago promised.'[29] For him, the principle that *Brown* stood for was decidedly asymmetric: the basic objective of those who wrote the Equal Protection Clause, he argued, was to forbid practices leading to racial exclusion: 'There is reason to believe that those who drafted an Amendment with this basic purpose in mind would have understood the legal and practical difference between the use of race-conscious criteria in defiance of that purpose, namely to keep the races apart, and the use of race-conscious criteria to further that purpose, namely to bring the races together.'[30]

The result has been increasing racial 'resegregation' in public schools in the US. In fact, schools are now more racially segregated than they were when the effort to achieve racial desegregation was at its height.[31] More worrying still is the clear influence of the intersection between race and poverty. According to the Harvard Civil Rights Project, 'the vast majority of intensely segregated minority schools face conditions of concentrated poverty, which are powerfully related to unequal educational opportunity. Students in segregated minority schools can expect to face conditions which students in the very large number of segregated white schools seldom experience.'[32] The Court in *Brown* assumed that integration was sufficient to achieve quality education. However, this focus on race alone failed to take into account the ways in which the right to education is deeply shaped by racialised poverty. This meant that no attention was paid to the poor quality of Black and Hispanic schools. The result of this blindness to the intersection of race and poverty in relation to the right to education has been that not only has the desegregation project failed in its aspirations to integration, but it has also failed to improve the conditions of disadvantaged schools, largely populated by American Hispanics and African Americans. Nor did it improve the ability of children and their parents in these areas to participate in the political process or the broader society, thus neglecting the participative dimension. As was seen in the *Rodriguez* case above, this meant that politicians were not held to account for lower budgetary allocations for inner-city disadvantaged schools. It was therefore necessary to take a further step and establish that the inferior quality of education, and in particular the lower budgetary allocations for inner-city disadvantaged schools, were a breach of the equality guarantee.

This was done by turning to state constitutions, which include express rights to education. Initially, litigators continued to focus on race rather than explicitly on poverty. Regarding race as an appropriate proxy for poverty, they aimed to reduce disparities in educational expenditure by claiming that school financing systems were discriminatory. However, the absence of a substantive approach to equality in the courts' response was glaring. Rather than redressing disadvantage, courts sanctioned solutions to inequalities which reduced the budgetary allocations of

---

[29] ibid 2800.
[30] *Parents Involved in Community Schools* (n 27) 2815.
[31] Minow (n 21) 5.
[32] ibid 7.

privileged groups rather than levelling up the allocation of the disadvantaged group. For example, Californian courts' finding that wealth-related dispari- ties among school districts must be reduced to insignificant difference led to a dramatic levelling down of educational expenditures. California's ranking fell from fifth in the nation's per pupil spending to forty-second in the three decades from 1964 to 1994.[33]

Taking this lesson to heart, litigators, rather than focussing on equity claims, turned to 'adequacy' claims based on the substantive right to education. This in effect makes it mandatory for budgetary allocations to be based on human rights rather than human rights being conditional on budgets.[34] Adequacy claims were launched in 45 out of 50 states, aimed at giving substance to the right to education in state constitutions. These are variously worded as the requirement to provide all students with an 'adequate public education', 'a thorough and efficient education', a 'high quality system of free public schools' or a 'sound basic education'.[35] These claims have had substantial success, with plaintiffs prevailing in over 60 per cent of the final liability decisions on this issue.[36] Such success was in part facilitated by the fact that the vast majority of states had already made a commitment to develop standards for quality education, identifying academic content, specifying requirements for teacher training, and providing curricula, books facilities and other resources necessary for proper instruction in accordance with the standards. Courts could then test educational provision against these criteria.

These developments are clearly reflected in a series of groundbreaking cases brought by the Campaign for Fiscal Equity (CFE) beginning in 1995, in which the New York courts upheld applicants' claims of a violation by New York of its obliga- tions under the New York State Constitution.[37] On the basis that the duty of the state required 'minimally adequate' physical facilities and teaching by adequately trained teachers, the New York State Court of Appeals held that New York City public schools had breached this duty.[38] In the second CFE case (*CFE II*), it added that students should have the opportunity for 'a meaningful high school educa- tion, one which prepares them to function productively as civic participants' and 'compete for jobs that enable them to support themselves'.[39] In *CFE II*, the Court concluded that the state had deprived schoolchildren of a sound basic education.[40] It upheld the trial court's finding that the 'inputs' into these children's education,

---

[33] Rebell (n 26) 511.
[34] S Fredman, *Human Rights Transformed: Positive Rights and Positive Duties* (Oxford University Press, 2008) 219.
[35] Cited in Rebell (n 26) fns 9–12.
[36] ibid 507.
[37] New York State Constitution, art XI, § 1.
[38] *Campaign for Fiscal Equity v State of New York (CFE I)* 86 NY2d 307 [1995] (New York State Court of Appeals); 100 NY2d at 908.
[39] *Campaign for Fiscal Equity v State of New York (CFE II)* 100 NY2d 893 (2003) (Court of Appeals of the State of New York), 903, 906.
[40] ibid 918–19.

in the form of teaching, facilities and instrumentalities of learning, were insufficient, as reflected by the deficiencies in the 'outputs', namely test results, graduation rates and dropout rates.[41] A causal link between the funding system and the failure to provide a sound basic education had therefore been established. In March 2006, the Appellate Division of New York State held that 'the State, in enacting a budget for the fiscal year commencing April 1, 2006, must appropriate the constitutionally required funding for the New York City schools'.[42] Accepting as rational the State's calculation of the sums required as consisting of additional operating funds of $1.93 billion,[43] the highest New York court refused to retain an ongoing supervisory role to ensure accountability. The decision in *CFE III* therefore terminated that litigation and no ongoing injunctive relief was given.

However, plaintiffs have had to commence renewed litigation, claiming that New York State has failed to carry out its commitment to provide the resources it itself had determined necessary to provide all its students with a sound basic education.[44] The New York State Court of Appeals in June 2017 allowed the claim that the State had not provided adequate funding for sound basic education in New York City and Syracuse to go forward to trial. Further stages of the process are awaited.

The move from the exclusive focus on race in *Brown* to the exclusive focus on disadvantage in the *CFE* cases has had some important advantages. In particular, it made the first steps towards recognising the central role of poverty in limiting the right to education. However, in failing to pay proper attention to the intersection between race and poverty, the *CFE* cases have not been able to advance either substantive equality or the right to education. The amended statement of claim in the *NYSER* case does not refer to race at all – the only indication is that 16 per cent of students are English-language learners.[45] Yet the intersection of poverty and race is incontrovertible in relation to the right to education. In 2016, as many as 31 per cent of Black children and 26 per cent of Hispanic children under the age of 18 were in families living in poverty, compared to 10 per cent of white and Asian children. This intersectionality is amplified in relation to the right to education, where public schools are highly segregated by race and class. In 2015, as many as 30 per cent of public students attended public schools in which the combined enrolment of minority students was at least 75 per cent of total enrolment. Well over half of Hispanic, Black and Pacific Islander students fell into this category,

---

[41] ibid 908.

[42] *Campaign for Fiscal Equity, Inc. v State of New York (CFE III)* 8 NY3d 14 (2006) (New York State Court of Appeals).

[43] ibid 31.

[44] *New Yorkers for Students' Educational Rights (NYSER) v State of New York*, New York State Court of Appeals, June 2017, http://nyser.org/wp-content/uploads/2017/06/75opn17-Decision-1.pdf0. For the plaintiffs' Amended Complaint to Supreme Court of the State of New York, see http://nyser.org/wp-content/uploads/2018/07/Third-Amended-Complaint-Filed-05-04-18.pdf.

[45] *NYSER v The State of New York* (Supreme Court of the State of New York) Plaintiffs' Third Amended Complaint (05/04/2018) [66], http://nyser.org/wp-content/uploads/2018/07/Third-Amended-Complaint-Filed-05-04-18.pdf.

whereas only 5 per cent of white students attended such schools. Instead, the majority of white students attended schools where minorities constituted less than a quarter of the school.[46]

In this context, the 'separate but equal' slogan is less true than ever. Rather, segregation has a negative multiplier effect, with poor school attainment concentrated in segregated schools, creating obstacles to pathways out of poverty. Although the white-Hispanic gap in reading achievement at Grade 8 has been narrowing since 1992, it remained at 19 points in 2017. Even more worryingly, both the reading and mathematical achievement gap between white and Black students did not budge in that period, remaining at 25 points for reading achievement and a shocking 32 points for mathematics. Similarly, the white-Hispanic achievement gap for mathematics at Grade 8 remained almost unchanged at 24 points between 1990 and 2017.[47]

Examining these figures through the lens of substantive equality reveals the importance of recognising the intersection between poverty and race in advancing human rights. While increased budgetary allocations for inner-city schools could contribute to redressing disadvantage in schooling (the first dimension), they do not address the stigma and stereotyping of segregated schools (the second dimension), a particularly problematic issue at the intersection of race and poverty. Some psychological research suggests that academic performance can be directly affected by the ways in which negative stereotypes trigger self-doubt, for example, in Black students in relation to stereotypes about academic inferiority, and in women in relation to stereotypes about inferiority in maths.[48] Thus, the insight of *Brown* into the recognition harms caused by segregation should not be lost.

But it is also important to go beyond the distributive and recognition dimensions of substantive equality and examine issues of voice and participation. The choices made by political elites on budget allocation are clearly more responsive to those with political power, which tends to exclude those who are marginalised by both race and poverty. The New York Court in the *CFE* cases made an important contribution by deriving the content of the duty to provide 'adequate' education directly from the underlying value which it attached to education, namely the ability to undertake civil responsibilities meaningfully. This allowed the Court of Appeals to set the standards for a 'sound basic education' as consisting of 'the basic literacy, calculating, and verbal skills necessary to enable children to eventually function productively as civic participants capable of voting and serving on a jury'.

At the same time, new litigation is being commenced to establish a similar point under the Federal Constitution. This case is pursuing a key point left open

---

[46] Figures in this section are taken from US Department of Education National Centre for Education Statistics, *Status and Trends in the Education of Racial and Ethnic Groups 2018* (NCES 2019–038) (Indicators 4, 7,10 and 11), https://nces.ed.gov/pubs2019/2019038.pdf.

[47] ibid.

[48] American Psychological Association, 'Stereotype Threat Widens Achievement Gap' (15 July 2006), https://www.apa.org/research/action/stereotype.

in the *Rodriguez* case, namely the issue of whether there may be a right to basic level of education needed for capable citizenship under the equal protection clause of the Fourteenth Amendment.[49] This very helpfully emphasises the participative dimension of substantive equality. However, a further step is still needed to highlight the ways in which poverty and race intersect to obstruct individuals' right to the kind of education which gives them real voice and participation in the political process. This brings the third dimension together with the first two – socio-economic disadvantage coupled with stigma and stereotyping to create a synergistic effect on participation.

It is the fourth dimension, which addresses structural obstacles, that is most often neglected in the intersectional arena. The segregation of inner-city areas, and the movement of white families to areas perceived to have better schools, is not the individual responsibility of any parent. Nor is the intergenerational transmission of educational disadvantage, where persistently disadvantaged parents are not in a position to support their children's education. Particularly important is the need to acknowledge that poverty and race are inextricably linked in the structural denial of the equal enjoyment of the right to education. It has been shown that the social class of low-income Blacks differs considerably from that of low-income whites: the history of racial discrimination and disadvantage materially affects the latter's experience of poverty. Sharkey's research shows that children whose mothers grew up in a poor neighbourhood score worse than other children, even if the latter have moved to a middle-class (non-poor) neighbourhood.[50] He further finds that Black families are much less likely to move out of the poorest neighbourhoods than whites. The result is that multi-generational exposure to poverty is much more likely to affect Black children than whites. The intersectionality of race and poverty is thus crucial to understanding continuing inequalities in the right to education. However, how structural change is to be affected remains contentious. While Sharkey focuses on urban regeneration, Rothstein is sceptical about their chances of success without also pursuing integration policies.[51] In either case, it is important to keep all dimensions of equality in mind in an intersectional sense in analysing different policy choices and in making decisions.

IV. South Africa

In South Africa, the intersection between race and poverty in relation to the right to education is deep-seated and long-standing. Under apartheid, this was

---

[49] MA Rebell, 'Major Federal Right to Education Lawsuit Filed in the US', *OxHRH Blog*, 12 December 2018, http://ohrh.law.ox.ac.uk/major-federal-right-to-education-lawsuit-filed-in-the-u-s.

[50] P Sharkey, *Stuck in Place: Urban Neighbourhoods and the End of Progress towards Racial Equality* (University of Chicago Press, 2013).

[51] R Rothstein, 'The Urban Poor Shall Inherit Poverty (*The American Prospect*, 7 January 2014), https://prospect.org/article/urban-poor-shall-inherit-poverty.

deliberate, with vastly inferior resources allocated to education for the Black majority as compared to their white counterparts, and segregated schooling was legally entrenched. The end of apartheid therefore brought with it the enormous challenge of achieving equity in a school system which had been both racially stratified and severely disadvantaged.[52] The strategy used by the newly elected government to achieve integration in public schools focused on preventing white flight from the well-resourced previously white or Model C government schools, while at the same time facilitating integration. Paradoxically, however, this has had the effect of maintaining class stratification in schools. This is because, in abolishing racially divided schooling and making education compulsory for the first time for Black South Africans, the newly elected government decided that school fees should be charged by public schools to supplement minimum state subsidies,[53] with fee waivers for those who could not afford to pay.[54] A school may not deny a learner admission because of their parents' failure to pay fees.[55] However, parents can be sued by the School Governing Body for non-payment.[56]

Partly because of the recognition that a two-tier education system had developed in South Africa, with disadvantaged schools remaining almost entirely Black, government policy was changed to designate the most disadvantaged schools as 'no-fee' schools.[57] Since 2007, the schools in the lowest two quintiles, and more recently also in the third quintile, were given the opportunity to apply to the Provincial Education Department to be declared no-fee schools.[58] No-fee schools receive larger state allocations per learner and a higher allocation for non-personnel, non-capital expenditure to compensate for lack of fee revenue.

While the no-fee policy has been welcomed as a pro-poor intervention, it remains the case that public schools which can bring in high levels of private income through fees attract better-qualified teachers, have smaller class sizes and can offer better infrastructural resources.[59] In their 2014 quantitative study, Mestry and Ndhlovu found that although the state was making concerted efforts to achieve equity in public schooling, the policy of increasing funds for no-fee schools in quintiles 1, 2 and 3 and reducing funding for quintile 4 and 5 schools

---

[52] This section is taken from Fredman (n 1) ch 11.

[53] E Fiske and H Ladd, 'Balancing Public and Private Resources for Basic Education: School Fees in Post-apartheid South Africa' in L Chisholm (ed), *Changing Class:Education and Social Change in Post-apartheid South Africa* (HSRC Press, 2004), 57; see also S Lewis and S Motala, 'Educational Decentralisation and the Quest for Equity, Democracy and Quality' in L Chisholm (ed), *Changing Class:Education and Social Change in Post-apartheid South Africa* (HSRC Press, 2004) 118.

[54] South African Schools Act, s 36(1).

[55] ibid s 5(3)(a).

[56] ibid s 41.

[57] Education Laws Amendment Act 2005; Amended National Norms and Standards for School Funding (Government Notice 869 in Government Gazette 261789 of 31 August 2006).

[58] R Mestry and R Ndhlovu, 'The Implications of the National Norms and Standards for School Funding Policy on Equity in South African Public Schools' (2014) 34 *South African Journal of Education* 1, 3.

[59] S Motala and Y Sayed, '"No Fee" Schools in South Africa' (Consortium for Research on Education, Access, Transitions and Equity (Create) Policy Brief No 7, 2009).

has not led to the improvement of educational outcomes and learner achievement, especially for rural, poor and illiterate children.[60] They argue that the reduction of state funding in affluent schools has been more than compensated for through school fees and other fundraising initiatives. Similarly, Transparency International found that, despite the laudable aims behind the no-fee schools policies, 40 per cent of educator respondents in their study believed that learners in no-fee schools received a lower quality of education than students in other types of school.[61] Mestry and Ndhlovu conclude that despite the emphasis on redress and equity, the school funding provisions 'appear to have worked thus far to the advantage of public schools patronised by middle-class and wealthy parents of all racial groups'.[62] Moreover, there are substantial variations in fee levels as between schools, with schools serving more affluent communities able to set higher fees and thereby protect and enhance their position. This is borne out by Fiske and Ladd's research. Even more seriously, they conclude that: 'Fees have reinforced the advantages enjoyed by the formerly white schools without at the same time increasing the resources available to schools serving historically disadvantaged students.'[63] Similarly, Motala and Sayed describe the South African public schooling system as 'characterised by a vast number of distinctly disadvantaged schools and a small pocket of highly privileged schools'.[64]

As in the educational adequacy cases in the US, litigation in South Africa has largely focused on disadvantage rather than race. There is a robust right to basic education, which is guaranteed in the Constitution.[65] Moreover, unlike other rights, such as housing and health, which are progressively realisable subject to maximum available resources, education is an immediate right. Litigators have therefore used the right to address the dire conditions in the poorest schools. In a series of cases relating to abysmal schooling environments, litigants have pressed the courts to establish that the right to education includes the conditions in which a child is educated. These cases have not reached the South African Constitutional Court, but in a development of potentially great importance, high courts and the Supreme Court of Appeal have been willing to find that the right includes basic conditions for learning, including proper buildings, textbooks, desks and chairs, and teachers.[66] Litigators have gone further and initiated legal processes aimed at compelling the government to enact standards stipulating the minimum infrastructure that all public schools should be provided with. This elicited an agreement by the Minister of Basic Education to publish norms and standards

[60] Mestry and Ndhlovu (n 58).

[61] H Døssing, L Mokeki and M Weideman, *Mapping Transparency, Accountability and Integrity in Primary Education in South Africa* (Transparency International, 2011) 41.

[62] Mestry and Ndhlovu (n 58) 2.

[63] Fiske and Ladd (n 53) 57–58.

[64] Motala and Sayed (n 59) 2.

[65] Constitution of South Africa, s 29.

[66] *Madzodzo v Minister of Basic Education* [2014] 2 All SA 339 (ECM) (South African Eastern Cape High Court).

regulations.[67] The resulting norms and standards have constituted an important foundation for ongoing litigation. Most recently, the High Court declared that key aspects of these regulations fall below the constitutional guarantee.[68]

However, in its overwhelming focus on poverty, this litigation has not captured the true intersectionality of race and poverty in relation to the right to education. There has been surprisingly little litigation in relation to education with specific reference to race. But it is here that the importance of a substantive approach to equality, which embraces intersectionality, becomes most salient. This can be seen by considering three cases relating to the right to education in section 29 of the Constitution. These cases have tended to emphasise either poverty or race rather than the synergistic effect of the two.

The first case, *FEDSA*, which concerned the exclusion of poor learners by better-off schools, was perhaps the most important recognition of poverty as interfering with the equal right of everyone to education. The case arose because fee exemptions for poor learners in non-poor schools are not compensated for by extra resources for the school, creating an incentive for School Governing Bodies (SGBs) to find ways to exclude poor learners. Fiske and Ladd show that although schools have to be careful not to discriminate unlawfully against students eligible for fee exemptions, 'there is little doubt that many schools consider a family's likely ability to pay their fees when making admissions policies'.[69] In an attempt to prevent discrimination based on the family's ability to pay fees, regulations were promulgated by the province of Gauteng, prohibiting schools from accessing confidential reports on applicant students during the admissions process. A 'confidential report' is defined in the regulations as 'a report containing information about the financial status of a parent, whether the parent can afford school fees and employment details of a parent or any other information that may be used to unfairly discriminate against a learner'. The Federation of School Governing Bodies challenged the regulation as infringing on the powers of school governing bodies to determine who to admit.[70] The South African Constitutional Court rejected the challenge, holding that the regulation served a legitimate purpose, namely to protect learners against the real prospect of unfair discrimination during the admissions process. Justice Moseneke stated:

> It is so that when a school fashions its admission policy it will be actuated by the internal interests of its learners. It is also quite in order that a school seeks to be a centre of excellence and to produce glittering examination and other good outcomes. But public schools are not rarefied spaces only for the bright, well-mannered and financially

[67] Regulations Relating to Minimum Uniform Norms and Standards for Public School Infrastructure promulgated under section 5A(1)(a) South African Schools Act 1996, Government Notice R920 in Government Gazette 37081 (29 November 2013).

[68] *Equal Education v Minister of Basic Education* Case No 276/2016 (High Court of South Africa) (19 July 2018).

[69] Fiske and Ladd (n 53) 72.

[70] *Federation of Governing Bodies for South African Schools (FEDSAS) v Member of the Executive Council for Education, Gautent* (CCT 209/15) [2016] ZACC 14 (South African Constitutional Court).

well-heeled learners. They are public assets which must advance not only the parochial interest of its immediate learners but may, by law, also be required to help achieve universal and non-discriminatory access to education.[71]

It is striking that the intersection between poverty and race is not part of this judgment. Yet statistics on educational achievement in South Africa show starkly how race and poverty map onto school achievement. Data show that while nearly 40 per cent of Black learners attended the poorest schools (quintile 1), negligible proportions of white learners attended schools in quintiles 1–4. By contrast, as few as 9 per cent of Black learners attended a quintile 5 school, as compared with over 90 per cent of white learners.[72] Quintile 1 schools have the worst educational outcomes, and the gap in average test scores between the bottom 80 per cent of schools in South Africa and the top 20 per cent is one of the widest in all the countries measured.[73] As the Institute of Race Relations concluded: 'It is clear that Black children are the ones who suffer the most from poor schooling that is provided by the government.'[74] Bearing in mind the importance of education as an accelerator right, this also means that those at the intersection of poverty and race will remain in the most disadvantaged groups, and the risk is that this will be perpetuated for their children and future generations.

While *FEDSA* referred primarily to discrimination on grounds of poverty without mentioning race expressly, identity and poverty were brought into the frame in *Ermelo* not as an intersectional issue, but rather as a conflict between poverty and the right to be educated in the language of one's choice, here Afrikaans. Section 29 of the Constitution gives everyone the right to be educated in the official language of their choice in state schools where 'reasonably practicable'. Once South Africa transitioned into a democracy, Afrikaners and the Afrikaans language became a minority, but one which retained much of the privilege and power of the apartheid regime. This is especially true of Afrikaans medium schools. The protection of Afrikaans as a minority language has therefore come to represent a clash of equalities. This is because the vast majority of Black South African parents prefer their children to be taught in English, even if this is not their mother tongue. As a result, Afrikaans medium schools are heavily undersubscribed, despite an acute shortage of space for English medium learners. On the other hand, many Afrikaners fear that the Anglicisation of Afrikaans schools will lead to the demise of the language and cultural and linguistic assimilation.[75]

---

[71] ibid [44].

[72] Figures from National Income Dynamics Survey, cited in M Roodt, *The South African Education Crisis: Giving Power Back to Parents* (South African Institute of Race Relations, 2018) 5.

[73] ibid 5.

[74] ibid 6.

[75] M Smit, '"Collateral Irony" and "Insular Construction": Justifying Single-Medium Schools, Equal Access and Quality Education' (2011) 27 *South African Journal on Human Rights* 398, 421; M Bishop, 'The Challenge of Afrikaans Language Rights in South African Education' in M Campbell, S Fredman and H Taylor (eds), *The Value of a Human Rights-Based Approach for Achieving Equality in Education: Comparative Perspectives on the Right to Education for Minorities and Disadvantaged Groups* (Policy Press, 2017).

Such was the position of Ermelo High School, which had an average of about 21 learners per classroom, as against the surrounding schools, where class sizes ranged from 33 to a staggering 62 learners per classroom. Despite many requests by the provincial government to create an English medium stream and thereby make more places available at Ermelo High School for the very disadvantaged local population, the School Governing Body (SGB) refused. This meant that 118 learners in their area would be unable to go to school at all for the year in question. The provincial head of the department of education (HoD) purported to suspend the SGB and appoint an interim SGB to put an alternative language policy in place. In the case of *Mpumalanga Department of Education v Hoërskool Ermelo*,[76] the SGB challenged the legality of this order.

The South African Constitutional Court has expressly recognised that 'the Afrikaans language is one of the cultural treasures of South African national life … In approaching the question of the future of the Afrikaans language, then, the issue should not be regarded as simply one of satisfying the self-centred wishes, legitimate or otherwise, of a particular group, but as a question of promoting the rich development of an integral part of the variegated South African national character contemplated by the Constitution'.[77] On the other hand, the Court was acutely aware of the risk that protecting the right to be educated in Afrikaans would maintain white privilege in the educational system. The potential for a compromise solution is to some extent found in the constitutional provision itself. Section 29(2) gives the right to receive education in the official language of their choice in state schools where 'reasonably practicable'. To ensure effective access to the right, the state should consider all reasonable educational alternatives, taking into account, as well as equity and practicability, the need to 'redress the results of past racially discriminatory laws and practices'.[78]

In *Ermelo*, the South African Constitutional Court held that the provincial authority had no power to remove the SGB and put another in its place to promulgate a new language policy. To that extent, the HoD acted unlawfully and the new language policy adopted by the interim SGB was void. On the other hand, the SGB did not have unlimited discretion as to the language policy it adopted. Instead, it was 'entrusted with a public resource which should be managed not just in the interests of those who happen to be learners and parents at the time but also in the interests of the broader community in which the school is located and in the light of the values of our Constitution'.[79] This led the Court to 'place substance above form' in devising a remedy, even though it had found in favour of

---

[76] *Mpumalanga Department of Education v Hoërskool Ermelo* (CCT40/09) [2009] ZACC 32 (South African Constitutional Court).

[77] *In Re Dispute Concerning the Constitutionality of Certain Provisions of the Gauteng School Education Bill of 1995* (1996) 3 SA 165 (South African Constitutional Court) [49].

[78] Constitution of South Africa, s 29(2).

[79] *Ermelo* (n 76) [80].

the SGB. It held that the SGB should reconsider its language policy in the light of dwindling enrolment numbers and in recognition of the great demand for admission of learners who prefer English as a medium of instruction. At the same time, the provincial authority should plan better to ensure sufficient places for learners who preferred English as their medium of instruction. This is a welcome endorsement of the importance of ensuring places for poor students. However, it does not factor in the other elements of substantive equality which would usher in a truly intersectional approach. In particular, paying attention to the third dimension – participation – would throw the spotlight on the composition of the SGB, which by its nature excluded non-Afrikaans-speaking parents. This meant that the voices of the excluded Black students would not be heard if the Court continued to defer to the SGB.

The most recent case of *Fundza Lushaka*[80] was one of the few education cases which relied on the right to equality in section 9 and where at least a gesture to substantive equality was made. The case concerned a scheme directly aimed at providing better-quality teaching to poor rural schools. It did so by giving bursaries to students undertaking teacher training courses if they committed to teaching in disadvantaged rural areas and were able to speak one of the local languages. The applicants relied on a formal equality approach to challenge the scheme, claiming that it discriminated against white students on the grounds of their race contrary to section 9 of the Constitution. The government explained the scheme on the grounds that there was a major teacher supply crisis, and particularly teachers who could teach learners whose mother tongue was an African language. It argued that it was an affirmative action scheme, aimed at advancing a group that had been disadvantaged by unfair discrimination in the past. This meant that it should be subject to a lighter standard of review under section 9(2) of the Constitution, which expressly permits schemes to advance under-represented groups.

However, the High Court rejected this approach, holding that an affirmative action scheme could only be upheld if the beneficiaries of the scheme constituted the same group as the scheme was designed to advance. Since the scheme was designed to advance rural learners, but benefited trainee teachers, it could not meet this criterion. On the other hand, the Court was prepared to depart from a strictly formal understanding of equality, as simply meaning that likes should be treated alike. Instead, it held that although the scheme was indirectly discriminatory against white candidates, since the criteria would generally exclude an overwhelming number of white students, this was justified by the need to redress disadvantage. It implicitly recognised both the first and fourth dimensions of substantive equality, namely the need to redress disadvantage and achieve structural change, enabling it to uphold this important scheme. It also paid attention to the second and third dimensions. Thus, it found that white Afrikaner students – the group that was disproportionately excluded – was not a group which had

[80] *Solidariteit Helpende Hand v Minister of Basic Education* Case No 58189/2015 (High Court of South Africa).

been subject to discrimination in the past. There were other ways in which white students could pursue further education. The distributive dimension was not relevant, nor did the Court find any evidence to support the allegation that white students' dignity was impaired. Moreover, it held that the scheme could not be unfairly discriminatory because 'it is aimed at addressing deep structural inequalities designed by apartheid'.[81] It therefore held that the scheme passed muster under section 9(3) of the Constitution. It rejected the applicants' challenge on the grounds of unfair discrimination.

V. Engendering Intersectionality: Excluding Pregnant Learners

Possibly the most urgent issue requiring an intersectional approach to the right to education concerns the widespread practice of excluding pregnant learners from school.[82] It is well known that there is a strong relationship between socio-economic deprivation and adolescent pregnancy. While early and unintended pregnancy affects young people in all classes and regions, a recent report emphasised that: 'In all countries, socio-demographic and educational factors, cultural norms around adolescent pregnancy and gender inequalities exacerbate the issues raised by early and unintended pregnancies.'[83] The report notes that: 'In all regions of the world poverty and socio-economic marginalization are the main determinants of early and unintended pregnancy.'[84]

The expulsion of pregnant learners has been an issue of growing concern among the human rights community. From her earliest report, Katerina Tomasevski, the former UN Special Rapporteur on Education, consistently drew attention to the pervasiveness of the exclusion of pregnant learners from school, highlighting the practice as a breach of the right to education and non-discrimination.[85] More recently, the Committee on the Rights of the Child, noting the pervasiveness of such practices, made it clear that 'discrimination based on adolescent pregnancy, such as expulsion from schools, should be prohibited, and opportunities for continuous education should be ensured'.[86] This has also been a common refrain on the part

---

[81] ibid [58].

[82] See further S Fredman, 'Procedure or Principle: The Role of Adjudication in Achieving the Right to Education' (2014) 6 *Constitutional Court Review* 165.

[83] UNESCO, 'Developing an Education Sector Response to Early and Unintended Pregnancy' (2014) 11, https://unesdoc.unesco.org/ark:/48223/pf0000230510.

[84] ibid.

[85] Statement by Special Rapporteur on the Right to Education, Commission on Human Rights, Geneva (22 March–30 April 1999), UN Commission on Human Rights, *Preliminary Report of the Special Rapporteur on the Right to Education, Ms Katarina Tomaševski* UN Doc E/CN.4/1999/49 (1999), https://digitallibrary.un.org/record/1487535?ln=en.

[86] Committee on the Rights of the Child, *General Comment No 15 on the Right of the Child to the Enjoyment of the Highest Attainable Standard of Health (art. 24)* UN Doc CRC/C/GC/15 (2013) [56].

of the Committee on the Elimination of Discrimination against Women (CEDAW Committee), which on numerous occasions has expressed concern at the exclusion of pregnant learners and urged states to ensure that such learners are able to stay in school. However, the practice has not abated.

The extent to which single parenthood, especially among adolescents, should be viewed through an intersectional lens is vividly illuminated through the prism of the four-dimensional approach. This is specifically true for the right to education. The distributive dimension is most glaring. Pregnancy has been the express reason for denial of the right to education for countless young women across many contexts and countries. Even when there is no formal policy of excluding pregnant learners, the failure to accommodate pregnancy, childbirth and parenthood leads to high rates of dropout for young women or, if they stay in education, a difficulty in engaging fully with detrimental effects on learning outcomes. This in turn leads to long-term disadvantage in the labour market and general wellbeing, not just for the young women themselves, but also for their children.[87] Because education is a key site for limiting specific adverse outcomes, the violation of the right of young pregnant learners is all the more problematic.

Yet it is not only the disadvantage; the second dimension – the racialised, gendered and poverty-based stigma that adolescent pregnancy brings with it – should also be brought into the frame in order to understand the extent to which the right to education is violated. Pregnancy at school frequently leads to highly punitive and stigmatic responses from teachers, authorities and parent communities. This, in itself, could lead to girls dropping out of school pre-emptively.[88] Others try to hide their pregnancy, thereby denying themselves necessary antenatal care. Nor is this limited to girls who become pregnant. Gendered stereotypes and prejudices can affect all girls, for example, in the form of mandatory pregnancy tests being carried out on girls at regular intervals or in an ad hoc manner, including through invasive, abusive and degrading means. According to a 2014 Report by the Centre for Reproductive Rights, mandatory pregnancy testing continues in a number of African countries, including Tanzania, Ghana, Kenya, Nigeria, Sierra Leone, Uganda and Zimbabwe.[89] Research from South Africa shows that the stigma surrounding adolescent sexuality means that few opportunities exist for open discussion about access to sex with either parents or partners. Similarly, access to contraception or prenatal care might itself be stigmatised, leading young people to forgo both contraception and prenatal care, resulting in risk to themselves.[90] Conversely, gender-based violence is itself frequently the cause

---

[87] UNESCO (n 83).

[88] ibid 16.

[89] Centre for Reproductive Rights, *Submission for Half-Day of General Discussion and Draft General Recommendation on the Right to Education* (2014), https://www.ohchr.org/Documents/HRBodies/CEDAW/WomensRightEducation/CenterForReproductiveRightsContribution.pdf.

[90] S Willan, 'A Review of Teenage Pregnancy in South Africa' (2013) 29, 31 and 49, https://www.hst.org.za/publications/NonHST%20Publications/Teenage%20Pregnancy%20in%20South%20Africa%20Final%2010%20May%202013.pdf.

of pregnancy. Shockingly, figures show that the perpetrators of sexual abuse leading to pregnancy are not infrequently teachers themselves, with figures from Cote
d'Ivoire showing that approximately 50 per cent of teachers had sexual relationships with students.[91]

The third dimension – voice and participation – is particularly easy to ignore.
Girls who are excluded from school are given no say in the ways in which their
young parenthood should be accommodated. The ostensible paternalism of
school authorities and others gives little or no credence to the young person's
own wishes and needs. As Austin vividly describes, it is paternalistic and wrong
to regard adolescent pregnancy through the lens of victimhood or to ascribe the
choices young women make as either immoral or misguided.[92] This is borne out
by recent research, which shows that up to 75 per cent of adolescent pregnancies
are intended and/or planned. For some young women, pregnancy could be viewed
as a way to satisfy the desire to feel needed, to obtain financial support or to keep
a male partner.[93] The choices young women make must be taken into account.
At the same time, the constraints under which such choices are made should be
factored in. There is also evidence of psychological pressure by male partners leading to pregnancy. In such situations, the right of women to voice their preferences
without coercion becomes paramount. Reshaping the right to education is a key
arena in which both these choices and their constraints can be addressed.

The fourth dimension of substantive equality requires particular attention to
be paid to the structural causes of pregnancy-related discrimination in relation
to education. Here too intersectional understanding is crucial. Addressing the
structural causes of obstacles to the right to education for poor, often racialised
pregnant learners requires a commitment to both the prevention of pregnancy,
through the provision of modern contraception, comprehensive sexual education
and the empowerment of young girls, and the accommodation and facilitation
of continuing education for those who, through choice or otherwise, do in fact
become pregnant. There is plenty of research indicating how this can be achieved.
But only if the specific gendered power relations and their intersection with poverty
and race are taken into account can such research be translated into real change.

The failure to recognise the intersectionality of pregnancy in relation to the
right to education can be seen by comparing two cases: one in the US and one in
South Africa. In her groundbreaking article 'Sapphire Bound',[94] Austin unravels
the intersectionality of race, gender and poverty through her analysis of the case
of Crystal Chambers, an arts and crafts instructor at the Girls Club of Omaha,
where 90 per cent of the programme participants were Black. Crystal Chambers
was dismissed when she became pregnant. Although this was a prima facie breach
of the Pregnancy Discrimination Act of 1978, the Club defended the dismissal

---

[91] UNESCO (n 83) 22.
[92] R Austin, 'Sapphire Bound!' (1989) 3 *Wisconsin Law Review* 539.
[93] UNESCO (n 83) 14.
[94] Austin (n 92).

on the grounds that she was unmarried and therefore constituted a 'negative role model' for Girls Club Members. The prima facie breach was therefore justified as a business necessity and a bona fide occupational qualification. The Nebraska District Court upheld the defence. In doing so, it fully subscribed to the stigmatic assumptions behind the view that, by becoming pregnant, a single Black teacher would constitute a negative role model for the young Black women attending the programme, encouraging them to follow suit. The many stigmatic allusions endorsed by the Court reflected a view of Black women as irresponsible, promiscuous, poor role models for their children, and unreliable as mothers. The fact that the dismissal of Crystal Chambers simply perpetuated the disadvantage experienced by single Black mothers was not seen to be a reason for upholding her rights, nor was any space given to the views of the Black community to which the Girls Club was meant to be catering. As well as paying no attention to the first three dimensions of substantive equality, the Court did not even begin to engage with the kind of transformational change indicated above.

The South African case of *Welkom* gave more credence to the extent to which exclusion of pregnant learners could violate their right to education.[95] However, little attention was paid to the equality issues. The case concerned the exclusion of two pregnant learners from the Welkom and Harmony schools in the Free State in South Africa. Both exclusions were pursuant to pregnancy policies requiring pregnant learners to remain out of school for a defined period. The policies were extremely invasive. For example, the Welkom school policy required a learner to inform a teacher as soon as she discovered she was pregnant. Furthermore, if a learner suspected that another learner might be pregnant, this should be brought to the attention of a member of staff. Moreover, the effect on the learner's schooling was drastic. The Welkom policy provided that the learner was not permitted to return to school in the year in which her child was born. It explicitly provided that 'a matriculant who falls pregnant and delivers her baby in June will not be allowed to write the matric final exams. If a learner delivers a baby in December, she will only be allowed to return to school in the second January following the birth, i.e. if the baby is born in December 2008, the learner may only return in January 2010'. The grade of the learner was irrelevant: 'Matriculants will not enjoy preferential treatment because it is their final year at school.' The age of the learner was also irrelevant, 'which means that if the learner, after the leave of absence is too old to attend school at a secondary school level, recommendations for adult education will be made'. So far as a learner's studies are concerned, the code stated that it would be 'the responsibility of the learner to keep up to date with the school work, and educators will assist only if they see that the said learner is doing her part'. The Welkom code ended with the declaration that 'this management policy does not suspend or expel a learner but ensures that learners take responsibility for their actions and make informed choices'.

---

[95] *Head of Department, Department of Education, Free State Province v Welkom High School* [2013] ZACC 25 (South African Constitutional Court).

Welkom and Harmony were not the only schools with pregnancy policies of this sort. This policy of excluding girls was one which was found in several schools in the area. There is a high prevalence of teenage pregnancy in South Africa. A review of teenage pregnancy in South Africa published in 2013 found that approximately 30 per cent of teenagers report 'ever having been pregnant'.[96] Of the teenage girls who fall pregnant, only about a third remain in school and return after giving birth. For the majority of teenage girls, as the report points out, 'falling pregnant has a devastating effect on their secondary schooling with consequent negative impacts on their lives'.[97] A recent study found that in Limpopo province, 3 per cent of learners were pregnant, the highest figure among the provinces. Matlala, Nolte and Temane cite newspaper figures, which they regard as a reliable source, as showing that one school in Mpumalanga had as many as 70 pregnancies.[98]

In the *Welkom* case, the provincial education department intervened to prevent the school from excluding a pregnant learner in conformity with the school's policy on pregnancy.[99] The Constitutional Court held that the Department of Education had no power to interfere with the decisions of the SGB and therefore upheld the school's position. However, it did state, obiter, that pregnancy exclusion was unlawful discrimination under the Constitution and urged the school to change its policy.

The majority decision, while acknowledging the prima facie breach of the rights to equality, privacy and education, nevertheless failed to engage with the full multi-dimensional requirements of substantive equality and therefore left out of account the intersectionality at the heart of exclusion of pregnant learners. It made some gestures towards the first dimension, the need to address disadvantage. As Khampepe J acknowledged, although in theory they are entitled to return to school, many learners simply cannot afford to add an extra year to their studies. This effect was clearly known to the schools. Khampepe J referred to statistics from Harmony which showed that two-thirds of the learners subject to the pregnancy policies before 2010 never returned to complete their secondary school education.[100] However, Khampepe J gave little attention to the second dimension, which is crucial to sustaining and perpetuating the breach of the right to education. This is the issue of stigma and stereotyping. There is well-established evidence that teenage pregnancy is considered morally wrong and stigmatised in South Africa.[101] South African studies have found that some educators perceive

[96] Willan (n 90).

[97] ibid.

[98] S Matlala, A Nolte and M Temane, 'Secondary School Teachers' Experiences of Teaching Pregnant Learners in Limpopo Province, South Africa' (2014) 34 *South African Journal of Education* 1, 2.

[99] *Welkom* (n 95).

[100] ibid [114].

[101] See, eg, S James, D van Rooyen and J Strümpher, 'Experiences of Teenage Pregnancy among Xhosa Families' (2011) 28 *Midwifery* 190.

pregnant learners to be a disturbance to the learning environment,[102] and this is backed up by Ngabazi and Shefer's research in 2013 showing that schools are intolerant of pregnant learners.[103] Some educators' negative attitude towards pregnant learners has even led them to mistreat these learners until they dropped out of school.[104] One serious implication is that learners do not disclose their pregnancies to teachers if they can help it.[105] The most recent study, carried out by Matlala et al, which examined teachers' experience of pregnant learners in three township schools in Limpopo province, found that pregnant learners' attempts to hide their pregnancies made it difficult for teachers to discern pregnancy and that once they did become aware, some teachers found it difficult to accept the pregnant learners in school.[106] There were some teachers who felt strongly that learners should be held accountable for their actions, for example, through suspension from school.

The approach of the *Welkom* majority to the third dimension – that of voice and participation – showed even greater lack of awareness of the power imbalances and marginalisation of pregnant learners. Khampepe J gave a central role to the SGB over that of the provincial authorities on the basis that it is this body that has been given the mandate of democratic governance of the school. In her view, the SGB was deliberately constituted so that decisions should be taken through a partnership involving the state, parents of learners and members of the local community. However, what is not clear is who represents the pregnant learners. Clearly, parents and members of the local community had ignored their interests for some years. It is for this reason that the learners turned to the 'state', which the South African Constitutional Court regarded as illegitimately intruding on the internal affairs of the school. This reflects a more general pattern. Tomasevski, in her reports as the UN Special Rapporteur on Education, observed that parents, teachers and community leaders in many regions tended to support the expulsion of pregnant girls from school, claiming that this upheld the moral norm prohibiting teenage sex.[107] Moreover, as Motala and Lewis argue, 'there does not appear to be recognition that the representative democracy being promoted through SGBs is a system of competition for power and influence, that is, a decidedly political one'.[108] Most saliently, they argue that the decentralisation of democratic governance could in practice deflect class, race and gender conflict from national or provincial arenas. For them, the Schools Act and the National Norms and Standards for School

---

[102] See, eg, D Bhana et al, 'South African Teachers' Responses to Teenage Pregnancy and Teenage Mothers in Schools' (2010) 12 *Culture, Health and Sexuality: An International Journal for Research, Intervention and Care* 871.

[103] S Ngabaza and T Shefer, 'Policy Commitments vs Lived Realities of Young Pregnant Women and Mothers in School, Western Cape, South Africa' (2013) 21 *Reproductive Health Matters* 106.

[104] N Mpanza and D Nzima, 'Attitudes of Educators towards Teenage Pregnancy' (2010) 5 *Procedia Social and Behavioural Sciences* 431.

[105] Ngabaza and Shefer (n 103).

[106] Matlala, Nolte and Temane (n 98).

[107] UN Commission on Human Rights, *Progress Report of the Special Rapporteur on the Right to Education* E/CN.4/2000/6 (2000).

[108] Lewis and Motala (n 53).

Funding (NNSF) are 'conspicuously silent on class, race and gender conflict, but ignoring conflict will not make it go away. This ignoring of conflict extends to the inaccurate conception of representative democracy as a benign collaboration of local actors as partners rather than competitors for power'.[109] They also point to well-documented evidence of lack of representativeness of SGBs in terms of race, class and gender.[110]

Conclusion

It is clear from these studies that policies focusing simply on race have not succeeded in addressing disadvantage in schools, but nor have policies which emphasise poverty to the exclusion of race. The same conclusion can be drawn with respect to gender and its intersection with race, age, class and poverty. It has been argued here that the true intersectionality of race and poverty in relation to the right to education requires a simultaneous emphasis on both redressing disadvantage and on addressing stereotyping, stigma, prejudice and violence, while also facilitating voice and participation and achieving structural change. Importantly, these dimensions need to buttress one another and if there is a conflict, this must be resolved by optimising all dimensions to the largest extent possible. We have seen that aiming to redress disadvantage on its own can cause stigma and stereotyping, while failing to facilitate participation and voice can both exacerbate stigma and undermine full political accountability. In order for funding to be properly directed, the participation of those involved should be encouraged.[111] Moreover, without fundamental structural change, including in the provision of housing, the zoning of schools, the structure of local taxation, the availability of transport and good-quality teachers, policies aiming to redress disadvantage will be short-lived. But structural change has to include both an emphasis on quality schooling and one which builds in recognition dimensions into the school environment and teaching. Simply using a 'white norm' has clearly not worked. Mother-tongue teaching, recognition of cultural values, and esteem need to be there as well. Similarly, facilitating voice without ensuring that this genuinely redresses disadvantage and contributes to structural change might be counter-productive. A recent report from the Institute for Race Relations in South Africa stridently argues for parental choice to send their children to fee-paying private schools as an answer to the problem. This is a well-known response. However, it has also been shown that the very poorest children will not be able to afford even low fees and the other supplementary expenses of private schooling. Not only that, but whether the outcomes are better is highly

---

[109] ibid 126.
[110] ibid 127.
[111] J Liebman and C Sabel, 'Changing Schools: A Public Laboratory Dewey Barely Imagined: The Emerging Model of School Governance and Legal Reform' (2003) 28 *NYU Review of Law and Social Change* 183, 213–39.

contested. This choice then has to be seen in the context of the other dimensions, which also require emphasis on recognition, redistribution and structural change.

It is now over 65 years since the US Supreme Court proclaimed: 'In these days, it is doubtful that any child may reasonably be expected to succeed in life if he [*sic*] is denied the opportunity of an education. Such an opportunity, where the state has undertaken to provide it, is a right which must be made available to all on equal terms.'[112] That promise will remain empty unless a truly intersectional approach to the right to education is adopted, based on a substantive conception of equality which recognises the deeply enmeshed ways in which poverty, race and gender intersect.

[112] *Brown* (n 3).

5

Class, Intersectionality, the Right to Housing and the Avoidable Tragedy of Grenfell Tower

GERALDINE VAN BUEREN QC

Introduction

The avoidable tragedy of Grenfell Tower starkly raises the issues of class and intersectionality, an area which has, until now, received insufficient analysis. This chapter excavates, inter alia, three issues surrounding class, intersectionality and the Grenfell Tower tragedy: the nature of class as a concept; its implications in constituting a ground of discrimination under the Equality Act 2010; and its relationship with intersectionality.

The reasons behind the insufficient attention to the cross-section of class, intersectionality and human rights may have to do with the many myths surrounding class and class discrimination in the UK,[1] which may also have contributed to the exclusion of class discrimination from protection under the Equality Act 2010. In particular, because of issues such as fluidity, and attributed and self-attributed identity, there are concerns with class being too loose a category to be capable of a satisfactory definition to constitute a category for protection. But in light of tragedies like Grenfell, there now needs to be serious consideration of whether reference to class as a concept in twenty-first-century legislation represents a novel departure at all in the UK. At the same time, there is also a need to analyse the reasons behind the apparent wariness of class amongst some feminists and race scholars, as well as the historical and rather unjustifiable exclusion of race, sex and gender from discussions of class. Finally, there is the right to adequate housing, which is a right guaranteed both under international law and in a growing number of national constitutions, including several European constitutions,[2] but is regrettably not a right yet guaranteed in the UK.

---

[1] These are examined in greater depth in G Van Bueren QC, *Class and Law* (Hart Publishing, forthcoming).

[2] These include France, the Netherlands and Spain. See below for a discussion of the French and Dutch legislation.

This chapter interrogates whether the hostility towards recognising socio-economic rights in England[3] is also a facet of class discrimination, and it explores how all of these matters fed into the avoidable tragedy of Grenfell Tower. It demonstrates that class has been considered in law on the basis of exclusion rather than equality of inclusion. It thus argues that law in the UK requires an express prohibition of class discrimination to deal with crosscutting issues like intersectionality and socio-economic rights such as the right to housing, because without such a prohibition of class discrimination, the situation that gave rise to the Grenfell Tower tragedy could re-occur.[4]

I. Class Discrimination: An Indefinable Concept or a Term Capable of Definition?

Class discrimination is perceived as being particularly complex because of the issues surrounding definition, resource distribution, stigma, wider participation and structural transformation. However, such complexity is often overstated. In fact, one of the assumptions behind the non-express inclusion of a prohibition of class discrimination in the UK is that it would disappear over time without the necessity of recognising it specifically, especially in law. Arguably, this has not occurred.[5] Class, with its different forms of economic, social and cultural capital, may accumulate a range of advantages and disadvantages similar to those associated with gender, race, religion, disability and sexual orientation. As with other recognised grounds of discrimination,[6] the effects of class discrimination extend beyond economic disadvantage. They include disadvantages which are not simply redistributive but go towards recognition in terms of stereotyping, stigma, prejudice, marginalisation etc, affecting access to basic goods like housing, education and healthcare. Seen this way, it is arguable that class, as well as race, age and disability,[7] played a significant role in the fire at Grenfell Tower and the ensuing responses of the local authorities and the government. It is only arguable at this stage, because the Moore-Bick Inquiry has not yet reported on this.[8] However, questions that ought to be considered include whether the socio-economic status of some of the residents had a bearing on the choice of cladding and whether

---

[3] This is arguably not the attitude to socio-economic rights in Scotland and Wales. On the right to food, see, eg, G Van Bueren QC, 'A Justiciable Right to Food: A Possibility for the United Kingdom?' [2019] *Public Law* 146.

[4] Argued more fully in Van Bueren QC (n 1).

[5] Within academia, see, eg, the creation of the Association of Working Class Academics in 2019, which is chaired by the author.

[6] Equality Act 2010, s 4. The following characteristics are protected characteristics under the Equality Act 2010: age, disability, gender re-assignment, marriage and civil partnership, pregnancy and maternity, race, religion or belief, sex and sexual orientation.

[7] See the discussion below in relation to poverty and socio-economic status or class.

[8] Grenfell Tower Inquiry, Phase 1 Report (October 2019), https://www.grenfelltowerinquiry.org.uk/phase-1-report.

socio-economic status played a role in ignoring the evidence produced in tragedies such as the Grenfell fire and the earlier Lakanal House fire in 2009.

In addition to being neglected in equality law, class has also been insufficiently connected to other human rights, as is illustrated by the example of life expectancy, which shows its link with the right to life vividly. So, in addition to the avoidable loss of life in Grenfell Tower, mortality and class discrimination seem fundamentally implicated and beyond the case of the right to housing. For example, there is a significant and unacceptable difference in life expectancy in the UK between different classes in boroughs of the same city.[9] Class is not, in Kincheloe and McLaren's terminology, 'antiseptically privileged'[10] and thus deserves equal consideration with other factors that impact individual life chances, especially the continuity and longevity of life. Despite its impact on life expectancy and, in turn, the right to life, there are a number of arguments raised against addressing class discrimination in the UK; these include an assumption that references to class are not a part of the British statutory tradition and that class is too difficult to define in law.[11]

Historically, legislative references to class and its position in England and Wales were intended to reinforce rather than remove class barriers. Sumptuary laws, such as the Statute Concerning Diet and Apparel 1363, prescribed who could wear specific styles of clothing and eat specific foods.[12] Sumptuary legislation also had significant consequences for different classes in terms of unequal access to property and restrictions on travel. Such detailed prescriptions may appear trivial or even absurd in the modern era, but they encompassed all the essentials of medieval life. Magna Carta (1215) focused on the rights of the baronial class and of freemen, and this was expanded in Carta de Foresta (1217) to those living in the royal forests and in Hwyl Dda to those serving specific nobility.[13] References to class, however, were not limited to the medieval period and continued well into the twentieth century. Voting restrictions, for example, applied to both class and gender through property ownership, and it was not until the Representation of the People (Equal Franchise) Act 1928 that class became formally invisible in the plebiscite.

---

[9] In relation to Glasgow, see World Health Organization, 'Closing the Gap in a Generation Health Equity through Action on the Social Determinants of Health' Commission on Social Determinants of Health Final Report (2009), https://www.who.int/social_determinants/thecommission/finalreport/en. See also SDS Fraser and S George, 'Perspectives on Differing Health Outcomes by City: Accounting for Glasgow's Excess Mortality' (2015) 8 *Risk Managed Healthcare Policy* 99.

[10] JL Kincheloe and P McLaren, 'Rethinking Critical Theory and Qualitative Research' in K Hayes, SR Steinberg and K Tobin (eds), *Key Works in Critical Pedagogy* (Sense Publishers, 2011) 285–326.

[11] An analysis of the literature on intersectionality and the capacity of the concept to embrace more fluid forms of discrimination can be found in Van Bueren QC (n 1); and S Atrey, 'The Intersectional Case of Poverty in Discrimination' (2018) 18(3) *Human Rights Law Review* 411.

[12] See further G Van Bueren QC, 'Socio-economic Rights and a Bill of Rights: An Overlooked British Tradition' [2013] *Public Law* 821.

[13] ibid.

Hence, historically, it has long been recognised that class is a legal relationship as well as a political, social and economic one, and it is therefore an appropriate area to legislate on. But the traditional ways in which class has been legislated on has been to service those who are relatively privileged, while being detrimental to those who are most vulnerable. The fact that class has a tradition of legislative protection in this very chequered way raises the question of whether class could still be a relevant factor in contemporary legislation. But it is in fact the consequence of continuing to ignore class discrimination in twenty-first-century legislation which ends up reproducing class discrimination, thus repeating the history of class discrimination through legislation, albeit in a different way. Now, it is discrimination by being excluded from protection, while previously it was discrimination by express inclusion.

Such 'instruments of exclusion', as Marshall described them,[14] continued at an informal level prior to Grenfell Tower. In both Rowntree's and Boothby's poverty maps of York and London, residents of streets were colour coded according to the moral standing of their inhabitants. It is beyond the scope of this chapter to explore the link between assumptions of morality and class;[15] however, it is appropriate to raise the question whether, amongst other things, portrayals of members of poorer classes feed into the lack of equal protection under both human rights and anti-discrimination laws.

Yet, the link between property ownership and class, although formally invisible in electoral law, as distinct from property residence, arguably played a significant and ultimately fatal role in Grenfell Tower, with perceptions concerning entitlement feeding into the way in which the Tower and its people were neglected and rendered vulnerable. Marshall's approach to class is relevant here because he regarded the essence of social class as 'the way a man is treated'. In the Royal Borough of Kensington, both Marshall's approach and Bourdieu's ideas of cultural, economic and social capital[16] played out clearly. Those perceived, wrongly or rightly, of having little economic, cultural and social capital – a perception based on residence – may have been deprived of equal consideration of their rights based on such perception, especially in relation to the lesser weight placed on the evidence reinforcing their safety concerns. The assumptions about the value and dignity of members of particular classes continue to shape how they are perceived, especially in law and by public services, and may have ultimately contributed to the deaths of Grenfell residents.

One of the challenges faced by those who confront class discrimination is that it is perceived as too difficult or more difficult to define than other prohibited grounds found in the Equality Act 2010. First, it is argued that, unlike other grounds, there

---

[14] TH Marshall (ed), *Class, Citizenship, and Social Development*, 2nd edn (Anchor Books, 1965).

[15] His analysis was in relation to the Elizabethan Statute of Artificers, which confined certain apprenticeships to social classes. See further Van Bueren QC (n 1).

[16] P Bourdieu, 'The Forms of Capital' in JG Richardson (ed), *Handbook of Theory and Research for the Sociology of Education* (Greenwood Press, 1986) 241–58.

is too much fluidity in defining class. This makes class too difficult as a ground of discrimination to be protected when it cannot be defined with clarity. However, such an argument is open to challenge. The right to change one's religion recognised in international law under the International Covenant on Civil and Political Rights (ICCPR)[17] and in regional treaties, including the European Convention on Human Rights (ECHR),[18] has not been regarded as an insurmountable obstacle to prohibiting religious discrimination. Similarly, there is also fluidity in definitions of gender, and a change in gender is not regarded as a bar to gender equality, but in fact a ground of protection in itself via transgender status. For example, the Court of Justice of the European Union in *P v S and Cornwall County Council*[19] recognised that discrimination on the basis of gender reassignment constituted discrimination under the EU Directive on equal treatment for men and women.

Despite the growing body of jurisprudence from national constitutional courts, beginning in Europe with the German Constitutional Court in particular,[20] contemporary human rights law has yet to come to terms with fluidity and self-definition of identity as a facet of autonomy. This is not to deny the complexities surrounding class and other forms of discrimination; however, human rights law has always, since its inception, grappled with complex and challenging cases in both domestic and international contexts; indeed, it is arguable that such complexity is the raison d'etre of human rights law. The *travaux préparatoires* of the UN Convention on the Rights of Persons with Disabilities 2006, for example, illustrate the challenges of defining 'disability' based on different conceptions or models of disability – medical, social and human rights.[21] Similarly, in drafting the UN Convention on the Rights of the Child, it took 10 years to agree upon a definition (as well as other matters), but the political will was such that a definition was eventually agreed.[22]

There is, in addition, an alternative approach; the prohibited grounds of race or sex have not been defined in their specific international or domestic instruments; rather, they have been defined and explored on a case-by-case basis. In defining class, guidance can therefore be sought from the approach to the definitions of race and sex. This is especially important because class is not merely an economic concept. It is, like race and sex, as much to do with the social, political and cultural dynamics of power as economic power. Moreover, it intersects with gender and sex to create uniquely gendered and sexualised forms of class capital. In 'The Forms

---

[17] International Covenant on Civil and Political Rights (opened for signature 16 December 1966, entered into force 23 March 1976) 999 UNTS 171, art 18.

[18] European Convention on Human Rights and Fundamental Freedoms (opened for signature 4 November 1950, entered into force 3 September 1953) ETS 5, art 9.

[19] Case C-13/94 *P v S and Cornwall County Council* [1996] ECR I-2143.

[20] German Constitutional Court, 1 BvR 2019/16 (10 October 2017). This judgment follows the line adopted by the European Court of Human Rights in *Van Kuck v Germany* [2003] 37 EHRR 51, which provides that the freedom to define one's gender identity is an essential aspect of self-determination.

[21] T Degener, 'Disability in a Human Rights Context' (2016) 5 *Laws* 35.

[22] The definition was, however, open ended. The author was one of the drafters.

of Capital', Bourdieu expanded the notion of capital beyond the economic definition, emphasising material exchanges, to include 'immaterial' and 'non-economic'
forms of capital, described as cultural and symbolic capital.[23] An understanding
of these multiple forms of capital helped elucidate the structure and functioning
of the social world.

In particular, the term 'cultural capital' represents the collection of non-
economic forces, such as family background, social class, varying investments in
and commitments to education, different resources, etc that influence academic
success. Bourdieu distinguished between three forms of cultural capital. The
embodied capital is directly linked to and incorporated within the individual
and represents what they know and can do.[24] Embodied capital can be increased
by investing time into self-improvement in the form of learning. As embodied
capital becomes integrated into the individual, it becomes a type of *habitus* and
therefore cannot be transmitted instantaneously. The objectified state of cultural
capital is represented by cultural goods, such as books, paintings, instruments and
machines. They can be appropriated both materially with economic capital and
symbolically via embodied capital. Finally, cultural capital, in its institutionalised
state, provides academic credentials and qualifications which create a 'certificate of
cultural competence which confers on its holder a conventional, constant, legally
guaranteed value with respect to power' and these academic qualifications can
then be used as a rate of conversion between cultural and economic capital.[25]

Class itself is intersectional and is not accurately described by reference only to
Caucasian males, as on occasion is portrayed by the media in the UK. Class is a rich
multi-dimensional concept, which embraces race, religion and gender, as well as
other fundamental aspects of identity. There is a need to further embrace intersectionality in the contemporary context when considering issues of class, otherwise
there is a danger in adopting inaccurate, narrow and exclusionary approaches to
class and also in isolating class from the social structure of society as a whole.
Intersectional approaches are necessary to move discussions of class beyond 'white
working-class men'. By adding the dimension of a prohibition on class discrimination, the law will be strengthened not only in relation to class discrimination but
also in relation to all the other protected characteristics and in turn the intersections that constitute them all.

It may be argued that because there was and continues to be a focus on social
exclusion in policies, the inclusion of class as a prohibited ground of discrimination
would not have had any impact on preventing the Grenfell Tower fire. Social exclusion, originally a French concept, is defined in the literature as applying to those
who are systematically excluded from participation in society.[26] Participation in

---

[23] P Bourdieu, 'The Forms of Capital' in Richardson (n 16) 241–58.
[24] ibid.
[25] P Bourdieu, 'Ökonomisches Kapital, kulturelles Kapital, soziales Kapital' in R Kreckel et al,
Soziale Ungleichheiten (Soziale Welt, Sonderheft 2, 1983) 183–98.
[26] Contemporary political interest in the concept began in 1974 when René Lenoir, then Secretary of
State for Social Action in a French Gaullist government, first popularised the term.

this context refers to four dimensions: the capacity to purchase goods and services; participation in economically or socially valuable activities; political engagement; and social interaction.[27] Social exclusion arises from a variety of causes, which are partly material, but also relate to other issues, such as living in a deprived area, suffering partnership breakdown, being a member of an ethnic minority, or being elderly or disabled. Social exclusion, as with class, is not just a temporary phase of poverty; it is systemic, often passed on from generation to generation and can be self-perpetuating. Although social exclusion is valuable in tackling poverty, by itself, it has not made a perceivable dent in addressing inequality and social mobility in the UK, as figures continue to show.[28] Nor has the focus on social exclusion created a binding obligation on local authorities to weigh the concerns and entitlements of people, such as the Grenfell Tower residents, equally and on a par with other more wealthy residents in the borough. This is not to argue that social exclusion policies or the concept of social exclusion itself should be abandoned; rather, it is to maintain that adopting both a social exclusionary approach reinforced by a prohibition on class discrimination would be more effective in tackling the complex nature of inequality associated with class rather than simply an aspect of it (ie, social exclusion).

A more cautionary approach is advisable in relation to socio-economic status, however. First, the term 'socio-economic status' does not provide positive definitions of identity, nor is it seen as autonomy-affirming in any way. For example, I may choose to describe my origins as working class, which is an important facet of my identity, but I do not self-identify as being from a low socio-economic status. There is nothing positive about low socio-economic status, whereas many of us are proud either: (a) to be living working-class lives; or (b) of coming from working-class backgrounds. There is also a risk that courts would not regard discrimination on the grounds of socio-economic status in the same light as racial discrimination and would instead adopt the approach of the US Supreme Court, which, as Sandra Fredman observes in Chapter 4 of this volume, sees such discrimination as less severe and as deserving of lighter scrutiny. In *San Antonio Independent School District v Rodriguez*,[29] the US Supreme Court rejected a claim that policies which discriminate against poor people can attract heightened judicial scrutiny. This was in part because the judgment did not classify poverty as similar to race.[30] In American jurisprudence, racial classifications were suspect because they concerned a discrete and insular minority, but poor people could not be regarded as discrete

---

[27] See J Mathieson et al, *Social Exclusion Meaning, Measurement and Experience and Links to Health Inequalities: A Review of Literature* (WHO Social Exclusion Knowledge Network Background Paper, 2008) 1.

[28] Social Mobility Commission, *State of the Nation 2016: Social Mobility in Great Britain* (16 November 2016), https://assets.publishing.service.gov.uk/government/uploads/system/uploads/attachment_data/file/569410/Social_Mobility_Commission_2016_REPORT_WEB__1__.pdf.

[29] *San Antonio Independent School District v Rodriguez* 411 US 959, 93 SCt 1919.

[30] In contrast, during the parliamentary debates on the inclusion of socio-economic status, there were a minority of Members of Parliament who appeared to equate socio-economic status and class; see, eg, discussions in HC Deb 11 May 2009, vol 492, col 614.

or insular. Hence, a system which funded local schools on the basis of local taxes and led to under-resourced schools in poorer areas could not, according to the US Supreme Court, be subject to heightened scrutiny, which would have been appropriate for a system which provided inferior schools to students of colour.

Broader attempts to address poverty also do not often connect issues of poverty with conceptions of class per se. Thus, class remains invisible even in the UK mission of the United Nations (UN) Special Rapporteur on Extreme Poverty and Human Rights, who explicitly argued for the need to combat extreme poverty with human rights, but failed to consider the impact of class on extreme poverty and human rights.[31] However, class is as relevant to poverty as it is to extreme poverty, as the recent UN Declaration on the Rights of Peasants 2018[32] makes clear. Its preamble states that peasants and other people working in rural areas suffer disproportionately from poverty, hunger and malnutrition, and Article 2(3) recognises 'the existing power imbalances' between peasants and those who make the decisions that affect their lives. These statements show awareness not only of poverty, but also of class in terms of the way in which class relations work in entrenching poverty and, in turn, the violation of human rights.

II. Class, Socio-economic Rights and the Right to Adequate Housing

In essence, the avoidable tragedy of Grenfell Tower concerned the right of everyone to adequate housing. Therefore, it is also necessary to explore the resistance shown by many, but not all, wealthier states to enshrining the right to adequate housing and other justiciable socio-economic rights into their constitutional structure, including the UK. In the UK, the resistance to recognising justiciable socio-economic rights has been shown by political parties both on the left and the right. Although the major statute on human rights is entitled the Human Rights Act 1998, it omits the express codification of socio-economic rights. The partial incorporation of the ECHR in the UK, along with the non-ratification of Protocol 12 on a self-standing non-discrimination guarantee, and the partial ratification of the European Social Charter 1961 with its omission of ratification of both the complaints procedure and newer substantive rights leave a gap in protections.[33] Although socio-economic rights, like civil and political rights, are symmetrical in nature such that everyone within the state's jurisdiction benefits from them,

---

[31] UN Doc A/HRC/41/39/Add.1 (23 April 2019).
[32] UN General Assembly, United Nations Declaration on the Rights of Peasants and Other People Working in Rural Areas, 73rd sess 2018–19, A/RES/73/165.
[33] Although the Human Rights Act 1998 is commonly referred to as incorporating the ECHR, this is not accurate because the Human Rights Act 1998 does not incorporate art 13 ECHR or all of the substantive rights in the ECHR Protocols.

socio-economic rights may be of particular value to members of social classes with less access to resources to realise their human rights.

In fact, symbolically and practically, justiciable socio-economic rights reduce class inequality directly. Symbolically, socio-economic rights reduce class inequality because they create a route for all classes to enjoy the right to adequate housing, nutrition and water, clothing and standard of living necessary for a good life. In practice, socio-economic rights reduce class inequality because they transform some members of the community, including those living in welfare states, from beneficiaries of social policies into social actors as rights bearers. This is the reasoning behind the Universal Declaration of Human Rights enshrining several socio-economic rights. Although it is commonly and erroneously assumed that rights, such as the right to adequate housing, were incorporated only at the urging of the Soviet states and therefore are an expression of communist values, an examination of the *travaux préparatoires* provides evidence that the socio-economic rights were included at the insistence of the Latin American states, and later reiterated in binding treaty form by a wide range of member states of the UN with diverse political systems.[34]

The International Covenant on Economic, Social and Cultural Rights (ICESCR)[35] paved the way for recognising socio-economic and cultural rights in additional human rights treaties aimed at protecting specific groups, such as the UN Convention on the Rights of Persons with Disabilities,[36] the Convention on the Elimination of All Forms of Discrimination against Women,[37] the Convention on the Rights of the Child[38] and the International Convention on the Elimination of All Forms of Racial Discrimination.[39] All of these may raise further questions in relation to the Grenfell Tower fire, for example, concerning the mobility challenges faced by disabled persons, older people, pregnant women and children. The class aspect of the right to housing in Grenfell is thus exacerbated by other intersectional vulnerabilities associated with disability, age, gender and pregnancy.

Because of the lack of incorporation of the ICESCR into domestic law, the right to housing has not been legally recognised in the UK. In addition, although the UK is bound by the Council of Europe's European Social Charter, which guarantees the right of the family to social, legal and economic protection, and

---

[34] For a fuller discussion, see Van Bueren QC (n 1). See, eg, UN Doc E/CN.4/W.8?Art 14/p18 submitted by Chile in relation to the right to work and the right to form unions. See also UN Doc E/CN.4AC.1/3/Add.1/p314 submitted by Chile, Costa Rica, Nicaragua, Paraguay, Peru and Uruguay.

[35] UN General Assembly, *International Covenant on Economic, Social and Cultural Rights*, 16 December 1966, United Nations Treaty Series, vol 993, p 3, art 11.

[36] UN General Assembly, *Convention on the Rights of Persons with Disabilities*, 24 January 2007, A/RES/61/106, art 28(1).

[37] UN General Assembly, *Convention on the Elimination of All Forms of Discrimination Against Women*, 18 December 1979, United Nations Treaty Series, vol. 1249, P 13, art 12(2)(h).

[38] UN General Assembly, *Convention on the Rights of the Child*, 20 November 1989, United Nations, Treaty Series, vol 1577, p 3, art 27(3).

[39] UN General Assembly, *International Convention on the Elimination of All Forms of Racial Discrimination*, 21 December 1965, United Nations Treaty Series, vol 660, p 195, art 5(e)(iii).

makes explicit reference to an obligation to protect family life and provide 'family housing',[40] the UK has not ratified the European Social Charter in full. The UK, in contrast to other states including Ireland, France and Portugal, has only ratified the barest minimum of the European Social Charter.[41] Full ratification would have offered the possibility for those living in Grenfell Tower to have the possibility of having their safety concerns attended to as a matter of right to housing recognised in Article 31(1) of the European Social Charter. This is evidenced by the interpretation of the Council of Europe's Committee of Social Rights, which requires states to both ensure an adequate supply of housing and to ensure that existing housing is of an adequate standard.[42]

The consideration of the UK's legal obligations in relation to the right to housing is thus limited in international law.[43] However, it is this failure to consider socio-economic rights as equal to and in fact related to civil and political rights, as a matter of indivisible and interdependent human rights, that further sidelines issues of class, which would prima facie make all socio-economic rights extend to all classes. Thomas Hammarberg, the former Council of Europe Commissioner for Human Rights, has stated that it is critical to support victims of housing rights violations, because access to housing is a precondition for exercising all other fundamental rights.[44] This approach is reinforced by the General Comment of the Committee on Economic, Social and Cultural Rights, which also provides that states, as a matter of legal obligation, are obliged to conceptualise adequate housing as not only equated with shelter, but equally, and importantly, as a facet of security, living in peace, and proximity to essential services such as schools and hospitals.[45] The Committee has begun to put this into effect through rulings on

---

[40] European Social Charter 1961, art 16.

[41] Ireland ratified the European Social Charter on 7 October 1964 and the Revised European Social Charter on 4 November, accepting 92 of the 98 paragraphs of the Revised Charter. It ratified the Additional Protocol providing for a system of collective complaints procedure on 4 November 2000. It has not yet made a declaration enabling national non-governmental organisations to submit collective complaints.

[42] Collective Complaint No 31/2005, *European Roma Rights Centre (ERRC) v Bulgaria* (European Committee of Social Rights, 18 October 2006).

[43] It is also limited in domestic law. Domestic law in England provides piecemeal rights and protections for tenants through the Housing Act 2004, the Landlord and Tenant Act 1985, the Environmental Protection Act 1990 and the Building Regulations 2010. In the wake of the Grenfell Tower tragedy in England, there is no general obligation to ensure that properties are fit for human habitation. In Wales, the Renting Homes (Wales) Act 2004 introduces a new requirement for rented dwellings to be fit for human habitation. In Scotland, the Housing (Scotland) Act 2006 gives tenants greater rights to enforce basic standards of habitability. After the Grenfell Tower fire, Karen Buck MP re-introduced the Homes (Fitness for Human Habitation) Bill, which would require residential rented accommodation to be provided and maintained in a habitable state. The Bill is currently before Parliament.

[44] T Hammarberg, *Recommendation of the Commissioner for Human Rights on the Implementation of the Right to Housing*, CommDH (2009) 5 (30 June 2009) 3.

[45] CESCR General Comment No 4 on the Right to Adequate Housing (Art 11(1) of the Covenant) Adopted at the Sixth Session of the Committee on Economic, Social and Cultural Rights on 13 December 1991, (Document E/1992/23) [9]. The principle is reiterated by the UN Special Rapporteur on the Right to Adequate Housing in 2016: 'The right to housing cannot be viewed in isolation from other human rights, in particular the rights to life, to respect for private and family life, and to property.'

complaints, such as the case of *IDG v Spain* in 2015,[46] which established that the state has an obligation to provide for effective remedies in foreclosure procedures related to defaulting on mortgage payments. Other European countries seem to have adopted strong protections around housing, having recognised a right to housing constitutionally.[47]

It may be tempting to conclude that if the UK had incorporated a right to housing, it would have prevented the fire, deaths and injuries in the Grenfell Tower tragedy. However, a right does not itself guarantee its own enforcement. France, for example, saw a similar tragedy to Grenfell unfold in Marseilles in 2018. France had previously, as a consequence of being found in breach of the European Social Charter,[48] adopted an enforceable right to housing.[49] Although fortunately fewer lives were lost in Marseilles, there are other similarities with Grenfell. These include the prior notice given to the authorities of the risk of fire and the rich ethnic diversity of the residents, including refugees and asylum seekers. Their right to adequate housing was still violated, even in the presence of an explicit recognition of the enforceable right. However, rights are not self-enforcing and the mere recognition of a legal right to housing does all but prevent tragedies of this nature.

Neither would a prohibition on class discrimination automatically guarantee that the tragedy of Grenfell Tower would have been avoided. But it would, in combination with a right to housing, make discrimination, such as that which arose in Grenfell, where those of a certain class received homes with poorer cladding, unlawful. Recognition of class discrimination in the enjoyment of legally recognised socio-economic rights would thus strengthen those rights as well as combat class inequality per se.

Although Brexit may, depending upon the nature of any future relationship (uncertain at the time of writing), release the UK from human rights obligations

See 'Adequate Housing as a Component of the Right to an Adequate Standard of Living' (8 August 2016) UN Doc No A/71/310 [5], [27], http://ap.ohchr.org/documents/dpage_e.aspx?si=A/71/310 a.

[46] Communication 2/2014, UN Doc E/C.12/55/D/2/2014.

[47] See, eg, art 22(2) of the Constitution of the Kingdom of the Netherlands 2008, which provides that 'it shall be the concern of the authorities to provide sufficient living accommodation'. This constitutional protection has its origins in the Dutch Housing Act 1901.

[48] In *FEANTSA v France* CC39/2006. The European Committee of Social Rights found that France violated art 31 by not making sufficient progress towards eradicating substandard housing, failing to pass legislation to prevent evictions, having an insufficient supply of social housing and having a poor social housing allocation system.

[49] Loi n° 2007-290 du 5 mars 2007 instituant le droit au logement opposable et portant diverses mesures en faveur de la cohésion sociale (1) NOR: SOCX0600231L Version consolidée au 27 mars 2019, which introduced an enforceable right to be housed (the DALO law) and charged prefects with the task of making the social housing application process more efficient by allocating accommodation to applicants deemed to have priority. This responsibility is exercised under the supervision of an administrative judge. Any person in difficulty, whose application for housing has not been satisfied, may apply to a mediation committee and then, in certain cases, lodge an appeal with an administrative court if they wish to pursue their application. In its first case, the court ruled that in order for the state to meet its obligation to protect the right to housing, 'families must not merely have a place to stay for the night but an adequate home'. See further K Olds, 'The Role of Courts in Making the Right to Housing a Reality throughout Europe: Lessons from France and the Netherlands' (2010) 28 *Wisconsin International Law Journal* 170, 171.

under EU law, including those arising out of the EU Charter of Fundamental Rights,[50] it would have no effect on the obligations which the UK has by virtue of being a party to the Council of Europe and thus under the ECHR. As well as providing for a right to life in Article 2, the ECHR provides in Article 14 a right not to be discriminated against on 'any ground such as sex, race, colour, language, religion, political or other opinion, national or social origin, association with a national minority, property, birth or other status'. This list of prohibited grounds of discrimination is not exhaustive and is prefaced by '*any* ground *such as*' (emphasis added). Arguably, this, together with 'other status', would mean that the right is a right not to be discriminated against on a ground other than those listed, when there is no rational relationship between the ground and the differential treatment based on that ground. An inclusion of class either through reading it into 'social origin ... birth or other status', as enshrined in the ECHR both in Article 14 and in its Protocol 12, is thus ostensibly possible in this context and, via this, in the UK. In fact, the European Court of Human Rights (ECtHR) is not bound by its earlier and current jurisprudential ranking of the grounds of discrimination with its consequential and regrettable exclusion of categories.[51] Similarly, it would be open to the courts in the UK under the Human Rights Act 1998 to go beyond the approach of the ECtHR.

Further, although there is no express right to housing under the ECHR, Article 2 of the Convention – which recognises that 'everyone's right to life shall be protected by law. No one shall be deprived of his life intentionally' – may provide an indirect method of redress in relation to extreme violations of the right to life in the context of housing. The ECtHR has found that there is a positive obligation on governments to take 'all appropriate steps' to safeguard life for the purposes of Article 2 ECHR.[52] These positive obligations must apply 'in the context of any activity, whether public or not, in which the right to life may be at stake'[53] and this clearly applies to the regulations concerning high-rise buildings. The ECtHR has in fact come up with these principles specifically in cases of loss of lives. For example, in *Oneryildiz v Turkey*,[54] the Court stressed that there was practical information available that the inhabitants were faced with a threat to their physical integrity on account of the technical shortcomings of the municipal rubbish tip. It found that the timely installation of a safety system before a situation became fatal would have been an effective preventative measure 'without diverting the State's resources to an excessive degree'.[55]

---

[50] European Union, *Charter of Fundamental Rights of the European Union* [2012] OJ C326/02, 26 October 2012.

[51] N Petersen, 'The Principle of Non-discrimination in the European Convention on Human Rights and in EU Fundamental Rights Law' in Y Nakanishi (ed), *Contemporary Issues in Human Rights Law Europe and Asia* (Springer, 2018) 129–42.

[52] *Oneryildiz v Turkey* (2005) 41 EHRR 20 [89].

[53] ibid [89]–[90].

[54] ibid.

[55] ibid [107].

Similarly, in the case of Grenfell, it would be open to a domestic court to consider whether, under the Human Rights Act 1998, the installation of safer cladding panels and the cost of a sprinkler system would have diverted the resources of the UK or the concerned local authority 'to an excessive degree'. It is unlikely that such a cost would have been found to be excessive in light of the danger associated with cheap cladding, ie, of loss of lives. Further, in *Budayeva v Russia*,[56] where an authority knew that a dam had been weakened but failed to tell the residents who would have been affected, the ECtHR has found that where lives are at risk, there is a smaller margin of appreciation given to states parties.

However, in respect of less serious violations, the ECHR's protection of the right to life has not provided a shield because, with some justification, the ECtHR has regarded this as protecting a right to housing through the back door without the express consent of the states parties. This justification is derived from a treaty regime, which does not focus on the inherent intersectionality of human rights, but rather on the sovereign decisions of states to ratify treaties with clear parameters and interpretations limited by the *travaux préparatoires*.

There is also the potential of applying Article 3 of the ECHR to the Grenfell Tower fire tragedy. In *Selcuk and Askar v Turkey*,[57] the ECtHR had found a violation of Article 3 ECHR when the applicants, who were over 50 years old and who had lived their entire lives in their village, were forced to watch their village being burnt and destroyed by members of the Turkish security forces. According to the Court, this had amounted to inhuman treatment under Article 3 ECHR. A similar finding may ensue in a case over the Grenfell Tower fire on the basis that it actually involved not only a loss of home and community, and the life associated with it, but also the actual loss of lives within that home and community.

However, piecemeal approaches to class discrimination, which may also include piecemeal approaches such as the incorporation of socio-economic rights in the UK,[58] would remain inadequate in terms of providing a shield against all the disadvantages associated with class inequality. Similarly, a prohibition of class discrimination alone would be insufficient to address all of the disadvantages of poverty. These approaches demonstrate the obstacles placed in the way of those seeking answers concerning the Grenfell Tower conflagration. Rather, an ideal intersectional approach would include all forms of necessary legal reform. One of the principal focuses of intersectionality has been on identities and the disadvantages associated with them; however, there is also an intersectionality of rights which in human rights language is not referred to as intersectional, but in terms of indivisibility and interdependence of rights. The lack of appreciation of intersectionality, as well as the indivisible and interdependent nature of human rights violations, lies at the heart of the avoidable tragedy of Grenfell Tower.

---

[56] *Budayeva v Russia* (2014) 59 EHRR 2.
[57] *Selcuk and Askar v Turkey* (1998) 26 EHRR 477.
[58] The author is a member of a small group who, at the time of writing, is drafting an Economic, Social and Cultural Rights Act for the UK.

Conclusion

Intersectionality is often applied to the interplay between different forms of equality, but there is also an important interplay, sometimes under-appreciated, between human rights in general and equality in particular, and the diverse bases on which they are violated. In human rights terminology, this interplay is described as indivisibility and it is arguable that by focusing only on the equality aspects of intersectionality, the human rights aspects of intersectionality have been ignored. It is also arguable that the very slow response of the human rights community in perceiving the fire in Grenfell Tower as a fundamental human rights issue was because of the complex intersectional issues it raised, concerning the loss of life in social housing affecting a diverse range of people, including primarily working-class people. In fact, the human rights dimension of the Grenfell Tower tragedy continues to be ignored, with the parliamentary inquiry into the tragedy even failing to grant the Equality and Human Rights Commission standing to appear. Its first report has also failed to address the tragedy as a matter of human rights violations per se.[59] But, as this chapter has shown, it is only when class discrimination is attended to, along with the right to housing, that one comes to appreciate Grenfell as an avoidable tragedy which would have been prevented had an intersectional approach been taken to appreciating how violations transpire because of multiple identities (including class) and how they affect the experience of multiple rights (such as the right to housing).

---

[59] A Nolan, 'Human Rights and the Grenfell Tower Inquiry', *London Review of Books Blog*, 4 November 2019, https://www.lrb.co.uk/blog/2019/november/human-rights-and-the-grenfell-tower-inquiry.

6

Intersectionality, Repeal and Reproductive Rights in Ireland

Introduction

Much has already been written about the 2018 referendum to repeal the Eighth Amendment of the Irish Constitution, as a result of which the near-total constitutional ban on abortion was removed from the Irish Constitution, paving the way for the legalisation of abortion in the Health (Regulation of Termination of Pregnancy) Act 2018.[1] From 1 January 2019, abortion has been legally available without restriction as to reason up to 12 weeks and on restrictive, medically indicated grounds after that point.[2] Although – as has widely been acknowledged[3] – this law has multiple and serious faults, it does bring Irish law far more closely into line with both comparative legal practice and best medical practice than was previously the case. The passage of the law and the winning of the referendum that enabled it were significant and rightly celebrated landmarks for reproductive rights in Ireland. For the 12,976 days of its operation – from 7 September 1983 to 18 September 2018, or all but 1,022 days of my life up until then – the Eighth

---

[1] See, eg, N Nic Ghabhann, 'City Walls, Bathroom Stalls and Tweeting the Taoiseach: The Aesthetics of Protest and the Campaign for Abortion Rights in the Republic of Ireland' (2018) 32(5) *Continuum: Journal of Media and Cultural Studies* 553; L Field, 'The Abortion Referendum of 2018 and a Timeline of Abortion Politics in Ireland to Date' (2018) 33(4) *Irish Political Studies* 608; S Calkin, 'Healthcare Not Airfare! Art, Abortion and Political Agency in Ireland' (2019) 26(3) *Gender, Place & Culture* 338; M Taylor, A Spillane and S Arulkumaran, 'The Irish Journey: Removing the Shackles of Abortion Restrictions in Ireland' (2020) 62 *Best Practice & Research in Obstetrics and Gynaecology* 36; R Fletcher, '#Repealedthe8th: Translating Travesty, Global Conversation, and the Irish Abortion Referendum' (2018) 26(3) *Feminist Legal Studies* 233; K Browne and S Valkin (eds), *After Repeal: Rethinking Abortion Politics* (Zed Books, 2019); 'Abortion in Ireland' (2020) 124 *Feminist Review*, the themed issue and edited by S Calkin, F de Londras and G Heathcote.

[2] Health (Regulation of Termination of Pregnancy) Act 2018.

[3] See M Enright, '"The Enemy of the Good": Reflections on Ireland's New Abortion Legislation' (2018) 8(2) *feminists@law*; F de Londras, '"A Hope Raised and Then Defeated?" The Continuing Harms of Irish Abortion Law' (2020) 124 *Feminist Review* 33; K Side, 'Abortion Im/Mobility: Spatial Consequences in the Republic of Ireland' (2020) 124 *Feminist Review* 15.

Amendment was a legal artefact of the misogynistic, proto-nationalist merging of church and state authority that lodged itself inside the body of everyone capable of pregnancy in Ireland. Following its repeal, this is no longer the case and this is, rightly, something to celebrate.

However, along the way – and especially during the formal politico-legal processes of referendum and law-making – the repeal campaign found itself confronted with significant challenges to the maintenance and enactment of the meaningful and reflective praxis of intersectionality. It is this that I focus on in this chapter. The law that emerged from these victories left many behind, especially those for whom multiple marginalities intersect to make domestic abortion travel difficult if not impossible, those whose gender presentation does not match a "female" marker assigned at birth, those with reduced access (for mobility or other reasons) to transportation and healthcare, and those racialised by both the containment practices of Irish refugee and immigration law and the persistent partition of the island of Ireland.

In this chapter, I reflect on the ways in which reproductive activism might be said to have failed in its intersectionality during the repeal campaign and, in particular, on the ways in which the formal processes of constitutional law reform that had to be negotiated in order to achieve meaningful reform and liberalisation of abortion law shaped these failures. In doing so, I write from the perspective of someone involved to some limited degree with the campaign (both informally with the civil society campaign and somewhat more formally with certain political and government figures who intervened in the referendum), someone who engaged in sustained campaigns of public legal education during the referendum campaign (primarily with my colleague Máiréad Enright)[4] and someone who continued to work following the referendum to try to improve the abortion legislation as it made its way through the Houses of the Oireachtas (primarily with colleagues in Lawyers for Choice).[5] I thus write – as others have already done[6] – from the strange insider/outsider position that both enforces an ethical obligation

---

[4] F de Londras and M Enright, *Repealing the 8th: Reforming Irish Abortion Law* (Policy Press, 2018); www.aboutthe8th.com.

[5] M Enright et al, 'Position Paper on the Updated General Scheme of the Health (Regulation of Termination of Pregnancy) Bill, 2018', https://lawyers4choice.files.wordpress.com/2018/08/position-paper-1.pdf; R Fletcher et al, 'Briefing Paper on the Health (Regulation of Termination of Pregnancy) Bill, 2018: Making the Legislation Work, Delivering on the Referendum', https://lawyers4choice.files.wordpress.com/2018/10/hrtop_briefing_final.pdf; F de Londras et al, 'Amending the Health (Regulation of Termination of Pregnancy) Bill: 5 Priority Issues for the Seanad', https://lawyers4choice.ie/2018/11/29/amending-the-health-regulation-of-termination-of-pregnancy-act-5-priority-issues-for-the-seanad.

[6] See Fletcher (n 1); Enright (n 3); S Duffy, 'The Regulation of Termination of Pregnancies Bill: An Argument for "Pregnant People" Wording', https://sandraduffy.wordpress.com/2018/07/18/the-regulation-of-termination-of-pregnancies-bill-2018-an-argument-for-pregnant-people-wording; E Burns, 'Intersectionality and the Irish Abortion Rights Campaign of 2018', https://emmaqburns.com/2018/09/19/10thdss-intersectionality-and-the-irish-abortion-rights-campaign-of-2018; S Redmond, 'It's Been Two Months Now', https://feministire.com/2018/07/27/its-been-two-months-now; H Stonehouse, 'Fuck You Simon Harris', https://learningtheworld.net/2018/11/29/fuck-you-simon-harris.

for critical self-refection[7] and potentially blinkers one from some important insights. I also write as someone who thinks it important to offer correctives to solely celebratory narratives of repeal, recognising that the rightly lauded success of the campaign carried with it significant costs.

My intention in this chapter is not to contribute in any substantial way to our evolving understanding of intersectionality and intersectional practice, but rather to reflect on the ways in which self-avowedly intersectional and intergenerational activism for abortion law reform in Ireland may have fallen short of that avowal within the formal process of constitutional law reform as it operates in Ireland. My contribution is, then, intentionally modest; it is a, not *the*, telling of the referendum campaign and it uses meaningful commitment to intersectionality as a benchmark for evaluating that campaign. In doing so, it does not disavow or seek to underplay the importance of formal constitutional and legal change; indeed, one might argue that since the early writings of Pauli Murray,[8] the germ-seeds of intersectionality as a form of legal argumentation were planted in formal constitutional argumentation and aspirations for legal change, notwithstanding our epistemological knowledge that legal change alone does not address structural and embedded disparities in power and agency and their multiple and variated instantiations in different lives.

In this chapter, the discussion is divided into three sections. In section I, I will reflect a little on the referendum campaign itself and particularly on some of the tactical manoeuvres of the campaign relevant to the question of intersectionality. In section II, I will illustrate some of the ways in which the new law and its operation fail adequately to deliver reproductive justice to all. Finally, in section III, I will reflect on the difficulties of intersectionality in constitutional referendum campaigns.

I. Repeal: The Referendum

The formal institutional story of the referendum to repeal the Eighth Amendment starts with the Programme for Partnership Government in May 2016, which led

---

[7] I am conscious, especially, of Patricia Hill Collins' conviction that Black Feminist Epistemology requires personal accountability and that knowledge does not require us to separate ourselves from the emotion and lived experience of that which we are studying or discussing. The same, I hope, is true of Irish pro-choice feminism. See P Hill Collins, *Black Feminist Thought: Knowledge, Consciousness, and the Politics of Empowerment*, 2nd edn (Routledge, 2000).

[8] Murray's briefs and other writings on the Fourteenth Amendment to the US Constitution can now be read as clearly intersectional in their tone and structure, and they ended up being deeply influential on the advocacy approaches of the National Association for the Advancement of Colored People (NAACP), although her contribution is perhaps not as well recognised as it might be. However, Serena Mayeri explored this in depth in *Reasoning from Race: Feminism, Law, and the Civil Rights Revolution* (Harvard University Press, 2014). See also S Azaransky, 'Jane Crow: Pauli Murray's Intersections and Antidiscrimination Law' (2013) 29(1) *Journal of Feminist Studies in Religion* 155; SD Elin Fisher, 'Pauli Murray's Peter Panic: Perspectives from the Margins of Gender and Race in Jim Crow America' (2016) 3 *Transgender Studies Quarterly* 95. For a biographical account, see R Rosenberg, *Jane Crow: The Life of Pauli Murray* (Oxford University Press, 2017).

to a Citizens' Assembly to consider, among other things, repeal of the Eighth Amendment. This Assembly, much lauded by some political scientists in particular, resulted in a wide-ranging set of recommendations including to repeal the Eighth Amendment and to introduce a new law that would make abortion lawfully available in a wide set of circumstances.[9]

Although the outcome of the Assembly was especially welcome, the proceedings themselves were problematic; there was very little engagement with the realities of reproductive life for women of colour, migrants, Traveller women, women with disabilities, trans people and women living in situations of reproductive coercion. Reflecting a fixation with law and legality, lawyers were invited to address the Assembly on every one of their four substantive meetings on the Eighth Amendment.[10] Nobody was ever asked to address questions relating to migration, race, ethnicity, language, sexuality, disability or gender identity as they apply to and arise in respect of access to abortion care. The Assembly was designed with a literal adherence to a notion of balance which meant that any lawyers who had expertise in abortion rights were not invited to address the assembled group of citizens. Instead, 'general' constitutional lawyers presented to them on questions of law. Furthermore, 'balance' was interpreted to ensure that anti-choice speakers received equal time as pro-choice speakers, even when their presentations were based on abortion myths or made by representatives of discredited organisations, such as Youth Defence, Every Life Counts and Women Hurt. However, the citizen members insisted in the end on a number of important interventions: they asked to be addressed by people with direct experience of the Eighth Amendment, ie, women who had and who had not accessed abortion.[11] They insisted on the rewording of some propositions at the time that votes were being taken, largely to make them less foetocentric and to attempt to break from the language and strictures of the Eighth Amendment that appeared to greatly influence the propositions being advanced by the Assembly's expert team. Ultimately, they made a set of recommendations that went far beyond what anyone had really expected,

---

[9] Citizens' Assembly, *Final Report on the Eighth Amendment of the Constitution* (Dublin: Citizens' Assembly, 2017), https://www.citizensassembly.ie/en/The-Eighth-Amendment-of-the-Constitution/Final-Report-on-the-Eighth-Amendment-of-the-Constitution/Final-Report-on-the-Eighth-Amendment-of-the-Constitution.html.

[10] Lawyers addressed the Assembly on its first (art 40.3.3 generally), second (art 40.3.3 and fatal foetal abnormalities, international human rights law and fatal foetal abnormalities, mechanisms of constitutional and legal reform), third (legal considerations in respect of a 'rape' ground) and fourth (art 40.3.3 and medical and parental decision-making, the protection of foetal rights in and beyond the Eighth Amendment, legal consequences of repeal) meetings. In total, it had five meetings; the fifth was dedicated to finalising its proposals.

[11] The Assembly addressed this by recording testimony from people who had and who had not accessed abortion during the time of the Eighth Amendment and playing those to the citizen members. This occurred in the third weekend of the Assembly's deliberations and can be accessed on its website: https://www.citizensassembly.ie/en/Meetings/Fourth-Meeting-of-the-Citizens-Assembly-on-the-Eighth-Amendment-of-the-Constitution.html.

including accounting for socio-economic deprivation as a basis upon which one ought to be permitted to access lawful abortion.[12]

Following the Assembly, a special parliamentary committee – the Joint Oireachtas Committee on the Eighth Amendment of the Constitution – was established to consider how to give effect to the Assembly's recommendations. This Committee also heard from a large number of experts and, unlike the Assembly, lawyers with well-established expertise on abortion law regulation were invited to address it and speak to questions raised by its members.[13] However, like the Assembly, it failed to hear from experts who could engage directly and, ideally, from a basis of experience with the difficulties faced by marginalised communities and with the intersectional effects of restrictive abortion laws.[14] Its recommendations were less radical than those of the Citizens' Assembly, but were nevertheless significant. Like the Assembly, it recommended constitutional change followed by a reasonably liberal legislative framework, and its recommendations were debated in the full Parliament before being sent to the Cabinet.[15]

At the Cabinet level, a further process of consideration was undertaken, resulting not only in an agreement to hold a referendum on the Eighth Amendment (to remove it and replace it with a text empowering the Oireachtas to pass abortion law), but also in a 'general scheme' for post-repeal legislation.[16] The General Scheme was intended to provide a reasonably coherent set of proposals to the electorate about how the government intended to legislate if the referendum was successful. Publishing such a scheme in the course of a referendum is not entirely unusual in Ireland; it is often considered an important step in assuring the electorate about what might follow constitutional change, although, of course, there is no *legal* (as opposed to political) obligation to propose law that tracks the published General Scheme. In the case of the Eighth Amendment, the General Scheme became an extremely important focal point in the campaign, especially for the 'No' side, which attempted to argue that the Scheme showed how repeal would lead, variously, to the legalisation of abortion on the basis of foetal disability (it would not), abortion 'up to birth' (it would not) and the introduction of a law comparable to the Abortion Act 1967, which operated in most of the UK (it did not).[17] The reality, though, was that the General Scheme included limitations that could

---

[12] For a critical reflection, see M Enright, 'Abortion and the Citizens' Assembly: Agonist Futures?', *IADC Symposium*, https://blog-iacl-aidc.org/blog/2018/12/5/abortion-and-the-citizens-assembly-ago nist-futures-xb2x6.

[13] Disclosure: I was invited to, and did, address the Committee in September 2018.

[14] The full list of witnesses is included as Appendix 2 to the Committee's Report: *Report of the Joint Oireachtas Committee on the Eighth Amendment* (Oireachtas, 2018), https://webarchive.oireachtas.ie/parliament/media/committees/eighthamendmentoftheconstitution/Report-of-the-Joint-Committee-o n-the-Eighth-Amendment-web-version.pdf.

[15] ibid.

[16] General Scheme of a Bill to Regulate Termination of Pregnancy 2018, https://health.gov.ie/wp-content/uploads/2018/03/General-Scheme-for-Publication.pdf.

[17] For analysis of the 'No' campaign's engagement in lawfare of this kind, see F de Londras and M Enright, '"The Only Lawyer on the Panel": Anti-choice Lawfare in the Battle for Abortion Law Reform' in K Browne and S Calkin (eds), *Post Repeal: Reflections and Futures* (Zed Books, 2019) 53.

not be traced back to either the Citizens' Assembly recommendations or the Joint Oireachtas Committee report. For example, under the proposed new law, women seeking abortion in early pregnancy would be required to undertake a mandatory waiting period. Furthermore, early pregnancy was to be defined as 12 weeks since the last menstrual period (LMP); a considerably shorter period than 12 weeks' gestation. In Cabinet, it seems, political realities had resulted in compromises designed to get key socially conservative members of government on board, especially the Tánaiste, Simon Coveney, who publicly supported repeal on the basis that these compromises assured him that the law would not be too liberal.[18]

Even before the Bill was finalised, then, there was a fairly good sense of what the new law would provide. It was, without question, welcome in many ways, especially in ensuring a period of abortion without restriction as to reason (up to 12 weeks LMP) and ensuring that potentially damaging provisions (like so-called 'rape grounds') were not included. It also did not include provisions that are well known to cause restrictions in practice elsewhere, like parental notification clauses, foetal remains disposal clauses or so-called 'informed consent' provisions requiring mandatory ultrasounds and the like.[19] However, even at that early stage, it was quite clear that the Bill posed real difficulties for numerous abortion seekers in Ireland. The mandatory waiting period combined with a very short window for early abortion (12 weeks LMP) was identified early on as a source of real concern, especially as it would likely pose significant challenges for people in Northern Ireland, young people, and people in abusive relationships who were sometimes unable to move freely even to go to the doctor.[20] But there were other concerns too, often discussed by activists on the ground, and in many cases reflecting suspicion borne out of experience about the willingness and the ability of the public healthcare system – much of which remains under the patronage of the Roman Catholic Church – to administer the law in good faith and in a way that maximised women's reproductive autonomy.

However, at the same time, the pro-choice activism of the previous 35 years found itself needing to adapt to the demands of the referendum form. The text of the Irish Constitution can only be changed by referendum of the people,[21] and activists had plenty of practice in abortion-related referenda. In 1983, they had resisted the insertion of the Eighth Amendment itself, without success. Then, in 1992, they had experienced three simultaneous referenda: one to establish a right to information about abortion (subject to legal regulation), one to affirm the right to travel in order to access abortion care abroad (albeit without state support) and one

---

[18] S Coveney, 'Here's How My Thinking Shifted on the Eighth Amendment' *Irish Independent* (28 March 2018).

[19] Importantly, after the referendum, anti-choice legislators repeatedly tried – without success – to have such clauses inserted. For an analysis, see de Londras and Enright (n 17).

[20] See, eg, the analysis in M Enright et al, 'Position Paper on the Updated General Scheme of the Health (Regulation of Termination of Pregnancy) Bill 2018', https://lawyers4choice.files.wordpress.com/2018/08/position-paper-1.pdf.

[21] Constitution of Ireland, art 46.

to reverse a Supreme Court decision – known as the *X Case*[22] – finding that a risk of suicide was a sufficient risk to life to allow for termination of a pregnancy under the Eighth Amendment. The rights to information and travel were affirmed, and the people rejected the attempt to reverse *X*. Then, in 2002, another referendum was proposed, again to reverse *X* and, uniquely in Irish constitutional history, to constitutionally entrench a piece of legislation regulating the availability of abortion. That was again rejected by the people.[23] Apart from these referenda expressly focused on abortion, numerous EU-related referenda had also developed an 'abortion-slant', with anti-choice organisers arguing that amendments to the treaties of the European Union (EU) – which Ireland can ratify only following constitutional amendment and thus a referendum – would expand EU competencies in a way that 'endangered' Ireland's 'pro-life' constitution. As a result, Ireland had, on numerous occasions, secured protocols from the EU affirming that its abortion law was a domestic matter only. While the abortion question was not, generally, very material in voters' decision-making in these referenda, it had nevertheless been on the agenda. As a result of all of this, as well as many activists' experience in other social justice referenda in Ireland (including securing divorce, children's rights, marriage equality and resisting (unsuccessfully) the removal of *jus soli* citizenship), pro-choice activists had extensive referendum experience. This included experience of deeply divisive and, in some ways, violent and damaging referendum campaigns.

In spite of some pre-referendum polling from Amnesty International Ireland suggesting majority pro-choice sentiment,[24] pro-repeal activists were nervous. Many, including myself, worried that even people who opposed the Eighth Amendment would be apprehensive about the extent of the new proposed law. While we knew that most Irish people were deeply uncomfortable and increasingly intolerant of the damaging impact of the Eighth Amendment, some of us were less convinced that they were ready to embrace the proposition that, as much as possible, the law should simply leave people to decide for themselves whether to continue with pregnancy. As many of the pro-choice groups organised themselves into a single, official campaigning organisation – Together for Yes – the tensions between the desired outcome (largely repeal, followed by decriminalisation and professional regulation only) and the perceived demands of a constitutional referendum (thought, through conventional wisdom, to be moderation, re-assurance and winning 'the middle ground') became clear. Together for Yes was a civil society platform, made up of more than 70 groups and organisations from across civil society. Its three co-directors, Gráinne Griffin, Ailbhe Smyth and Orla O'Connor, represented three major organisations: the Abortion Rights Campaign (ARC);

---

[22] *Attorney General v X* [1992] 1 IR 1.

[23] For a comprehensive analysis of these referenda and the shaping and reshaping of abortion law after the Eighth Amendment was inserted in 1983, see F de Londras, 'Constitutionalizing Fetal Rights: A Salutary Tale from Ireland' (2015) 22(2) *Michigan Journal of Gender and the Law* 243.

[24] Amnesty International Ireland, 'What You Need to Know about Attitudes to Abortion in Ireland' (February 2016), https://www.amnesty.ie/poll/#. Raw polling data is also accessible through links on that webpage.

the Coalition to Repeal the Eighth; and the National Women's Council of Ireland (NWCI). While ARC and the Coalition were specifically organised to secure abortion law reform, the NWCI is a much broader organisation, which had not always supported reproductive rights reform and was, comparatively, something of a latecomer to advocacy for repeal. The Together for Yes executive consisted of the co-directors with experienced reproductive rights and health campaigners: the chief executive and director of advocacy of the Irish Family Planning Association, Niall Behan and Maeve Taylor, experienced activists and abortion-reform scholars with long associations with the Coalition and ARC (like Sinéad Kennedy and Sarah Monaghan) and a communications specialist from the NWCI (Silke Paasche). The campaign also had a 'Campaign Platform' with which it engaged as needed, although the Platform did not have decision-making roles; rather, strategic decisions seemed to be made primarily by the Executive. The Platform had dozens of member organisations, including those formed specifically to campaign for a 'yes' vote, longer-standing advocacy groups, trades unions and non-governmental organisations (NGOs).[25] The Campaign Platform was the most representative part of the campaign infrastructure and included groups that advocate for the (general and reproductive) rights of migrant and ethnic minority persons in Ireland (such as MERJ, AkiDwA, National Traveller Women's Forum and the Anti-Racism Network), and those that advocate for trans (reproductive and general) rights in Ireland (such as Transgender Equality Network Ireland, NXF National LGBT Federation and LGBT+ for Choice).

Together for Yes focused, deliberately, on so-called middle-ground concerns; cases where women had received diagnoses of fatal foetal anomalies were foregrounded, the harms of a rape ground were advanced as a key argument in favour of a 'protected period' of abortion without restriction as to reason, medical professionals were advanced as key promoters of repeal, abortion was presented as a matter primarily of medical care and rarely as a matter of personal choice, the (considered by many as liberating) practice of self-managed abortion was (often implicitly) presented as dangerous and risky,[26] and nationalist tropes were subtly engaged with as the reality of abortion travel and reliance on 'English' abortion law were presented as state failures.[27] Drawn into engaging with the General Scheme

---

[25] The full platform membership is available at: https://www.togetherforyes.ie/about-us/campaign-platform-members.

[26] Together for Yes, "'As She Was Losing Consciousness, I Couldn't Call a Doctor' – Mother of Woman Who Took Abortion Pills' (23 May 2018), https://www.togetherforyes.ie/as-she-was-losing-consciousness-i-couldnt-call-a-doctor-mother-of-woman-who-took-abortion-pills. *cf* Together for Yes, 'Briefing on the Proposal to Regulate Termination of Pregnancy in Early Pregnancy (12 Weeks): Medical Abortion', https://www.togetherforyes.ie/medical-abortion, which stated that: 'While the option of medical abortion is generally safe and effective, it cannot be considered acceptable healthcare as it does not reflect an active preference, but the lack of safe options and alternatives.'

[27] Importantly, as politicians seemed to respond well to the claim that without repeal, 'English abortion law is Irish abortion law' given dependence on abortion travel to the mainland UK, I too pressed this message in both press briefings and newspaper columns. See, eg, F de Londras, '"Yes" Can End Primacy of English Law' *The Times: Ireland Edition* (4 May 2018).

by the 'No' campaign's insistent focus on this proposed legislation, the official Yes campaign found itself endorsing or supporting the General Scheme either expressly or by deliberate and choreographed engagements with the Minister for Health, who was its primary proponent. Indeed, Together for Yes released a policy paper in which it concluded that the General Scheme, as proposed, constituted 'workable and reasonable proposals to allow women and girls to access the abortion services which they need, in a safe and regulated medical environment within the Irish health system'.[28] Nowhere in that policy paper were the shortcomings of the General Scheme acknowledged; understandably so, as to do so would have been to present the 'No' campaign with ammunition to ground claims detrimental to the 'Yes' movement.

While these strategic moves were driven by a desire to win the referendum and a sense, ever present and reinforced by very tight opinion polling, that the referendum was going to be extremely close and might well be the last opportunity for repeal for a decade or more, they reduced the space for nuance and sophistication in the campaign, including for bringing to the fore the inadequacy of the proposed reforms especially seen from marginalised perspectives. They also reduced the space to acknowledge and support people who had 'everyday' abortions, who did not fall into the 'hard cases' categories but instead were the embodiment of everyday reproductive life. The right to choose was rarely discussed; there seemed to be a reluctance to insist in public discourse on autonomy and choice as fundamental to agentic reproductive life, just as there had been in 1983.[29] There was little talk of 'trusting women', but much discussion of trusting women *and their doctors*.[30] Immigrant women, women in direct provision and trans people became almost invisible in official campaign activities, and even when concerns were raised inside the movement about their exclusion, the response tended to be that the campaign *of course* cared about them, but that it had to focus on what voters cared about: Irish women in hard cases. Others involved in the referendum have already written about how the narrowness of the official campaign was circumvented at times: some organisations refused to come on board and instead ran their own campaigns, usually insisting on more explicitly pro-choice and feminist talk,[31] and some 'on the ground' activists began simply to ignore the messaging from Head Office and did their own thing instead.[32] But there was, of course, discomfort too in the official campaign. Some of the co-directors, like Ailbhe Smyth, were rooted in an explicitly intersectional, all-island, feminist commitment to choice,

---

[28] Together for Yes, 'Position on Bill to Regulate Termination of Pregnancy' (5 April 2018), https://www.togetherforyes.ie/12-weeks.

[29] See the account of the 1983 referendum in L Connolly and T O'Toole, *Documenting Irish Feminisms: The Second Wave* (Woodfield Press, 2005).

[30] For example, during live TV debates, Together for Yes tweeted: 'We need to trust women and trust doctors to do their jobs'; https://twitter.com/Together4yes/status/989998165616185344.

[31] See, eg, Solidarity People before Profit.

[32] Burns (n 6).

autonomy and abortion without restriction, and the Abortion Rights Campaign – one of the three organisations that merged into Together for Yes – was explicitly intersectional in its design and commitments.[33] For them, no doubt, the strictures of the official campaign were difficult but necessary; for others, continuing their support for the campaign was difficult, not least because of the feeling that '[i]t would have taken less energy to include migrants in the campaign than it did to actively exclude us and fight with us'.[34] For all of us, there was an uncomfortable tension between what we believed in and what we thought we needed to do or say to win the referendum. The apprehension of a loss was weighty and sometimes overbearing; in truth, many of us did, wrote and said what we thought would work to secure a 50.1 per cent vote for 'yes' on 25 May 2018.

In the end, though, the victory was far greater than what almost any of us expected or could have predicted. The exit poll suggested that the pre-referendum polling done by Amnesty International Ireland had been right – the single greatest reason people gave for voting 'yes' was the right to choose.[35] Most people said that the referendum campaign had had no impact on their decision.[36] Middle Ireland, it turned out, was pro-choice after all, and by a huge majority. It is difficult to know whether those exit polls reflect real sentiment or the reconstructed sentiment of voters on a day when, at least in Dublin where I was, one could feel that the 'Yes' campaign would be victorious from very early on. But at the very least, the figures make us pause for thought about the compromises that were made in the referendum campaign, compromises that felt to many people and organisations committed to intersectional abortion rights activism like betrayal rather than pragmatism and that laid the foundation for the sharpest edges of the legislation that followed repeal.

---

[33] Abortion Rights Campaign, 'Abortion Rights Campaign Values and Inclusivity Statement', https://www.abortionrightscampaign.ie/2016/11/21/abortion-rights-campaign-values-and-inclusivity-statement: 'ARC aspires to be inclusive and representative of the varied groups of people affected by Ireland's restrictive abortion laws. We believe this requires a particular focus on those groups that are disproportionately affected by these laws including women who are marginalised by poverty, racism, immigration status and disability. However, we acknowledge the significant structural barriers at a societal and organisational level, which prevent marginalised groups participation and involvement in ARC. As a result ARC commits to actively address these barriers so as to support the meaningful involvement of people from all socio-economic backgrounds, minority ethnic groups or cultures, including Travellers and Roma, people of colour, the LGBTQI community, sex workers and people with disabilities. ARC aims not only to be inclusive within our organisation but also in how we work with others. We aim to work in solidarity with other groups who are experiencing oppression and develop meaningful partnerships to advance our collective struggles across social justice movements in Ireland and internationally.'

[34] Tweet from Emily Waszak (@waszaaaaak) of MERJ, https://twitter.com/waszaaaaak/status/1180216647468105728.

[35] RTE & Behaviour and Attitudes, 2018, Exit Poll on the Referendum on the 36th Amendment to the Constitution.

[36] ibid.

II. The Health (Regulation of Termination of Pregnancy) Act 2018 and Incomplete Reproductive Justice

The Health (Regulation of Termination of Pregnancy) Act 2018 finally came into operation on 1 January 2019. The Act, broadly speaking, divides access to abortion into three temporal stages. Up to 12 weeks LMP, a woman can access abortion without restriction as to reason provided she undertakes a mandated three-day wait from the time at which the gestation of the pregnancy is certified by a medical practitioner.[37] In practice, this usually means that women access medication abortion through a GP practice up to nine weeks and then abortion in hospital settings from nine to 12 weeks LMP.[38] Gestational dating is usually quick and based on a woman's own reported dates, but if someone is over nine weeks' gestation based on her own dates or there are otherwise reasons for doing so, an ultrasound may be used,[39] usually introducing further delays while the scans are scheduled and awaited. There is no facility to waive the waiting period where it would put someone over the 12-week limit or, in other cases, such as domestic violence, where ability to undertake a second visit might be diminished. At the time of writing this chapter, it was reported that all but two counties have GP practices that have publicly signed up to the provision of abortion care,[40] but in-county travel to access care is often needed. A central, government-run telephone and online advisory service – My Options – is in operation and women can ring this service for advice on GPs in their area who provide care. Abortion care is free for Irish residents and, if someone is in possession of a medical card (a card providing free GP care, usually on the basis of income), it is one of the few treatments for which a patient is permitted to attend a doctor other than the doctor with whom the medical card is registered.

After 12 weeks, abortion becomes tightly constrained. From 12 weeks to foetal viability, it is permitted only where there is a risk to the life of the pregnant person[41] or a risk of serious damage to her health.[42] Two medical practitioners, one of whom is an obstetrician,[43] must certify that such a risk exists. Where that is the case, and if the pregnant woman chooses it, abortion is provided in a hospital setting. Viability is determined on a case-by-case basis, but usually considered to be around 23 weeks; the statute defines it as 'the point in a pregnancy at which,

---

[37] Health (Regulation of Termination of Pregnancy) Act 2018, s 12.

[38] Institute of Obstetrics and Gynaecologists, *Interim Clinical Guidance: Termination of Pregnancy under 12 Weeks* (December 2018) 13.

[39] ibid 9–10.

[40] C McQuinn, 'Two Counties Still without Any GPs Offering Abortion as Just 13pc Sign up to the Service' *Irish Independent* (10 September 2019).

[41] Health (Regulation of Termination of Pregnancy) Act 2018, s 9.

[42] ibid.

[43] ibid.

in the reasonable opinion of a medical practitioner, the foetus is capable of survival outside the uterus without extraordinary life-sustaining measures'.[44] The only situations in which later abortion is permitted is where there is an emergency[45] or where the foetus has been diagnosed with a condition that is likely to result in its death before or within 28 days of birth.[46] This diagnosis must be certified by two medical practitioners, at least one of whom is an obstetrician. Because the foetus never reaches viability – statutorily defined – in these cases, there is no upper limit on when abortion might take place. Again, these later terminations take place in hospital settings. In all cases other than emergencies, medics may refuse to provide abortion on conscience grounds, but in those cases, they must refer a woman to a willing provider.[47]

On the face of it, there is much to commend in this law. The provision for abortion without restriction as to reason in the first 12 weeks LMP is considerably more liberal than in many countries – including the UK – and medics' only role is to certify gestation. The health ground after 12 weeks is uniquely constructed; what matters is that there is a risk of serious harm to health, not a *serious* risk, and not a risk of permanent or grave injury to health. This wording is of course a double-edged sword: it both empowers doctors to assess the nature of the possible injury to health in a way that centres the pregnant person's perspective *and* empowers doctors to install insurmountably high standards for an apprehended injury to health to be considered sufficiently serious. In other words – and in keeping with the tone of the campaign – it very much centres medical professionals as critical decision-makers in the administration of abortion law, creating spaces for caution and conservatism. The fact that medics who provide abortion care outside of the terms of the Act are still committing a serious criminal offence[48] means that the 'chilling effect'[49] of criminalisation continues to cast a shadow over those medical decision-making processes. That this is so can be acknowledged even while one notes, positively, that the new law does in fact make abortion available primarily in local, primary care settings for most people who need it.

However, what this hides are the ways in which the law continues to deliver incomplete reproductive justice and how that impacts particularly on marginalised communities whose reproductive lives were largely ignored in the attempt to bring the electorate 'on board' in the referendum campaign. On a systematic level, the law imposes what I call both dignitary and constitutional costs on all those who attempt to avail of it.[50] The dignitary costs comprise mostly the costs imposed by the law on women seeking abortion care – the mandatory waiting period, the multiple certifications and so on. The constitutional costs refer to the fact that

---

[44] ibid s 8.
[45] ibid s 10.
[46] ibid s 11.
[47] ibid s 22.
[48] ibid s 23.
[49] *A, B & C v Ireland* [2011] 53 EHRR 13.
[50] De Londras (n 3).

the law does not foresee or provide for any remedies in situations of wrongly denied abortion, for example, where a woman presents in the first 12 weeks, but is denied – by the running down of the clock through delayed or refused certifications, refusal to refer etc – because the 12-week time limit runs out, and she does not have a health risk associated with pregnancy that suffices to allow for abortion lawfully to be provided after 12 weeks. The implication of this is that the Act reflects a legislative failure to recognise that the general constitutional rights of pregnant women – including rights to privacy, bodily autonomy and freedom from torture or inhuman and degrading treatment – might *entitle* a woman to access an abortion in at least some circumstances.[51] All abortion seekers, then, suffer at least some harms under the Act. This, of course, is not unique to Ireland, but its ubiquity is not its excuse.

Nevertheless, some pregnant people suffer the sharp edges of the abortion law in exacerbated and particular ways. Let me illustrate this by two examples: trans and non-binary people who seek abortion care; and migrants in Ireland, including those seeking asylum and residing in direct provision accommodation.

A. Trans and Non-binary Abortion Seekers

Irish law recognises only two genders: male and female.[52] However, no medical interventions are required for someone to apply for legal recognition of gender; in other words, self-certification is permitted and quite unproblematic.[53] Following a review of the operation of the Gender Recognition Act 2015,[54] there is now a policy commitment to recognise 'non-binary' as a gender identity. For the most part, the practice of statutory interpretation ensures that legal gender is not a barrier to the equal application of the law, with words importing the feminine gender importing the male and vice versa.[55] However, in the Health (Regulation of Termination of Pregnancy) Act 2018, the terms 'woman' and 'pregnant woman' are used exclusively to refer to those persons to whom abortion care may be provided and for whom abortion outside the terms of the law is not a crime. Furthermore, 'woman' is defined as 'a female person of any age'.[56] From very early on in the legislative process, it was clear that members of the Oireachtas were uncomfortable with this, first, because of a concern that it would legally exclude men or non-binary people in need of abortion care and, second, because of a concern that even if all people were included in the legal category of 'woman' for the purposes

---

[51] ibid.
[52] Gender Recognition Act 2015.
[53] ibid pt II.
[54] Review of the Gender Recognition Act 2015: Report to the Minister for Employment Affairs and Social Protection (2018), https://www.gov.ie/pdf/?file=https://assets.gov.ie/69547/dd757168e2e44d-3faa7196b4b17fc4d8.pdf#page=1.
[55] Interpretation Act 2005, s 18(b)(1).
[56] Health (Regulation of Termination of Pregnancy) Act 2018, s 2.

of this Act, this would result in significant dignitary harm to non-women seeking care. Ruth Coppinger TD addressed this directly at the Second Stage, saying that: 'Transgender people genuinely fear they could be refused an abortion under the legal definition provided here, which makes clear the person must be a woman. This could be changed very simply by replacing the word "woman" with either the word "person" or the words "pregnant person" or inserting the words "and pregnant person" in the legislation.'[57]

It was absolutely clear that the government's policy was to ensure that the law was inclusive of all people who needed abortion care. The Minister for Health made this clear from the start,[58] and both he and Members of Parliament frequently used trans-inclusive language, moving easily between 'woman', 'girl' and 'pregnant person' in debates, referring to our 'trans siblings' and speaking directly of the need to ensure that this law serves their needs not least because trans and non-binary people were at the forefront of reproductive rights activism throughout and before the referendum.

In Ireland, the pro-choice movement is, and long has been, trans-inclusive. This is neither controversial nor contested within the community; as Louise O'Reilly TD put it at the Second Stage debate on the Bill in the Dáil: 'Trans people, particularly trans women, are an inextricable part of the feminist community and it would be remiss of us if the legislation providing for the provision of services was to leave them out.'[59] We all know the weight of law on our bodies and want to lift it from one another, recognising that reproductive freedom for some does not have to come at the cost of sexual, gender and reproductive freedom for others. However, in spite of this, the legislative language used in the Health (Regulation of Termination of Pregnancy) Act 2018 is clearly exclusionary in sentiment, even if not in legal application. Although some of us continued to press the Oireachtas to add 'or pregnant person' to the term 'woman' and 'pregnant woman' when it appeared in the Bill,[60] Together for Yes itself appears not to have intervened, even though the proposed fix (to add 'person' and keep 'woman') seemed to meet the needs of both acknowledging that the Eighth Amendment's weight was primarily borne by women and girls and that trans people already experience exclusion and violence within the health system.[61] In other words, such an approach might have ensured both express trans-inclusivity and linguistic acknowledgement that the burdens of the Eighth Amendment fell almost entirely on women and girls in Ireland. This failure can be seen as a continuation of the failures of the referendum

[57] R Coppinger TD, *Dáil Debates* (4 October 2018).

[58] See, eg, Simon Harris TD's comments at the Committee Stage: 'I want this legislation to be inclusive. I want it to be trans-inclusive. I want a very clear message to go out from these Houses that this legislation is inclusive of transgender people.' Select Committee on Health (6 November 2018).

[59] L O'Reilly TD, *Dáil Debates* (4 October 2018). At the Second Stage on the same day, this point was also made by Brid Smith TD, Clare Daly TD and Joan Collins TD.

[60] See the sources referred to in n 5 above.

[61] TENI, *Speaking from the Margins: Trans Mental Health and Wellbeing in Ireland* (TENI, 2013).

campaign itself – failures that at least some parts of the trans community insisted on naming and having acknowledged. On 26 May 2018, the day after the referendum, Trans Voices for Repeal released the following statement and demand:

> A group of independent trans people have called on Together for Yes to formally apologise to the trans people of Ireland, and to acknowledge the pain caused by the trans exclusionary campaign ran by the group in the referendum to repeal the eighth amendment of the constitution.

> We had been informed that, during the course of the campaign, directors and representatives of Together for Yes stated that their exclusion of trans people from the campaign, and campaign messaging, was done purposely to reach the 'middle ground'. Not only is the idea that trans people, and their lives, are confusing or repugnant to voters extremely offensive but, judging by the tallies and exit polls being released, it seems that it was entirely unnecessary.

> …

> Trans Voices for Repeal would like the national Together for Yes campaign, as well as its individual co-directors, to formally acknowledge the pain their actions have caused trans people in Ireland, the negative effect their campaign has had on the mental health of trans people and the unnecessary nature of this exclusion.[62]

To the best of my knowledge, no apology was forthcoming, even though the campaign platform for Together for Yes included a trans rights group (TENI) and even though it was a queer organisation with strong trans representation – Radical Queers Resist – that put their bodies on the line, using oversized 'wings' and sheets to cover up giant pictures of dismembered foetuses erected outside of maternity hospitals and on street corners by the Irish Centre for Bioethical Reform during the referendum. We do not yet know how many trans and non-binary people have sought abortion under the Act because the reporting processes refer to women only. But what we do know is that for many, including those who support trans rights but are themselves cisgender, this was a significant failure in the visioning and articulation of reproductive justice during and after the campaign.

B. Migrants and Asylum Seekers

It has always been the case that Ireland's abortion law disproportionately impacted migrants, especially non-EU migrants and those without travel documents.[63] The tolerance of abortion travel provided escape hatches only for those easily able to

[62] Trans Voices for Repeal, 'Trans Voices for Repeal Call on the Together for Yes Campaign to Formally Apologise to Trans People for the Exclusionary Campaign Ran' *Medium* (26 May 2018), https://medium.com/@transvoicesforrepeal/trans-voices-for-repeal-call-on-the-together-for-yes-campaign-to-formally-apologise-to-trans-people-84931f0fa85d.
[63] See, eg, E Luibhéid, 'Sexual Regimes and Migration Controls: Reproducing the Irish Nation-State in Transnational Contexts' (2006) 83 *Feminist Review* 60; C O'Brien, 'Dozens of Migrant Women Unable to Travel for Abortions' *Irish Times* (15 December 2014).

cross borders; for others, it introduced new traps – the need to seek single-entry visas or special travel documentation especially for asylum seekers, the financial burdens of both visas and travel, the delay this created with attendant consequences of abortion type and complication etc.[64] For undocumented migrants, transnational travel is almost entirely excluded; Brexit preparedness mean that modes of transportation between Ireland and the mainland UK – such as ferries – that are usually used without document checks by people perceived to be Irish or British are locations of real border trouble for people of colour and undocumented migrants.

Although transnational 'travel' is no longer the default route for abortion access in Ireland, abortion travel is still prevalent. In some cases, that travel is domestic, with people needing to travel to find a willing provider; in others, it continues to be transnational – when someone misses the 12-week window or if a foetal diagnosis is insufficiently serious to meet the statutory threshold, for example. Given the operation of mandatory waiting periods, people must be able to undertake domestic travel twice to access abortion care in the first 12 weeks: once for the certification of gestation and once to receive the prescribed medications or have the surgical intervention that results in the abortion. If someone is unlucky enough to attempt to access care from a doctor who refuses it on the basis of conscience, that number increases to three trips (refusal + new certification + medication/surgery) and more if an ultrasound needs to be scheduled for the purposes of certifying gestational age.

It may be true that, in some ways, domestic abortion travel is not the same as transnational abortion travel,[65] but this ought not to be taken to mean that domestic abortion travel is accessible. Asylum seekers in Ireland cannot work for a living, mostly live in direct provision centres (many of which are in isolated rural locations) and are provided only a paltry weekly allowance of €38.80 by the Irish state. How exactly are they supposed to afford to travel to the doctor even if public transport is available (and it almost always is not in rural Ireland)? For asylum seekers in particular, Ireland's racialised architecture of confinement intersects with poor public services and the new abortion law to impose and exacerbate a fixity and immobility[66] that easily pushes people out of the 12-week window and often into the necessity of transnational travel and all of the complications that come with this. Further, service provision failures exacerbate this: the My Options

---

[64] K Side, 'A Geopolitics of Migrant Women, Mobility and Abortion Access in the Republic of Ireland' (2016) 23(12) *Gender, Place & Culture* 1788.

[65] The fact that travel will not generally involve taking a plane to another jurisdiction has been pressed by a number of commentators to suggest that abortion travel under the new law cannot be compared to abortion travel under the Eighth Amendment. See the comments of Dr Peter Boylan: 'There may be some degree of travel, but the important thing is that women won't be travelling outside the country, using Ryanair and Aer Lingus and all the expense and so on that's involved with that.' Reported in E Edwards, 'Abortion Services Will Be "Unrecognisable" in Year's Time – Peter Boylan' *Irish Times* (16 December 2018).

[66] Side (n 3).

information is available in English and Irish only,[67] and people with limited English-language skills who find themselves in hospital settings being assessed for qualification after 12 weeks may especially struggle to be heard and to access or challenge the jargonistic medical assessments that the legislation treats as determinative of access to lawful abortion. This new law may meet the needs of most Irish women, but in many cases its failures and limitations bear most severely on migrants. This, of course, was predictable and predicted, but once again the referendum campaign ignored or minimised these risks, failing to place the needs and realities of migrants to the forefront of arguments for repeal and, post-repeal, for legislative reform. As MERJ write:

> We warned about these problems and unfortunately we are seeing them being played out. Let's not make the same mistakes and continue to ignore migrant women. The specific barriers that borders, racism and financial precariousness impose on those who make up to 20% of the population of Ireland cannot be ignored. We cannot talk about reproductive justice, we cannot talk about intersectional feminism, we cannot talk about free, safe, legal and local until we ensure that the voices of all those affected by lack of abortion access are heard and their needs are met.[68]

Two years after the referendum, MERJ and others continue to try to 'challenge the narrative surrounding Together for Yes as a model of intersectional feminism and to address the continued exclusion of migrants and ethnic minorities from Irish feminist discourse in order to move past the dominance of liberal white feminism and build a more radical and inclusive feminist movement in Ireland'.[69]

III. The Referendum Form and Failures of Intersectional Praxis

Iris Marion Young starts *Inclusion and Democracy*[70] with an anecdote about the passage of a referendum petition to establish a Police Civilian Review Board based largely on the need to address the racially oppressive use of police power against Black Americans in Pittsburgh. There, as in Together for Yes, a wide coalition was built so that in the end, the call for change was not only about injustice experienced by African Americans, but was also about the unjust application of police power to the LGBT community and other non-Black racial groups. Building such a coalition required a narrative, a way of telling the story of injustice and change

---

[67] MERJ Ireland, 'Migrants and Ethnic Minorities Being Left Behind by Ireland's Abortion Legislation', http://merjireland.org/index.php/2019/09/09/migrants-and-ethnic-minorities-being-left-behind-by-irelands-abortion-legislation.

[68] ibid.

[69] Event description for MERJ, 'Challenging White Feminism: Moving Beyond the Exclusionary Politics of Together for Yes' (Dublin, 13 October 2019).

[70] I Marion Young, *Inclusion and Democracy* (Oxford University Press, 2002).

to a broad range of people so that all would connect with it and, ultimately, vote in support. This was, she says, 'ordinary democracy in action'.[71] But what I am interested in here is the role of 'the narrative', which she shows us matters beyond securing the vote; it matters because it plays a role in how the vision of justice that emerges is shaped and in the extent to which the change that follows is seen as responding to the injustice that motivated it.

In campaigning for repeal, we also built a narrative during the official referendum campaign in Ireland. In contrast to the commitments and arguments of decades-long, intersectional pro-choice activism in Ireland that saw abortion law reform as part of a broader commitment to sexual emancipation and gender justice, that campaign was narrow, focused and modest in its claims. For those (including most politicians) whose entry point to abortion law reform in Ireland was the formal institutional setting of repeal – the 2016 election, the Citizens' Assembly, the Joint Oireachtas Committee and the campaign itself – these visionary, intersectional, emancipatory and radical underpinnings were easily invisibilised. In the official campaign, repeal was about 14-year-old rape victims, women who received diagnoses of fatal foetal anomalies, teenagers endangering their health taking abortion pills unsupervised, women whose health was seriously compromised in pregnancy and doctors unable to give the medical care they thought appropriate because of the limitations imposed by the Eighth Amendment. The woman for whom repeal was needed was, in this narrative, not brown. She was not trans or non-binary. She was not in direct provision. She was decidedly 'Irish'. She was not, as Tara Flynn so aptly put it, 'a filthy slut' who got pregnant after disappointing sex on a bean bag.[72] She was virtuous, sad, torn and in need of our help and support. She was the person we thought people would vote for. She was the paradigm around which so much of the argumentation we made or supported revolved. I used these same arguments and messages myself in public debates, newspaper columns, on the radio and knocking on doors. The priority was to win on 25 May 2018; nothing else would be possible without that, and in this blunt and one-off mechanism of constitutional change (the referendum), many of us worried that the intersectional realities of reproductive oppression were beyond the concern of too many 'average voters' to justify putting them at the centre of our argumentation.

This kind of narrative pragmatism is what a referendum-based campaign for change pushes us into, but what did it produce? What did we do when we built that narrative? We set expectations of what would suffice as 'justice' once the Eighth Amendment was gone. We conceded – though we perhaps did not allow ourselves to see it – that the change we so hoped for was one that would contain what Wendy Brown calls '"hidden cruelties" behind its sunny formulations of freedom and equality'.[73] And in those expectations we forgot to make sure that real people with

[71] ibid 3.
[72] Taken from Tara Flynn's monologue in *Not a Funny Word*, a one-woman testimonial play about accessing abortion in the Netherlands.
[73] W Brown, 'Suffering Rights as Paradoxes' (2000) 7(2) *Constellations* 208.

real and often deeply complex experiences of life, who did not fit the paradigm that we thought the electorate would care enough about to vote for, would also find justice within that frame. Even when we reflected on it, in corners of meetings and over anxious glasses of wine, we – certainly *I* – felt entrapped by the constitutional conditions that shaped our claim for legal emancipation, unable to imagine a way to overcome the limitations of the constitutional form and political imagination. We operated, in short, within Patricia Hill Collins' 'matrix of domination'[74] rather than in resistance to it, pushed into that position by the promise but the limited emancipatory capacity of constitutional rights work, and by the history of Irish feminism's 'alchemy of rights'[75] as the things that oppress us, when attributed to the foetus, but offer some promise of reproductive emancipation if re-ascribed to our bodies.

Would a more deliberate and self-aware commitment to the manifested praxis of intersectionality have changed this? In all honesty, I am not sure that it would. We would still have had to convince the electorate (to come out and vote, and to vote 'yes' to this particular proposition) and, more importantly, we would still had have to start from scratch in educating and on-boarding the vast majority of politicians to support a 'yes' vote. And so how then could we, as human rights lawyers and feminists, build a truly intersectional vision of reproductive justice and maintain our fidelity to it when we had to try to advance it through a politics that is so poor at complexity, so short in its attention span and so lacking in truly visionary leadership? The truth is that I don't know the answer to this question. Maybe the answer is that we simply were not brave enough to try. But maybe the answer is that we couldn't – that the mechanism of the referendum is radically unsuited to it. Perhaps we must just proceed with the battles that we believe we can win, apologise, recognise what is at stake and recommit ourselves to trying once again to improve the law that we now can, tentatively, say instantiates imperfect reproductive justice for some in Ireland. Maybe that is part of the cost of trying to advance justice through constitutional rights, but if it is, we must own that. We must remember 'that liberal individualism is a violating enablement'[76] and that constitutional rights as a discourse and a framework of rights protection is founded on liberal individualist grounds. Perhaps too the work of constitutional change was so depleting that our collective resources were diminished and we were less able to impact decisively on the legislative process, ushered in by politicians who in many ways wanted to retreat to the pre-repeal position of dealing with abortion as quickly and as 'neatly' as possible,[77] and seemed unwilling to continue to engage with the complexity and labour of making a law that maximises reproductive agency for all, focusing instead on 'delivering on the referendum'

---

[74] Hill Collins (n 7).

[75] Here I draw of course on Patricia Williams: P Williams, 'Alchemical Notes: Reconstructing Ideals from Reconstructed Rights' (1987) 22 *Harvard Civil Rights-Civil Liberties Law Review* 401.

[76] G Spivak, *Outside in the Teaching Machine* (Routledge, 2008).

[77] M Fox and T Murphy, 'Irish Abortion: Seeking Refuge in a Jurisprudence of Doubt and Delegation' (1992) 19 *Journal of Law and Society* 454.

and 'getting the law done' on time for a self-imposed 1 January 2019 deadline for service rollout.[78]

It is difficult to name and see what was unwon in the victory of repeal. We do not want to criticise those who worked so hard and gave so much over many years to bring us to 25 May 2018, and ultimately to the initiation of lawful abortion provision on 1 January 2019. We also want to be able to hold on to some of the exhilarated, relieved, astounded and – yes – proud delight that coursed through our bodies and poured its way out onto the streets of our towns and cities, onto Twitter and Facebook, and into the embraces and tears of activists gathered together in silent anxiety when the exit poll results were announced late in the evening of 25 May 2018. But unless we name what was unwon and recommit ourselves to working to improve the law from a base of intersectional understanding of its oppressiveness, we will fall into the trap of seeing constitutional change as success and of failing to remember that reproductive justice is a process, not an event. In Ireland, this process has only just begun. This will require us to continue the 'feminist law work'[79] of legal consciousness formation and raising, to advance and try to secure traction for interpretations and applications of the law that better reflect an intersectional commitment to and envisioning of reproductive justice, as well as to continue our engagement with the formal processes of law reform itself. Three years after the legislation came into force, there will be a statutory review of its operation.[80] This review will be our opportunity to recentre those who are most extremely and oppressively marginalised and damaged by that law; the people who continue to rely on abortion travel, generosity, importation of medication, self-managed abortion and feminist activist networks to free themselves, when they can, from a pregnancy that they feel they cannot proceed with.

Mara Clarke, the CEO of Abortion Support Network which supports women from Ireland, Northern Ireland, Malta and Gibraltar to access abortion care in the UK, recently tweeted 'Hey Ireland? Your new abortion law is sometimes a real piece of shit. Signed, @AbortionSupport, the people sick of getting phone calls from the people falling through the cracks'.[81] She is right. It is sometimes a real piece of shit and this cannot easily be disaggregated from (nor is it primarily attributable to) the failures of intersectional praxis in the referendum campaign. These failures

---

[78] This is subject to the recognition that some politicians worked hard to try to improve the draft, but the Minister for Health generally refused to accept any amendments and, even where he declared himself in sympathy with the arguments about access, intersectionality and marginalisation, claimed either that the General Scheme was to be treated as if binding or that the Attorney General had advised that a desired course of action was not constitutionally permissible or legally wise. For analyses of the legislative process, see, for example, de Londras and Enright (n 17); de Londras (n 3); Enright (n 3); Fletcher (n 1).

[79] M Enright, K McNeilly, F de Londras, 'Abortion Activism, Legal Change, and Taking Feminist Law Work Seriously' (2020) 71(3) *Northern Ireland Legal Quarterly* (forthcoming).

[80] Health (Regulation of Termination of Pregnancy) Act 2018, s 7.

[81] Mara Clarke, Twitter (9 September 2019), https://twitter.com/maraclarke/status/11709701541 77613824.

and their particular implications for marginalised pregnant people also subject to racism, nationalism, misogyny, transphobia, homophobia, unregulated capitalism, socio-economic inequality, partition and ableism demand our renewed attention if a truly intersectional commitment to reproductive justice is to be realised in Ireland and if we are to redeem our failures of intersectional praxis during the referendum campaign.

7

The Distance Between Us

Sexual and Reproductive Health Rights of Rural Women and Girls

MEGHAN CAMPBELL*

Introduction

Geography impacts the realisation of sexual and reproductive health rights. Sexual and reproductive health is the 'complete physical, mental and social well-being ... relating to the reproductive system and to its functions and processes'.[1] It includes, inter alia, comprehensive sex education, freedom to decide if and when to reproduce, access to a range of contraceptive methods and abortion services, comprehensive maternal healthcare and freedom from gender-based violence. A constellation of human rights is engaged in matters of sexual and reproductive health, including the right to life, health, privacy, bodily security, education and the prohibition against discrimination.[2] In human rights law, little attention is given to how the rural–urban divide affects the realisation of sexual and reproductive health rights of women and girls. The neglect of rurality is unwarranted. It is a meaningful, often lynchpin explanatory factor for rural girls and women's lack of access to sexual and reproductive health rights. The lack of public investment in rural areas means that women and girls must routinely travel long distances to access sexual and reproductive health services. Their economic dependence upon family can make overcoming distances particularly difficult, and tragically the cost of travelling can have life-and-death consequences. The close-knit, traditional, patriarchal nature of many rural communities makes accessing sexual and reproductive health services humiliating and creates risks of social ostracism. Living in a rural community also increases vulnerability to serious bodily harm and operates to isolate and silence the voices of women and girls.

* A warm thank you to Michele Statz and Lisa Pruitt for their helpful comments on earlier drafts of this chapter.
[1] International Conference on Population and Development, 'Programme of Action' (1994) [7.2], https://www.unfpa.org/sites/default/files/event-pdf/PoA_en.pdf.
[2] ibid [7.3].

The role of rurality is not formally recognised in many human rights instruments. It is not normally recognised as a ground of discrimination or as the common legal method to take account of discrimination, intersectionality or both. There are no specific rights targeting rurality. In fact, some jurisdictions have explicitly rejected 'place of residence' as a ground of discrimination.[3] The unspoken assumption is that rural life mirrors the characteristics of urban life and that geography plays little role in the enjoyment of human rights. But differences between urban and rural settings make a crucial difference in terms of how rights materialise in rural life. The metro-normativity of human rights law and policy results in an insensitivity to lived experiences and creates obstacles or exacerbates violations of sexual and reproductive health rights. Without due regard to the complexities of rural life and the role they play in undermining sexual and reproductive health, the rights of rural women and girls continue to be violated.

An exception to this overall global trend is the United Nations Convention on the Elimination of All Forms of Discrimination against Women (CEDAW).[4] CEDAW is unique among United Nations (UN) treaties in that Article 14 protects the equal rights of rural women in various fields of life, including 'access to adequate health care facilities, including information, counselling and services in family planning'.[5] Lisa Pruitt observes that CEDAW 'moves beyond the implicit focus on urban populations that characterizes a great deal of contemporary law making'.[6] There are also provisions in CEDAW that apply to rural and urban women alike that, both in theory and practice, take account of rurality in sexual and reproductive health rights, including Article 5 (negative cultural stereotypes and attitudes), Article 10 (equality in education), Article 12 (equality in access to healthcare) and Article 16 (equality in family life). CEDAW is asymmetric in that it only protects the rights of women and girls.[7] Echoing this asymmetry, the focus here is only on the sexual and reproductive health rights of rural women and girls. Zoning in on rural women and girls is further warranted as 'globally, and with few exceptions, on every gender and development indicator ... rural women fare worse than rural men and urban women and men'.[8] However, the analysis pays attention to how gender and rurality interact with other more well-recognised intersectional identities. This chapter explores how the Committee on the Elimination

[3] *R v Turpin* [1989] 1 SCR 1296 (Supreme Court of Canada).
[4] United Nations Convention on the Elimination of All Forms of Discrimination against Women (adopted 18 December 1979; entry into force 3 September 1981) 1249 UNTS 13.
[5] CEDAW, art 14(b). See also Protocol to the African Charter on Human and Peoples' Rights on the Rights of Women in Africa (adopted 13 September 2000, entered into force 25 November 2005) CAB/LEG/66.6, arts 14 and 12; African Youth Charter (adopted 2 July 2006), arts 13, 14, 16 and 22; Convention on the Rights of Persons with Disabilities (adopted 13 December 2006, entered into force 3 May 2008) 2515 UNTS 3, arts 9(1), 25(c) and 26(1)(b).
[6] L Pruitt, 'Deconstructing CEDAW's Article 14: Naming and Explaining Rural Difference' (2011) *William and Mary Journal of Women and the Law* 247, 352.
[7] CEDAW, art 1.
[8] CEDAW Committee, 'General Recommendation No 34 on the Rights of Rural Women' (2016) CEDAW/C/GC/24 [5].

of Discrimination against Women (CEDAW Committee), the body tasked with monitoring the implementation of CEDAW, has developed the treaty in relation to rural women and girls' sexual and reproductive health rights.

Drawing on cutting-edge scientific and sociological research, Section I demonstrates the role that rurality plays in undermining sexual and reproductive health rights. Section II turns to CEDAW. It begins by placing CEDAW in context, explaining its obligations, aims and accountability mechanisms. It then proceeds to analyse the structure and the drafting history to shed light on the purposes of protecting rural women's equal rights under Article 14. Section II concludes by canvassing CEDAW's approach to intersectionality to understand how the non-rural-specific provisions of CEDAW can account for rurality. Section III analyses the CEDAW Committee's key outputs on rural women's sexual and reproductive health. This evaluation points out strengths of the CEDAW Committee's approach and marks out areas for a more fine-grained analysis of rurality and women and girls' sexual and reproductive health rights. The analysis in this chapter serves as a call for action to conceptualising rurality as an identity characteristic under an intersectional human rights framework and a springboard for deeper engagement with the difference rurality makes to all human rights in both international and domestic human rights law.

I. Rurality Matters for Gender Equality

The CEDAW Committee estimates that 'rural women represent a quarter of the world's population'.[9] Rural communities are 'characterized by social and geographic isolation'.[10] The core features of rural life inherently shape the sexual and reproductive health rights of women and girls. The empirical evidence from a range of states in the Global North and South indicate that the chronic under-investment in rural communities, the distance and the financial implications of distances, the stubborn strength of traditional patriarchal norms in rural communities and the absence of privacy undermine the cluster of sexual and reproductive health rights throughout the life cycle of girls and women. These barriers may be present in urban settings, but in rural communities they are often more prevalent and severe, with more limited options for overcoming these barriers. There are differences in rural life for women and girls in different parts of the world, but their lives are disproportionately marked by poverty and by limited education and employment opportunities.[11] Rural areas are not homogeneous. Migrants, Indigenous peoples,

---

[9] ibid [3].
[10] TK Logan, R Walker and C Leukefeld, 'Rural and Urban Women's Perceptions of Barriers to Health, Mental Health and Criminal Justice Services: Implications for Victim Services' (2001) 16 *Journal of Interpersonal Violence* 266.
[11] CEDAW Committee (n 8) [5]–[6].

religious and ethnic minorities, women, children, older people, disabled persons, diverse sexual orientations and gender identities make their homes in rural communities. Some rural communities are at the coalface of climate change, while others are recovering from the trauma of conflict. This section is not a comprehensive assessment of the role of rurality on all sexual and reproductive health rights. Instead, it acts as a survey to demonstrate that living in a rural community is an explanatory factor that demands consideration for fully understanding the sexual and reproductive health rights of women and girls.

This lays the foundation for arguing that rurality is an intersectional issue for women's sexual and reproductive health rights. Conceptualising rurality as an identity characteristic builds upon the pioneering insights of Kimberlé Crenshaw, Patricia Hill Collins and other Black feminists whose work demonstrates that it is essential to fully grasp how multiple identities intersect to produce disadvantage.[12] Intersectionality and intersectional theory were initially developed to challenge the normative conceptions of women as white and Blacks as male.[13] Crenshaw argued that 'sometimes Black women experience discrimination as Black women – not the sum of race and sex discrimination, but as Black women'.[14] There is something unique and synergistically different when discrimination involves multiple identity characteristics.[15] Intersectionality has expanded to question how a plethora of identity characteristics – race, gender, age, disability, sexual orientation, migrant status and poverty – interact with each other to create webs of power, subordination and vulnerability. Rurality needs to be added to the canon of intersectional identities and, indeed, to intersectionality itself, as this section demonstrates that it is crucial for diagnosing the failure to realise women and girls' sexual and reproductive health rights.

Risks to sexual and reproductive health rights are more pronounced for girls in rural areas. The UN has found that female genital mutilation (FGM) is more prevalent in rural areas.[16] A World Health Organization (WHO) study found that in Egypt, where half of the girls between 10 and 18 years old have undergone FGM, a disproportionate number of girls in rural schools have been subjected to FGM (61.7 per cent of rural girls compared to 46.2 per cent of urban girls).[17] Girls in rural areas are 'more likely to become child brides than their urban counterparts'.[18]

---

[12] K Crenshaw, 'Demarginalising the Intersection of Race and Sex' (1989) *University of Chicago Legal Forum* 139; P Hill Collins, *Black Feminist Thought*, 2nd edn (Routledge, 2009); bell hooks, *Feminist Theory: From Margin to Center*, 2nd edn (SEP, 2000).

[13] S Atrey, 'Fifty Years on: The Curious Case of Intersectional Discrimination in the ICCPR' (2017) 35(3) *Nordic Journal of Human Rights* 220, 239.

[14] Crenshaw (n 12) 149.

[15] S Fredman, *Discrimination Law*, 2nd edn (Oxford University Press, 2011) 139.

[16] UN Population Fund, 'Demographic Perspectives on Female Genital Mutilation', https://sustainabledevelopment.un.org/content/documents/19961027123_UN_Demograhics_v3%20(1).pdf.

[17] MA Tag-Eldin et al, 'Prevalence of Female Genital Cutting among Egyptian Girls' (2008) 86(4) *Bulletin of WHO* 269.

[18] UNCIEF, 'Ending Child Marriage: Progress and Prospects' (2014), https://www.unicef.org/media/files/Child_Marriage_Report_7_17_LR.pdf.

In Bangladesh, Pakistan, India and Nepal, rurality is a key predicator of early forced marriage. This may be due to limited access to schools, fewer employment opportunities, prevalence of girls and women doing unpaid work on family farms, and the strength of traditional practices.[19]

There is evidence that rural teachers and administrators perceive a chilling effect in teaching sex education in rural communities. One study in the US found that the lack of anonymity in rural areas made teachers feel more vulnerable to criticism or social ostracism when sex education deviated from community expectations.[20] In rural Australia, 'stakeholders delivering sexual health interventions reported fear of community backlash'.[21] A similar trend is evident in Lesotho, where rural teachers who discuss sex education have been labelled as 'corrupting children's innocence'.[22] American teachers felt it was difficult to adopt a progressive, inclusive sex education curriculum in rural communities due to socially conservative beliefs.[23] As Sandra Fredman notes in Chapter 4 in this volume, in some schools in South Africa, sex education is reinforcing traditional gender norms and stereotypes on women's roles and sexual activity.[24] This finding is echoed in studies from Australia and Lesotho, which noted that sex education in rural areas did not adequately focus on diverse sexuality or address the needs of rural LGBTQI students.[25] The Australian study also found that the lack of anonymity affected students who reported feeling uncomfortable having sex education from their regular teacher who they would often see throughout the community.[26] Rurality impacts multiple actors within the community. The intersecting vulnerabilities of young women as well as the service providers in rural areas both have a disproportionate impact on how sexual and reproductive health rights are attended to and experienced.

The lack of privacy, anonymity and confidentiality in rural communities also perpetuates the stigma commonly associated with sexual and reproductive health, and particularly with respect to contraception. Being seen in the waiting room of sexual and reproductive health service clinics can be acutely embarrassing in

---

[19] A Marphatia, G Ambale and A Reid, 'Women's Marriage Age Matters for Public Health: A Review of the Broader Health and Social Implications in South Asia' (2017) 5 *Public Health* 269.

[20] L Blinn-Pike, 'Sex Education in Rural Schools in the US: Impact of Rural Educators Community Identities' (2008) 8(1) *Sex Education* 77.

[21] C Heslop, S Burns and R Lobo, 'Stakeholder Perceptions of Relationships and Sexuality Education, Backlash and Health Services in Rural Town' (2020) 20(2) *Sex Education* 170, 175.

[22] M Khau, 'Sexuality Education in Rural Lesotho Schools: Challenges and Possibilities' (2012) 12(4) *Sex Education* 411, 417.

[23] Blinn-Pike (n 20).

[24] See also K Alison Smith and A Harrison, 'Teachers Attitudes towards Adolescent Sexuality and Life Skills Education in Rural South Africa' (2013) 13(1) *Sex Education* 68.

[25] Khau (n 22); C Heslop, S Burns and R Lobo, '"Everyone Knows Everyone": Youth Perceptions of Relationships and Sexuality Education, Condom Access and Health Services in a Rural Town' (2019) 19(6) *Sex Education* 1.

[26] Heslop, Burns and Lobo (n 25).

close-knit communities.[27] This is accentuated for girls and young women who feel 'their sexual reputations were closely monitored'.[28] This is not the only barrier to accessing contraception. Negative attitudes on the part of medical professionals can prevent women, particularly adolescent girls, from accessing contraception. Rural Canadian women report being refused contraception by a doctor 'who will not prescribe birth control because he doesn't believe in it … for religious reasons'.[29] In many of these rural communities in Canada, the conservative views of doctors act as a de facto contraception ban as there is no other doctor within easy reach of the community.[30] In Ethiopia, distance from health centres negatively impacted contraceptive use among rural women and limited the range of contraceptive choices.[31]

Legal regimes in places that criminalise or heavily regulate abortions operate to increase the financial, social, physical and emotional costs for rural women. If these costs are too great, the laws, in essence, compel women to remain pregnant or risk unsafe abortion. The protection of conscientious objection means that in rural Italy, there is virtually no access to abortion.[32] In Texas, over-regulation resulted in the closure of abortion clinics.[33] The US Supreme Court found that the effect of these laws was 'to force women to travel long distances to get abortions in crammed-to-capacity' clinics where they received poor healthcare.[34] Pruitt and Statz go a step further than the Court in their analysis of the Texas abortion regulations and illuminatingly show the intricate and often invisible intersecting impact of rurality, gender, poverty and immigration status on women.[35] This situation seems to exist around the world for rural women from Canada to New South Wales, Australia.[36] There are costs in travelling large distances: fuel, public transport, overnight accommodation, meals, time off work and potential childcare arrangements. These costs 'are unaffordable and inaccessible for rural

[27] K Johnston, 'Increasing Access to Sexual Health Care for Rural and Regional Young People' (2015) 23(5) *Australian Journal of Rural Health* 257, 260.

[28] D Warr and L Hillier, '"That's Problem with Living in a Small Town": Privacy and Sexual Health Issues for Young Rural People' (1997) 5(3) *Australian Journal of Rural Health* 132.

[29] J Hulme et al, 'Barriers and Facilitators to Family Planning Access in Canada' (2015) 10(3) *Healthcare Policy* 48, 56.

[30] ibid.

[31] S Shiferaw, 'Does Proximity of Women Facilities with Better Choice of Contraceptives Affect Their Contraceptive Utilization in Rural Ethiopia?' (2018) 13(1) *PLOS ONE* e0192258.

[32] European Parliament's Policy Department for Citizens' Rights and Constitutional Affairs, 'Sexual and Reproductive Health Rights and the Implication of Conscientious Objection' (2018), www.europarl.europa.eu/RegData/etudes/STUD/2018/604969/IPOL_STU(2018)604969_EN.pdf.

[33] L Greenhouse and R Siegel, 'The Difference a Whole Woman Makes: Protection for Abortion Right after *Whole Woman's Health*' (2016) 126 *Yale Law Journal Forum* 149.

[34] *Whole Woman's Health v Hellerstedt* 136 S Ct 2292, 2318 (US Supreme Court).

[35] M Statz and L Pruitt, 'To Recognise the Tyranny of Distance: A Spatial Reading of *Whole Woman's Health v Hellerstedt*' (2018) 51(5) *Environment and Planning A: Economy and Space* 1106.

[36] L Vogel, 'Abortion Access Grim in English Canada' 2015 187(1) *Canadian Medical Association Journal* 17; F Doran and J Hornibrook, 'Rural New South Wales Women's Access to Abortion Services' (2014) 22(3) *Australian Journal of Rural Health* 121, 121.

women especially those on lower incomes'.[37] The financial costs associated with travelling long distances to abortion clinics mean that women cannot return for any 'follow-up care and [results in] poor continuity of care'.[38] The intersection of gender, poverty and rurality also explains the health outcomes. Women who seek abortion services in rural areas risk being exposed to scrutiny. In the Maldives, young unmarried, rural women resort to unsafe abortions due to fears of public humiliation.[39] Canadian women report doctors questioning their decision to obtain an abortion and even 'blocking passage of the plane destined to a referral centre for therapeutic abortion'.[40] In Chapter 6 in this volume, Fiona de Londras similarly observes that women and girls, particularly individuals within Ireland's asylum system, experience difficulties in travelling to abortion services, which are only available in urban centres.

The 'geographical position intensifies and compounds social determinants' to maternal health.[41] From Ghana to the US and from Canada to Mozambique, the lack of public investment in maternal health services in rural areas means that women must again travel.[42] Rural women may not have the time to travel the long distances, there might not be good-quality infrastructure to travel to health centres, and public transport options can be limited and extremely costly. This negatively impacts pre- and post-natal care and creates difficulties in accessing emergency maternal healthcare with devastating consequences. This is the underlying factual matrix to one of the CEDAW Committee's most famous decisions, *Da Silva Pimental Teixeira v Brazil*, which is discussed below in Section III.[43]

Rurality also plays a role in gender-based violence against girls and women. In the UK, 'rurality and isolation are used as weapons by abusers. Financial control, removal from friends, isolation from family are all well-understood tools of abuse'.[44] Men hold positions of power in rural communities and this makes 'women more vulnerable to coercion, control, prevent[ing them] from speaking out and accessing support'.[45] There is a similar pattern in Canada. The UN Special

---

[37] Doran and Hornibrook (n 36).

[38] ibid.

[39] S Hameed, 'To Be Young Unmarried, Rural and Female: Intersections of Sexual and Reproductive Health and Rights in the Maldives' (2018) 26(54) *Reproductive Health Matters* 61.

[40] Vogel (n 36), 57.

[41] Northern Secretariat of the BC Centre of Excellence for Women's Health, University of Northern British Columbia, 'The Determinants of Women's Health in Northern Rural and Remote Regions', https://www.unbc.ca/sites/default/files/assets/northern_fire/WmNorth.PDF.

[42] ibid; G Buruwaa Nuamah et al, 'Access and Utilization of Maternal Healthcare in a Rural District in the Forest Belt of Ghana' (2019) 19 *BMC Pregnancy and Childbirth* 1; D Maron, 'Maternal Health Care is Disappearing in Rural America' (*Scientific America*, 15 February 2017), https://www.scientificamerican.com/article/maternal-health-care-is-disappearing-in-rural-america; T Firoz, 'Community Perspective on the Determinants of Maternal Health in Rural Southern Mozambique' (2016) 13(2) *Reproductive Health* 112.

[43] *Da Silva Pimental Teixeira v Brazil* (2011) CEDAW/C/49/17/2008.

[44] Rural National Crime Network, 'Domestic Abuse in Rural Areas' (2019), https://www.ruralabuse.co.uk/wp-content/uploads/2019/07/Domestic-Abuse-in-Rural-Areas-National-Rural-Crime-Network.pdf.

[45] ibid.

Rapporteur on violence against women observed that rural women in Canada 'lack confidentiality when reporting abuse'.[46] There are also limited gender-based violence shelters in rural spaces, thus trapping women in abusive settings with men who often control the means of transportation and hence of escape.[47] In the US, cultures of rural masculinity are identified as playing a negative role in maintaining violence.[48] The economic conditions of rural life are also under stress from climate change and globalisation; this has resulted in a further embedding of rural patriarchy and violence against rural women.[49]

The lack of investment in rural spaces, the distances and difficulties in overcoming distances, the power of social norms and the lack of privacy undermine the sexual and reproductive health rights of millions of rural women and girls. More empirical evidence is needed for an in-depth analysis of the impact of rurality, as common factors unifying rural life can play out in various permutations in different rural communities. The current understanding of how rurality and other intersectional identities – minority status, sexual orientation, disability, socio-economic status, age and religion – combine to influence the realisation of sexual and reproductive health rights is under-researched. Clarity is also required on how urban stakeholders perceive rurality to better understand any stereotypes and attitudes that attach to rural women and girls. Despite these research gaps, the available evidence strongly indicates that the unique conditions in rural life can create obstacles to the sexual and reproductive health rights of women and girls.

Returning to intersectionality, the original theory and its praxis were developed by Black women and women of colour in the US in response to their oppression. Intersectionality revealed that Black women's experience of racism and sexism 'cannot be captured by looking at the race or gender dimensions of those experiences separately'.[50] The subordination of Black women was thus to be understood as unique, distinct or synergistic.[51] Black feminist scholars and advocates have observed the dangers of being blind to the reality to intersecting identities. For example, Crenshaw argues that 'where systems of race, gender and class domination converge … intervention strategies based solely on the experiences of women who do not share the same class or race backgrounds will be of limited help to women who because of race and class face different obstacles'.[52] However, intersectionality theory and practice has not been collapsed to only race and gender. Patricia Hill Collins observes that 'Black women's struggles are part of a wider

[46] UN Special Rapporteur on Violence against Women, its Causes and Consequences, 'Visit to Canada' (2019) A/HRC/41/42/Add.1 [94].

[47] National Advisory Committee on Rural and Health and Human Service, 'Intimate Partner Violence in Rural America' (2015), https://www.hrsa.gov/advisorycommittees/rural/publications/partnerviolencemarch2015.pdf.

[48] A Hall-Sanchez, 'Intimate Violence against Rural Women: The Current and Future State of Feminist Empirical and Theoretical Contributions' (2016) 10(4) *Sociology Compass* 272.

[49] ibid.

[50] K Crenshaw, 'Mapping the Margins: Intersectionality, Identity Politics and Violence against Women of Color' (1991) 43(6) *Stanford Law Review* 1241.

[51] Hill Collins (n 12).

[52] Crenshaw (n 50) 1246.

struggle for human dignity, empowerment and social justice'.[53] Intersectionality has thus been used to map the role of age, disability, sexual orientation, poverty and migrant status, inter alia, in creating reinforcing webs of disadvantage. The analysis in this section reveals the webs of disadvantage created by the intersection of rurality with sex, gender, poverty, pregnancy, age, disability etc in the context of the sexual and reproductive rights of women and girls. It thus shows that rurality is an identity characteristic that is crucial in diagnosing and remedying the violation of sexual and reproductive health rights of women and girls who live in rural communities. The next section investigates the extent to which international human rights law has handled the intersectional nature of rurality.

II. Recognising the Significant Role of Rural Women

There is rich promise within CEDAW to grasp how geographical and social isolation shapes the realisation of sexual and reproductive health rights. Article 14 of CEDAW stands alone among the core UN human rights treaties in that it explicitly 'takes into account the particular problems faced by rural women'. This is an overt, textual recognition that geography plays a meaningful role in the realisation of women's human rights. Article 14 emphasises 'the significant roles which rural women play in the economic survival of their families including their work in the non-monetized sectors of the economy'. The various subsections of Article 14 protect rural women's equal rights in different fields of life. The remaining obligations in CEDAW also apply to rural women. States must ensure the equality of rural (and urban) women in political life, nationality, education, employment, health, access to justice and family life.[54] Thus, CEDAW has a twin-tracking approach to rurality. This section analyses the text of CEDAW, the drafting history of Article 14 and CEDAW's approach to intersectionality in order to understand the potential contained within the text of the treaty to address the unique context of the sexual and reproductive health rights of rural women and girls.

A. A Landmark Treaty

CEDAW requires states to eliminate discrimination against women so that women can enjoy, on the basis of equality, their human rights and fundamental freedoms.[55] Equality, non-discrimination and human rights are the intertwined core of CEDAW.[56] The impetus for CEDAW arose from the failure of the mainstream

---

[53] Hill Collins (n 12).
[54] CEDAW Committee (n 8) [2].
[55] CEDAW, art 1.
[56] A Byrnes, 'Article 1' in M Freeman, C Chinkin and B Rudolf (eds), *CEDAW: A Commentary* (Oxford University Press, 2012) 52; CEDAW Committee, 'General Recommendation No 28 on the Core Obligations' (2010) CEDAW/C/GC/28 [4].

UN human rights treaties to take gender discrimination seriously.[57] While there are 'numerous ways that human rights can be violated', CEDAW zones in on how gender inequality and discrimination limit women's human rights.[58] The substantive obligations in CEDAW require states to eliminate discrimination and achieve equality in political, civil, social and economic rights. Along with Article 14 on the equal rights of rural women, there are several other unique provisions in CEDAW. Article 3 obliges states to ensure women's full advancement and development. Article 4 requires states to undertake temporary special measures to advance women's equality and Article 5 explicitly calls on states to remedy negative socio-cultural stereotypes and prejudices that disadvantage women. The CEDAW Committee explains that the text of the treaty anticipates 'the emergence of new forms of discrimination that had not been identified at the time of drafting'.[59] Through an evolutionary interpretation of the text, the CEDAW Committee has redressed gaps in the treaty, most notably through interpreting gender-based violence as a pernicious form of discrimination against women.[60]

The implementation of the Convention is monitored by the CEDAW Committee, which is a body of independent experts from diverse professional backgrounds, including law, politics, sociology and even dentistry.[61] Overwhelmingly, throughout the CEDAW Committee's history, it has been composed of women.[62] To date, there has been no investigation into the urban-rural background of treaty body members. The CEDAW Committee monitors states' progress in eliminating discrimination through a series of accountability mechanisms. Its flagship accountability procedure is the periodic reporting process.[63] Every four years, states parties submit a written report to the CEDAW Committee on the steps they have taken to achieve gender equality, including for rural women under Article 14. Civil society and international organisations submit shadow reports to overcome any gaps or biases in the state reports. There is a written and oral dialogue between state representatives and the CEDAW Committee. The *Concluding Observations* draw this wealth of knowledge together to pinpoint areas of concern and recommendations to achieve equality in women's rights.

Under the Optional Protocol to the Convention (OP-CEDAW), an individual can allege violations of the treaty.[64] The CEDAW Committee considers these

---

[57] UN Women, 'Short History of CEDAW Convention', www.un.org/womenwatch/daw/cedaw/history.htm.

[58] M Campbell, *Women, Poverty, Equality: The Role of CEDAW* (Hart Publishing, 2018) 127.

[59] CEDAW Committee (n 56) [8].

[60] CEDAW Committee, 'General Recommendation No 19 on Gender-Based Violence' (1992) CEDAW/C/GC/19 and CEDAW Committee, 'General Recommendation No 35 on Gender-Based Violence against Women' (2019) CEDAW/C/GC/35.

[61] A Byrnes, 'The Committee on the Elimination of Discrimination Against Women' in P Alston and F Megret (eds), *The UN and Human Rights*, 2nd edn (Oxford University Press, 2020).

[62] ibid.

[63] CEDAW, art 18.

[64] Article 2 (adopted 10 December 1999, entered into force 22 December 2000) 2131 UNTS 83; J Connors, 'Optional Protocol' in M Freeman, C Chinkin and B Rudolf (eds), *CEDAW: A Commentary* (Oxford University Press, 2012).

Individual Communications, which entail a series of written submissions from the individual and the state. If it concludes that there has been a violation, it makes a series of specific and general recommendations to redress the individual and systemic harms raised by the communication. In addition, under the OP-CEDAW, upon receipt of reliable information, the CEDAW Committee can conduct an *Inquiry Procedure* to investigate grave or systemic violations of CEDAW.[65] This process is designed to tackle structural barriers to women's equality.[66] For each inquiry to date, the CEDAW Committee has conducted a fact-finding mission and dialogued with a wide range of relevant stakeholders. The *General Recommendations* synthesise the CEDAW Committee's knowledge and expertise. It interprets and evolves the legal obligations in the Convention, shares best practices on gender equality and provides guidance to states on the periodic reporting process.[67] Through these various mechanisms, the CEDAW Committee has developed 'a substantial body of interpretive material on specific articles of the Convention'.[68] Section III below will evaluate how all of these different accountability mechanisms engage with rural women's sexual and reproductive health rights.

B. Article 14 of CEDAW

CEDAW 'evinces a concern about gender as it intersects with rurality'.[69] Article 14(1) holds:

> States Parties shall take into account the particular problems faced by rural women and the significant roles which rural women play in the economic survival of their families, including their work in the non-monetized sectors of the economy, and shall take all appropriate measures to ensure the application of the provisions of the present Convention to women in rural areas.

There is consensus that Article 14(1) is meant to spotlight the uniqueness of rural women and girls.[70] Rural women are routinely invisible to 'official statistics relating to GDP and employment and have very often been ignored in development planning'.[71] A legal obligation in an international human rights treaty on rural woman is a significant milestone.

---

[65] OP-CEDAW, art 8.
[66] M Campbell, 'Beyond the Courtroom: Accountability for Grave and Systemic Human Rights Abuses' (2019) 1 *University of Oxford Human Rights Hub Journal* 55.
[67] H Keller and L Grover, 'General Comments of the Human Rights Committee and Their Legitimacy' in H Keller and G Ulfstein (eds), *UN Human Rights Treaty Bodies: Law and Legitimacy* (Cambridge University Press, 2012).
[68] A Byrnes, 'The Committee on the Elimination of Discrimination against Women' in A Hellum and H Singding Aasen (eds), *Women's Human Rights: CEDAW in International, Regional and National Law* (Cambridge University Press, 2013) 39.
[69] Pruitt (n 6) 350.
[70] ibid; N Burrows, 'The 1979 Convention on the Elimination of All Forms of Discrimination against Women' (1985) 32 *Netherlands International Law Review* 419, 446; F Banda, 'Article 14' in M Freeman, C Chinkin and B Rudolf (eds), *CEDAW: A Commentary* (Oxford University Press, 2012).
[71] Burrows (n 70) 447.

Article 14(2) guarantees specific equal rights for rural women:

States Parties shall take all appropriate measures to eliminate discrimination against women in rural areas in order to ensure, on a basis of equality of men and women, that they participate in and benefit from rural development and, in particular, shall ensure to such women the right:

(a)   To participate in the elaboration and implementation of development planning at all levels;
(b)   To have access to adequate health care facilities, including information, counselling and services in family planning;
(c)   To benefit directly from social security programmes;
(d)   To obtain all types of training and education, formal and non-formal, including that relating to functional literacy, as well as, inter alia, the benefit of all community and extension services, in order to increase their technical proficiency;
(e)   To organize self-help groups and co-operatives in order to obtain equal access to economic opportunities through employment or self-employment;
(f)   To participate in all community activities;
(g)   To have access to agricultural credit and loans, marketing facilities, appropriate technology and equal treatment in land and agrarian reform as well as in land resettlement schemes;
(h)   To enjoy adequate living conditions, particularly in relation to housing, sanitation, electricity and water supply, transport and communications.

Article 14(2) of the Convention speaks directly to rurality (agricultural loans and land reform) and repeats provisions already in CEDAW (healthcare). The drafters, however, felt this repetition was important in 'stressing the situation of rural women'.[72]

Article 14(2)(b) of the Convention obliges states to ensure access to healthcare services as well as access and information to family planning services. During the drafting process, the representative from Bangladesh 'proposed expanding the scope of coverage [for rural women] to include receiving adequate nutrition during pregnancy and lactation'.[73] There was wide support for this proposal and it was moved to Article 12 (equal access to healthcare) so that urban and rural women are entitled to appropriate maternal healthcare.[74] Comparing Articles 12 and 14(2)(b), there are textual differences that provide clarity as to how CEDAW protects the sexual and reproductive health rights of rural women and girls. Pruitt observes that Article 12 guarantees equal access to healthcare, while Article 14(2)(b) only guarantees '*adequate* healthcare facilities' (emphasis added) or seemingly 'a minimal standard of healthcare – for rural women'.[75] Recalling that Article 12 applies to rural and urban women, Pruitt concludes that Article 14(2)(b) is not a minimal standard, but rather emphasises geographical inequality in health services.[76]

---

[72] L Rehof, *Guide to the Convention on Discrimination against Women* (Brill, 1993) 159.
[73] Banda (n 70) 363.
[74] ibid.
[75] Pruitt (n 6) 367.
[76] ibid 368.

There is a debate on the drafter's intentions on the geographical scope of 'rural' in Article 14 of the Convention. Examining the drafting history, there is an argument that 'rural' should be equated with rural development in the Global South. The impetus for protecting rural women's rights in CEDAW came from a representative of the Food and Agricultural Organization, drawing on commitments made throughout the UN on gender and rural development.[77] Representatives from India, Egypt, Indonesia, Thailand, Iran, Pakistan and the US proposed the initial draft of Article 14.[78] Burrows argues that Article 14 is 'a manifestation of the impact of delegates of women from the Third World' and is 'perhaps an inevitable culmination of the work of the UN linking questions of development with those of women'.[79] Pruitt observes that the obligations in Article 14(2) echoes UN development documents on rural women.[80] Article 14 could thus be read as directed towards rurality in the Global South. However, on a plain reading of Article 14, it applies to any rural area in the Global North and South. Section III will demonstrate that the CEDAW Committee has been attentive to the intersection between gender, rurality and sexual and reproductive health rights in all parts of the world.[81]

C. CEDAW and Intersectionality[82]

The other provisions in CEDAW – Article 5 (negative cultural attitudes), Article 10 (education), Article 12 (health) and Article 16 (family life) – apply to all women, including rural women and girls. The question investigated in Section III below is whether the CEDAW Committee addresses the intersection between gender and rurality in these and other obligations in CEDAW. It is necessary first to establish how CEDAW addresses intersectionality.

There are no specific provisions in CEDAW recognising women's intersectional identities. CEDAW has been accused of not protecting against intersectional discrimination.[83] Reading the text reveals glimmers of an intersectional approach. The preamble refers to poverty, racial discrimination and colonialism, Article 4 (temporary special measures) and Article 11(2) protect women based on pregnancy and motherhood, and Article 9 prohibits discrimination based on the intersection of gender and nationality.

A deeper textual analysis of CEDAW reveals an implicit commitment to eliminating intersectional discrimination. CEDAW adopts a fluid and expansive

---

[77] Burrows (n 70) 446.

[78] Banda (n 70) 362.

[79] Burrows (n 70) 447.

[80] Pruitt (n 6) 364.

[81] CEDAW Committee (n 8) [88]–[92].

[82] This subsection is drawn from M Campbell, 'CEDAW and Women's Intersecting Identities: A Pioneering New Approach to Intersectional Discrimination' (2015) 22 *Revista Direito GV* 479.

[83] J Bond, 'International Intersectionality: A Theoretical and Pragmatic Exploration of Women's International Human Rights Violations' (2003) 53 *Emory Law Journal* 71, 95.

conception of women's lives that allows an appreciation of the various identity characteristics, factors and experiences that interact with sex and gender to prevent women from enjoying their human rights. Article 2 of CEDAW condemns discrimination in 'all of its forms' and this provides the textual basis for recognising intersectional discrimination as a form of discrimination.[84] If women's rights are denied through the intersection of gender and other aspects of women's identity, they can be addressed through CEDAW. The CEDAW Committee explains that 'discrimination of women based on sex and gender is *inextricably linked* with other factors that affect women, such as race, ethnicity, religion or belief, health status, age, class, caste, sexual orientation and gender identity' (emphasis added).[85] CEDAW does not confine itself to the traditional canon of intersectional identities recognised in discrimination law, but includes a wide variety of identity markers and experiences, including prisoner status, literacy, poverty and rurality.[86] CEDAW's approach recognises that 'categories of discrimination cannot be reduced to watertight compartments'.[87] All aspects of identity, including rurality, are relevant in diagnosing and remedying women and girls' disadvantage.

III. The CEDAW Committee and Gendered Rurality

In all its accountability mechanisms, the CEDAW Committee engages with gendered rurality. As a set of examples, this section examines the Concluding Observations from the CEDAW Committee's July 2019 session, Individual Communications, Inquiry Procedures and General Recommendations. Many typical criticisms of UN treaty bodies apply to gender, rurality and sexual and reproductive health rights. Most prominently, there is a lack of consistency and in-depth engagement.[88] In many of the Concluding Observations examined here, under Article 14, the CEDAW Committee simply expresses concern on the 'limited access for rural and indigenous girls to health services, in particular sexual and reproductive health' without any further detail.[89] For Qatar, no specific mention is made of rural sexual and reproductive health rights.[90] Despite these limitations, the CEDAW Committee has a twin-tracking approach to the intersection of gender, rurality and sexual and reproductive health rights: it focuses on sexual and reproductive health on the basis of Article 14(2)(b) *and* identifies

---

[84] CEDAW Committee, 'General Recommendation No 19' (n 60).

[85] CEDAW Committee (n 56) [18].

[86] CEDAW Committee, 'General Recommendation No 27 on Older Women and the Protection of Their Human Rights' (2010) CEDAW/C/GC/27; Campbell (n 58) 23.

[87] *Egan v Canada* [1995] 2 SCR 513, 561–64 (dissenting judgment of Justice L'Heureux-Dube) (Canadian Supreme Court).

[88] Banda (n 70) 364.

[89] CEDAW Committee, 'Concluding Observations: Guyana' (2019) CEDAW/C/GUY/CO/9 [43(d)].

[90] CEDAW Committee, 'Concluding Observations: Qatar' (2019) CEDAW/C/QAT/CO/2.

rurality as an identity factor that limits sexual and reproductive health on the basis of the other obligations in CEDAW. Casting a wide net for analysing, the CEDAW Committee's approach to gender, rurality and sexual and reproductive health rights demonstrates that it is sensitive to many of the interlocking systemic issues that plague rural communities. There is one aspect of rural and sexual and reproductive health that the CEDAW Committee is not giving enough attention to: the impact of living in a small socially isolated community where 'everyone knows everyone', which numerous studies demonstrate can limit sexual and reproductive health rights.[91] To more fully respond to the intersection of gender and rurality, the CEDAW Committee's recommendations need to encourage states to take measures to respect the confidentiality of rural girls and women when exercising their sexual and reproductive health rights and transform rural cultural attitudes that perpetuate shame and stigma.

Before turning to analyse how the CEDAW Committee engages with specific aspects of sexual and reproductive health, it is helpful to map the CEDAW Committee's concerns and recommendations that go to the heart of the geographical and social isolation in rural areas. The CEDAW Committee advocates for temporary special measures, sustained investment in rural spaces and rural women's economic empowerment and participation.[92] Although not always directly linked to sexual and reproductive health rights, they reflect the realities of rural life and, if adopted, could have a positive impact. Urban policy-makers and rural (often male) leadership do not allocate sufficient budgets for rural sexual and reproductive health services.[93] To correct this imbalance, the CEDAW Committee encourages states to 'increase its health expenditure ... in rural and remote areas'[94] and ensure that all rural healthcare services are of high quality, staffed with trained medical personnel, physically accessible, affordable and culturally acceptable.[95]

Even with greater urban–rural equality in health budgets, the realities of geography mean that distances will always be a factor for many rural women and girls. States are recommended to 'analyse sex-differentiated demands for transport services in rural areas, ensure that transportation ... policies ... reflect the mobility needs of rural women and provide them with safe, affordable and accessible means of transport'.[96] The CEDAW Committee also focuses on rural women and girls' economic empowerment and participation. Strengthening programmes on rural women's economic empowerment can guarantee that rural women and girls have the resources to travel the distances to urban-based sexual and reproductive health centres.[97] In order to empower the voices of rural women and girls and to demand accountability for

---

[91] Heslop, Burns and Lobo (n 25).
[92] CEDAW Committee, 'Concluding Observations: Austria' (2019) CEDAW/C/AUS/CO/9 [19(a)].
[93] CEDAW Committee (n 8) [37].
[94] CEDAW Committee, 'Concluding Observations: The Democratic Republic of the Congo' (2019) CEDAW/C/COD/CO/8 [37(a)].
[95] CEDAW Committee (n 8) [39(a)].
[96] ibid [87].
[97] ibid [9(e)], [15], [17(b)].

violations of their sexual and reproductive health rights, states must increase rural
women's access to justice through increasing legal literacy, supporting legal aid and
establishing courts in rural areas.[98] In a similar vein, rural women's participation
'in all decision-making at all levels and in community-level discussions with high
authorities' can ensure that there is the political will and action for rural sexual and
reproductive health rights.[99] Increasing rural women's participation 'in the assessment, analysis, planning, design, budgeting, financing, implementation, monitoring
and evaluation of all … rural development strategies' is crucial.[100]

Recognising the diversity of rural spaces, the CEDAW Committee is sensitive
to intersectionality of rural life. It stresses that migrant, Indigenous and minority
women, as well as women in poverty, experience intersecting forms of discrimination in rural areas,[101] and rurality is commonly included in the CEDAW Committee's
list of other vulnerable grounds.[102] Unfortunately, there is less recognition of older
rural women, disabled and LBTQI women living in rural communities. Thus,
there is space for a more comprehensive intersectional analysis still, once rurality
has been factored in.

In the specific case of sexual and reproductive health rights, the CEDAW
Committee highlights the prevalence of cultural norms in rural communities that
underpin FGM and early forced marriage.[103] In the inquiry into 'bride-kidnapping'
in Kyrgyzstan, the CEDAW Committee found that a disproportionate number of
rural men 'believed the victim of bride-kidnapping should marry the abductor'.[104]
The 'social acceptance of bride-kidnapping, especially in rural areas' makes it difficult for women to leave the forced marriage.[105] To end these gross violations of
sexual and reproductive health rights, the CEDAW Committee encourages states
to target awareness raising on such harmful cultural practices in relation to traditional leaders, men and boys, and to enforce the laws prohibiting FGM and early
forced marriage.[106]

There is less awareness of the role of rurality in sex education. The CEDAW
Committee does advocate for comprehensive, scientifically accurate, gender
responsive sex education which applies to both urban and rural girls.[107] However,
it is not attentive to the unique factors that arise in delivering sex education in

[98] ibid [9(c)]; CEDAW Committee, 'General Recommendation No 33 on Women's Access to Justice'
(2015) CEDAW/C/GC/35 [13], [14(e)], [16(a)] and [17(f)].
[99] CEDAW Committee (n 8) [53].
[100] ibid [54(d)].
[101] CEDAW Committee (n 8) [15], [25(b)], [26],]27], [59], [77(c)], [89] and [90].
[102] CEDAW Committee (n 98) [13]; CEDAW Committee, 'General Recommendation No 35' (n 60)
[12] and [30(c)]; CEDAW Committee, 'General Recommendation No 36 on the Right of Girls and
Women to Education' (2017) CEDAW/GC/C/36 [29], [32], [33], [35(c)] and [65(j)].
[103] CEDAW Committee (n 8) [22].
[104] CEDAW Committee, 'Report of the Inquiry Concerning Kyrgyzstan of the CEDAW Committee
under Article 8 of OP-CEDAW' (2018) CEDAW/C/OP.8/KGZ/1, [21].
[105] ibid [59] and [70].
[106] CEDAW Committee (n 8) [23].
[107] M Campbell, 'The Challenge of Girls' Right to Education: Let's Talk about Human-Rights Based
Sex Education' (2016) 20(8) *International Journal of Human Rights* 1219.

rural communities. The analysis under either Article 10 (education) or Article 14(2) does not touch upon social isolation and social conservatism that limits sex education. There are a few examples of the CEDAW Committee making passing references to increasing information on sexual and reproductive health rights in rural areas, but this falls short of fully appreciating the impact of rurality.[108] Similarly, the recommendations on rural education are predominantly focused on access and improving literacy.[109] The inattention to the intersection of rurality and sex education is a missed opportunity to provide tailored recommendations that speak to the lived reality of rural women and girls.

On a more positive note, the CEDAW Committee consistently advocates that rural women and girls must be able to access affordable modern contraception.[110] In General Recommendation No 34 on the rights of rural women, it pinpoints poverty, lack of information and limited availability as obstacles to accessing contraception.[111] Unfortunately, the CEDAW Committee does not acknowledge the role of stigma in accessing contraception in rural communities, particularly close-knit rural communities. Its recommendations could be strengthened by harmoniously encouraging states to protect girls and women's privacy and to tackle negative attitudes surrounding the use of contraception so that rural women and girls can use contraception without public shaming.

The lack of investment in rural sexual and reproductive health rights increases the risk that rural women and girls will resort to unsafe abortion. The CEDAW Committee observes that 'rural women are more likely to resort to unsafe abortion than urban counterparts'.[112] In the Inquiry into Northern Ireland (taking place prior to the recent decriminalisation of abortion), the CEDAW Committee observed that in the extremely limited circumstances where abortion is legal, the two facilities are located in the region's main city (Belfast) and concluded that accessibility is limited by geography.[113] It held that the risk factors undermining access to abortion in Northern Ireland are exacerbated by rurality. Rural poverty, conservative sex education, limited access to contraception, the costs of travelling to England for an abortion (where the laws on abortion are more permissive), the negative health impacts of being unable to afford the associated costs of post-abortion care in England and the high levels of secrecy around abortion all increase rural women and girls' 'susceptibility to turning to unsafe abortion'.[114] Where abortion is decriminalised, the legal regimes that regulate access to abortion can

---

[108] CEDAW Committee (n 8) [39(f)].

[109] CEDAW Committee, 'Concluding Observations: Cabo Verde' (2019) CEDAW/C/CPV/CO/9 [40(b)]; CEDAW Committee, 'Concluding Observations: Cote d'Ivoire' (2019) CEDAW/C/CIV/CO/4 [39(a)]; CEDAW Committee: Mozambique' (2019) CEDAW/C/MOZ/CO/3-5 [31(b)].

[110] CEDAW Committee (n 8) [38]; CEDAW Committee, 'Concluding Observations: Cote d'Ivoire' (n 109) [44(d)]; CEDAW Committee, 'Concluding Observations: Mozambique' (n 109) [38(c)].

[111] CEDAW Committee (n 8) [38].

[112] ibid.

[113] CEDAW Committee, 'Report of the Inquiry Concerning the UK and Northern Ireland of the CEDAW Committee under Article 8 OP-CEDAW' (2017) CEDAW/C/OP.8/GBR/1 [13].

[114] ibid [69].

significantly impact rural women and girls. Abortion has recently been decriminalised in Northern Ireland, in part in response to the Inquiry, and it remains to be seen how the new regime will ensure access for rural women and girls.[115] The CEDAW Committee identifies that waiting periods for access to abortion can 'impede access for rural women' who cannot afford to travel multiple trips to healthcare clinics or overnight accommodation (a problem also identified by Fiona de Londras in Chapter 6 in this volume).[116] The synergy between distance from health services and financial costs also negatively impacts post-abortion care, as rural woman often cannot return to health clinics. In its Concluding Observations, the CEDAW Committee repeatedly encourages states to guarantee post-abortion care for rural women.[117] In the Concluding Observations for Mozambique, the CEDAW Committee stresses the importance of rural women and girls being able to access confidential abortion services, a recognition of the lack of privacy many rural women and girls experience in exercising their sexual and reproductive health rights.[118] Somewhat surprisingly, the CEDAW Committee does not explicitly engage with the role of conscientious objection and access to abortion, which is an oversight, as protecting the beliefs of medical professionals can act as a de facto abortion ban for rural women and girls.

The CEDAW Committee expresses concern that 'maternal mortality and morbidity are disproportionately high in many rural areas'.[119] Again, the CEDAW Committee diagnoses poor maternal health outcomes as linked to the lack of investment in rural health services. Rural communities do not have the same access to 'the presence of skilled birth attendants and medical personnel'.[120] Along with the overarching recommendations to increase health budgets and improve transport links, the CEDAW Committee recommends improving access to skilled birth attendants, community health workers and mobile health units to end rural maternal mortality.[121] There is some innovative research on the value of having a birth companion (partner, friend or family member) for the physical and emotional health of women during childbirth.[122] The CEDAW Committee could consider recommending that states fund birth companions for rural women who must travel with the pregnant person to safely deliver.[123] Tragically, in the case of *Da Silva Pimental Teixeira v Brazil* (already addressed by Gauthier de Beco in Chapter 2 of this volume), despite evidence of haemorrhaging, it took eight hours

---

[115] Northern Ireland (Executive Formation etc) Act 2019, s 9.

[116] CEDAW Committee (n 8) [38].

[117] ibid [39(a)]; CEDAW Committee, 'Concluding Observations: Cabo Verde' (n 109) [34(b)]; CEDAW Committee, 'Concluding Observations: Cote d'Ivoire' (n 10) [44(d)]; CEDAW Committee (n 94) [45(c)].

[118] CEDAW Committee, 'Concluding Observations: Mozambique' (n 109) [36(d)].

[119] CEDAW Committee (n 8) [38].

[120] ibid.

[121] ibid [39(h)].

[122] J Perkins et al, 'Humanized Childbirth: The Status of Emotional Support in Rural Bangladesh' (2019) 27(1) *Sexual and Reproductive Health Matters* 228.

[123] ibid.

to transport Ms da Silva Pimental Teixeira to an urban hospital as the local centre refused to provide ambulance transport.[124] The CEDAW Committee alludes to regional disparities, but when applying the intersectional lens to the individual communication, it does not explicitly refer to rurality, but only to Ms da Silva Pimental Teixeira's African descent and socio-economic background.[125] Her mother argued that due to the uneven geographical distribution of health services, the nearest hospital was two hours away, requiring 'travel time equal to the amount of time an average woman in [Ms da Silva Pimental Teixeira's] condition had to live'.[126] The lack of investment in emergency healthcare services is a death sentence for rural women, especially poor rural women. Further, this case raises questions on the quality of care in rural health centres, as warning signs of miscarriage were ignored. Again, this is a missed opportunity to address the endemic lack of investment in non-urban maternal health services and emergency transport that contributed to her death.

The frequently subordinate role of women in rural communities perpetuates gender-based violence.[127] The Inquiry Procedure into missing and murdered Indigenous women in Canada emphasises the interaction between rural and Northern remoteness, Indigenous status and gender. The CEDAW Committee found that 'the intersectional discrimination suffered by Indigenous women living on reserves is exacerbated by their living in a rural environment, because of their geographical isolation and limited mobility, the lack of safe transportation and their limited access to law enforcement, protection and counselling services'.[128] Due to lack of public transport, Indigenous women in rural and Northern communities resort to hitchhiking, which exposes them to serious risks of violence.[129] A 724-km highway in British Columbia is commonly referred to as the 'Highway of Tears' because of the murders and disappearances of Indigenous women in its vicinity.[130] The neglect of rural communities creates obstacles to breaking free from cycles of violence. In Long Point First Nation in Canada, the nearest shelter from gender-based violence is 100 km away and in the Yukon there are no state-funded shelters.[131] In General Recommendation No 34 on the rights of rural women, the CEDAW Committee recommends raising the awareness of men, boys, and local, religious and community leaders to eliminate discriminatory social attitudes that underpin and condone gender-based violence; to prevent, investigate, prosecute, punish and remedy acts of violence; and to ensure integrated services for including emergency shelters and healthcare that enhance the privacy and dignity of

---

[124] *Da Silva Pimental Teixeira* (n 43) [7.3].
[125] ibid [7.4].
[126] ibid [3.10].
[127] CEDAW Committee (n 8) [24].
[128] CEDAW Committee, 'Report of the Inquiry Concerning Canada of the CEDAW Committee under Article 8 of OP-CEDAW' (2015) CEDAW/C/OP.8/CAN/1 [204].
[129] ibid [106].
[130] ibid.
[131] ibid [176].

victims in rural communities.[132] It also advocates for increased access to information communication technology which can be crucial in overcoming the social isolation that contributes to gender-based violence and empowers the voice of girls and women to end violence.[133] Again, this reflects the CEDAW Committee's twin-tracking approach to intersectionality. The rights of vulnerable groups such as Indigenous women must be examined through a high-precision intersectional lens that accounts for rurality (and other identity characteristics) within specific rights, such as the right to be free from gender-based violence.

Conclusion

Rural girls and women are far too often invisible and their sexual and reproductive health rights are routinely violated. CEDAW shines the international spotlight on the intersection of rural, gender and sexual and reproductive health rights. The CEDAW Committee uses the recognition of intersectionality in Article 14 (equality for rural women) and applies it across the Convention in relation to other identity characteristics and in the context of different rights to highlight how living in a rural community can act as an obstacle to rural women's human rights. It also proposes recommendations to guide states in achieving rural women and girls equal sexual and reproductive health rights. The recommendations are targeted towards many of the structural inequalities in rural communities – investment in rural health services and transportation links, and increasing women's economic independence and participation in rural decision-making. While the CEDAW Committee is attentive to rural women and girls' lived experiences, there are still gaps in its approach to rurality. The lack of privacy and the social isolation combined with traditional gender attitudes in rural areas can make exercising sexual and reproductive health rights challenging. However, the CEDAW Committee's recommendations should reflect this reality. It should encourage states to develop health services that protect women and girls' privacy over intimate areas of their lives and transform rural cultural attitudes that perpetuate shame and stigma. Overall, CEDAW's sensitivity to rurality is to be commended and other domestic and international human rights bodies should similarly take account of the role of geography in shaping the realisation of human rights.

---

[132] CEDAW Committee (n 8) [25].
[133] ibid [75]–[76].

Epilogue

As noted at the outset, this book is about understanding how the complexity of human identity and disadvantage affects the articulation, realisation, violation and enforcement of human rights. Through seven substantive chapters – drawing upon a range of disciplinary, subject and methodological perspectives – this book has advanced the central argument: that intersectionality has a theoretical and practical appeal in human rights law and that, by engaging with intersectionality theory, properly understood and applied, human rights actors can better address entrenched and systemic forms of disadvantage.

The book does not establish (nor does it purport to recommend) an intersectional 'model' for human rights adjudication. Rather, the various contributions help illuminate what Atrey calls 'the workings of human rights, i.e. on what basis they matter (intersectional universality), and on what basis they transpire (realised or violated in intersectional terms)'.[1] As such, the book seeks to encourage greater understanding within this emerging area of academic discussion and practice, both in terms of how the intersections of identities, conditions and context may complicate access to human rights, as well as the 'considered and creative solutions' which are required to achieve transformational reform.[2]

This brief Epilogue identifies four key themes which have arisen from the discussions thus far and considers what these ideas tell us about the current position of intersectionality within human rights theory and practice. The goal here is neither to provide a detailed summary of the arguments made in the individual contributions nor to relitigate issues of particular sensitivity or dispute. Rather, by focusing on just four themes – existing jurisprudence, structural change, poverty and class, and the right to education – the Epilogue spells out some of the crosscutting questions that emerge from the chapters taken as a whole.

Looking, first, to the *existing interventions by human rights adjudicators*, the contributions to this book illustrate the extent to which, at both the international and regional levels, human rights adjudicators have already begun to incorporate intersectional analyses into their assessments.

In recent years, this trend has been increasingly evident in the jurisprudence of the UN human rights treaty bodies. In *Djazia and Bellili v Spain*,[3] the Committee

---

[1] See Shreya Atrey, ch 1 in this volume.
[2] ibid.
[3] *Djazia and Bellili v Spain*, Views Adopted by the Committee under the Optional Protocol to the International Covenant on Economic, Social and Cultural Rights with Regard to Communication No 5/2015, UN ESCOR, Comm on Econ, Soc & Cult Rts, 61st Sess, ¶ 11.5, UN Doc E/C.12/61/D/5/2015 (2017).

on Economic, Social and Cultural Rights (CESCR Committee) held that Spain had failed to adequately secure the housing rights of socio-economically deprived individuals who were under the threat of being evicted. In *Da Silva Pimental Teixeira v Brazil*,[4] the Committee on the Elimination of Discrimination against Women (CEDAW Committee) concluded that a pregnant woman had been discriminated against 'not only on the basis of her sex, *but also* on the basis of her status as a woman of African descent and her socio-economic background' (emphasis added).[5] The Committee on the Rights of Persons with Disabilities (CRPD Committee) has observed that people 'do not experience discrimination as members of a homogenous group but rather as individuals with multidimensional layers of identities, statuses and life circumstances'.[6]

At the regional level too, adjudicators are more willing to acknowledge discrimination arising from a combination of grounds. In *BS v Spain*,[7] the European Court of Human Rights (ECtHR) emphasised the 'particular vulnerability' (owing to the intersections of gender, ethnic origin and work) of an African woman engaged in sex work. In *JD and A v UK*,[8] the ECtHR was equally conscious of the ways in which the UK's infamous 'bedroom tax' impacted those who both depended on social welfare and suffered serious domestic abuse. The European Committee on Social Rights (ECSR Committee) has emphasised the historic marginalisation of Roma populations, owing to the intersection of their ethnicity and socio-economic vulnerability.[9] In a series of decisions since 2000, it has condemned states parties for failing to sufficiently accommodate the unique status and needs of Roma communities in terms of housing and healthcare.[10]

There is thus reason to applaud what O'Cinneide describes as 'avenues [opening] up within human rights law for the application of intersectionality analysis'.[11] Such developments encourage and facilitate a more rigorous understanding of the ways in which individuals are denied basic human rights. However, we cannot overstate developments of this kind. As the chapters in this book highlight, while intersectionality is much discussed within academic literature, its application by international, regional and national adjudicatory bodies remains patchy, lacking a consistent or coherent approach.

---

[4] CEDAW Committee, *Da Silva Pimental Teixeira v Brazil*, 2011, CEDAW/C/49/D/17/2008 [7.5].
[5] ibid [7.7].
[6] CRPD Committee, *General Comment No 3 on Article 6: Women and Girls with Disabilities*, 2016, CRPD/C/GC/3 [16].
[7] *BS v Spain* App No 47159/08 (ECtHR, 24 July 2012).
[8] *JD and A v UK* App Nos 32949/17 and 34614/17 (ECtHR, 24 October 2019).
[9] Decision on the merits of 7 February 2005.
[10] See Complaint No 27/2004, *ERRC v Italy* (Decision on the merits of 21 December 2005); *ERRC v Portugal*, Complaint No 49/2008 (Decision on the merits of 1 July 2011); Complaint No 31/2005, *ERRC v Bulgaria* (Decision on the merits of 1 July 2011); Complaint No 58/2009, *Centre on Housing Rights and Evictions (COHRE) v Italy* (Decision on the merits of 6 July 2010); Complaint No 63/2010, *COHRE v France* (Decision on the merits of 13 July 2011); Complaint No 67/2011, *Médecins du Monde v France* (Decision on the merits of 20 September 2012).
[11] Colm O'Cinneide, ch 3 in this volume.

In his chapter, de Beco particularly critiques the 'partial use of intersectionality theory's theoretical framework leaning on identity politics'.[12] He shows that international and regional actors continue to rely on identity-focused analyses when addressing claims of discrimination, even as they acknowledge how multiple characteristics, circumstances and vulnerabilities shape inequality in a structural sense. Citing cases such as *Kell v Canada*[13] and *RPB v The Philippines*,[14] de Beco argues that adjudicators must go beyond the mere recognition that numerous identities and attributes can influence experiences of discrimination. Rather, they must substantively explore how the intersections of these characteristics can themselves constitute unique and complex 'infringements of human rights in a way different than just a matter of discrimination on the basis of the different grounds'.[15]

In this respect, the CRPD Committee may already have provided a roadmap for reform. As both Atrey and de Beco note, in its landmark General Comment No 6 on Equality and Non-discrimination,[16] the CRPD Committee describes intersectional discrimination as 'several grounds operat[ing] and interact[ing] with each other at the same time in such a way that they are inseparable and thereby expose relevant individuals to *unique types of disadvantage and discrimination*' (emphasis added).[17] Under this framework, the goal is not simply to identify the ways in which belonging to multiple groups or characteristics can negatively impact fundamental rights; instead, human rights actors must reflect upon whether intersectional disadvantage 'produces forms of oppression that an exclusive focus on identity-categories does not allow them to detect'.[18]

While the CRPD Committee is writing in the context of disability protections, the underlying reasoning is applicable to a broader scope of human rights adjudication. In *Da Silva Pimental Teixeira v Brazil*, for example, an intersectional lens would go beyond the CEDAW Committee's acknowledgement of mistreatment arising from race *and* socio-economic status. Rather, it would interrogate the uniquely disadvantaged position of poor women of colour in Brazil and it would challenge state (in)action leading to women, such as Ms da Silva Pimentel, being denied life-saving medical treatment. As de Beco remarks, 'the question is not only about the possible consequences of belonging to one or more groups ... but also about shortcomings in social institutions' per se.[19]

Turning, second, to questions of *transformation and structural change*, a key theme running through the chapters is the limited extent to which human rights actors consider structural factors that limit the enjoyment of human rights. In the

---

[12] Gauthier de Beco, ch 2 in this volume.
[13] CEDAW Committee, *Kell v Canada*, 2012, CEDAW/C/51/D/19/2008.
[14] CEDAW Committee, *RPB v The Philippines*, 2014, CEDAW/C/57/D/34/2011.
[15] De Beco, ch 2 in this volume.
[16] CRPD Committee, General Comment No 6 on Equality and Non-discrimination (2018) UN Doc CRPD/C/GC/6.
[17] ibid [19].
[18] De Beco, ch 2 in this volume.
[19] ibid.

same vein, intersectionality theory too is often invoked in 'international human rights law as simply focusing on identity-categories instead of the structures of disadvantage associated with one or several of them simultaneously'.[20] The collective uptake from the authors is that, rather than approaching human rights analysis through a narrow lens of comparison based on attributes associated with identity-categories, courts and policy-makers should consider the broader systems of disadvantage associated with them. It is only the latter that can enable transformative or structural change.

In her chapter, Atrey suggests that '[i]ntersectionality ultimately aspires to transformation or social change by dismantling the complex structures of disadvantage it reveals'.[21] In adopting an intersectional lens of analysis, the point is not to deny that individual attributes, such as race and gender, exist or to claim their irrelevance in the enjoyment of human rights. Instead, intersectionality enhances collective understandings of how 'identities, conditions and contexts'[22] form part of wider systems which limit access to fundamental guarantees. As such, it plays a vital role in identifying those structures which require transformation. Although, as Atrey notes, '[t]his does not quite tell us *what* it takes to subvert those dynamics',[23] intersectionality nevertheless provides important insights into the nature of the dynamics that need subverting, thus enabling transformative change.

Fredman too emphasises the importance of structural transformation for guaranteeing the enjoyment of fundamental human rights.[24] Drawing upon the fourth dimension of her substantive equality analysis[25] – accommodating difference rather than demanding assimilation – she observes a need to both go 'beyond formal equality's demand that outgroups conform to existing structures as a condition of inclusion' and to require 'a recognition and celebration of difference and a transformation of existing social structures to incorporate diverse identities'.[26] In the specific context of education, she observes that judicial and policy efforts to combat systemic disadvantage 'will not succeed unless placed in the context of tackling ... structures of racialised poverty'.[27] However, such structural approaches are frequently lacking. This is particularly evident in the American and South African case law, which reveals a striking failure to engage with core concerns, including racialised housing patterns, economic inequality and the absence of employment opportunities. Unless adjudicatory bodies confront the intersectional roots of systemic disadvantage, there can only be limited progress in guaranteeing core human rights.

[20] ibid.
[21] Atrey, ch 1 in this volume.
[22] ibid.
[23] ibid.
[24] Sandra Fredman, ch 4 in this volume.
[25] S Fredman, *Discrimination Law*, 2nd edn (Oxford University Press, 2011) 25.
[26] Fredman, ch 4 in this volume.
[27] ibid.

Yet, at the same time, intersectional praxis may be easier said than done in terms of bringing about transformative change. As de Londras' chapter shows, intersectionality is both strategically relevant *and* challenging in social movements. Writing in the context of Ireland's recent abortion referendum, de Londras notes how the structures of the constitutional reform process, a national referendum, limited the potential for intersectional politics.[28] Despite the historically broad coalition advocating for reproductive justice in Ireland, the political dynamics of the 2018 referendum campaign ultimately required a more unidimensional engagement with the electorate. The rich diversity of narratives representing the demand for abortion in the Together for Yes campaign was thus eschewed in favour of a more publicly digestible message, emphasising medicine, grief, family and Irishness. De Londras recognises the implicit erasure, both within the campaign and subsequent legislation, of trans individuals and those within Ireland's asylum system. Transformative change in the Irish abortion laws thus seems to have come about selectively and with a less than transformative intersectional politics focusing on complex systems of disadvantage.

Third, the intersection of *poverty and class* with other systems of disadvantage, such as sexism, racism and ableism, is another recurring motif in the chapters in this collection. Whether in the sphere of education (de Beco and Fredman), reproductive health (Campbell and de Londras) or access to housing (O'Cinneide and Van Bueren), class and economic disadvantage, understood within broader social and political structures, impede the enjoyment of basic rights.

O'Cinneide opens with the observation that 'human rights law in general – and equality law in particular – has historically provided little or no meaningful legal protection against the socially exclusionary impact of poverty and material inequality'.[29] Seeing poverty as a largely political rather than legal consideration, adjudicatory bodies have preferred to bypass concerns of material inequality. This has had two consequences: it has resulted in courts failing to properly acknowledge the particular impact of economic inequality, especially poverty; and it has also obscured the ways in which poverty and class shape other kinds of disadvantage – what O'Cinneide describes as 'poverty and material inequality amplify[ing] the impact of other forms of inequality'.[30] O'Cinneide shows how these trends could be subverted within the emerging European social rights jurisprudence. For example, the focus on 'group vulnerability' has proven to be an useful tool in channelling intersectional concerns in social rights adjudication.

That said, while greater awareness of poverty and class has obvious potential for human rights, there are reasons to be cautious. O'Cinneide himself acknowledges the risk in emphasising social groups and inequality over more baseline enquiries, such as the minimum standard of treatment that all individuals must enjoy.[31]

---

[28] Fiona de Londras, ch 6 in this volume.
[29] O'Cinneide, ch 3 in this volume.
[30] ibid.
[31] ibid.

Focusing on intersectionality alone can thus take away from concerns that are more central to the logic of social rights, such as minimum core or progressive realisation. Though this is no reason to abandon intersectionality, it may still be worthwhile to consider how intersectionality could be tapped into without compromising other issues in human rights analyses.

Van Bueren also warns against any intersectional approach which foregrounds considerations of poverty to the exclusion of class.[32] The protected characteristic or ground of 'poverty' may potentially address a number of the disadvantages (particularly economic) which those experiencing class discrimination encounter. However, poverty alone may fail to capture how class prejudice often lies at the root of human rights violations. Citing the impact of class on the avoidable tragedy of Grenfell Tower, Van Bueren thus argues that class 'deserves equal consideration with other factors that impact individual life chances, especially the continuity and longevity of life'.[33]

Finally, a fourth common theme running throughout the book is the importance of intersectional analysis in understanding and defending the *right to education*. As Fredman observes, education is an 'accelerator' guarantee – a key determinant for enjoying other human rights and exiting broader systems of disadvantage. Barriers to adequate education thus amplify human rights violations. The impact is particularly acute for those who experience intersecting vulnerabilities to do with gender, race, class, poverty, age and disability.

Campbell reflects on the particular difficulties for women in rural environments, who are often unable to access reliable and evidence-based sex education.[34] Conservative social mores and the closeness of rural communities can inhibit educators from offering (and students from seeking) information regarding sexual and reproductive health. This places young women and queer students in positions where they have inadequate knowledge to make informed choices about their bodies and sexual development. The contributions also speak to the challenges of pregnant students,[35] who may be involuntarily removed from education when their pregnancy is revealed. Drawing upon examples from South Africa and the US, Fredman exposes the 'racialised, gendered and poverty-based stigma that adolescent pregnancy brings with it', reproducing and exacerbating existing structures of gendered and racialised inequality.[36]

In the context of the right to education of children with disabilities, de Beco underlines the importance of a multi-dimensional approach.[37] It is vital that human rights actors engage with the lived experience of disability, appreciating the various ways in which disabilities arise and are lived. At the same time, one

---

[32] Geraldine Van Bueren, ch 5 in this volume.
[33] ibid.
[34] Meghan Campbell, ch 7 in this volume.
[35] Fredman, ch 4 in this volume.
[36] ibid.
[37] De Beco, ch 2 in this volume.

must also be conscious of the ways in which disability intersects with other characteristics, including how different disabilities intersect with different personal characteristics differently. Each of these positions of intersection has to be carefully studied and revealed in order to understand how disabled children's right to education is limited.

Fredman advocates an intersectional approach to rights that is grounded in substantive equality.[38] The substantive equality framework, with its distinctive focus on redistributive, recognition, participative and structural forms of disadvantage, can provide adjudicators a template for delineating 'the synergism of race, gender, poverty and any other identity'.[39] Instead of asking whether the right to education has been impaired in comparison with other students or groups, the focus would be on foregrounding the particular experiences of students whose right to education is denied on the basis of their membership across several disadvantaged groups. The particular forms of disadvantage they face (redistributive, recognition, participative and structural) then illuminate the dynamics of how the right to education actually plays out in their lives.

These are some of the themes that emerge consistently throughout the book. While this is no definitive account of intersectionality and human rights, we hope that it is a conversation starter in beginning to theorise, conceptualise and implement intersectionality's contribution to human rights law. International, regional and comparative legal contexts will all benefit from this conversation. A range of rights cutting across the civil-political and socio-economic divide will benefit too. Most importantly, the greatest benefit yet may be to those intersectionally disadvantaged, to whom this intervention can make a real difference in accessing their human rights. It is with this hope in mind that the relationship between intersectionality and human rights law should continue to be explored.

---

[38] Fredman, ch 4 in this volume.
[39] ibid.

INDEX

www.ingramcontent.com/pod-product-compliance
Lightning Source LLC
Chambersburg PA
CBHW050443280326
41932CB00013BA/2222